To Ian and Marion
from
Bill & Carol
Barker
For "Aro Lang Syne"

Shaped by Vision

A Biography of
Theodore Austin-Sparks
1888 – 1971

by
Rex G. Beck

Shaped by Vision

A biography of
Theodore Austin-Sparks
1888 – 1971

Rex G. Beck

Greater Purpose Publishers
www.greaterpupose.net
Cleveland, Ohio

Published by
Greater Purpose Publishers
2207 Grandview Ave.
Cleveland Heights, OH 44106
www.greaterpupose.net

Email: rex_beck@worldnet.att.net

Library of Congress Control Number: 2004096425

International Standard Book Number 0-9766358-0-1

Printed in the United States of America

First Printing

Printed and Bound by Publishers' Graphics, LLC

CONTENTS

Note on the Cover Graphics

The Lampstand on the front cover is the symbol that appeared on every cover of Mr. Sparks' journal *A Witness and a Testimony* from 1933 until 1971. The symbol on the back cover, the circle with the Greek letters "En Christo" (meaning "In Christ") appeared in the January 1932 issue of *A Witness and a Testimony*.

"God's intention, God's proclamation is that all things are in His Son."

—*Stewardship of the Mystery I*

Introduction

My interest in Theodore Austin-Sparks began a few years ago when a close Christian friend encouraged me to read some of Mr. Sparks' books. Being familiar with some ministries on deeper Christian life, I was struck by the depth and spiritual insight that Mr. Sparks conveyed in his writings. As I read more, I found that my own vision of the heavenly Christ and His Body was uplifted, my prayer life was strengthened and my desire to live for God's purpose and to see God's purpose fulfilled was increased. I realize the spiritual impact the writings of Mr. Sparks can have on believers seeking a deeper walk with God.

Not long after, thanks to some very kind Christian friends, I acquired copies of Mr. Sparks' journal, *A Witness and a Testimony*. Through the many reports and editor's letters in this journal, I was able to gain more insight into Mr. Sparks as a man, in addition to knowing the revelation that he had apprehended. In this man I saw a pattern of a servant of the Lord who travailed for God's heavenly testimony to be firmly established on this earth. It seemed that Mr. Sparks was a rare example of a man who cared more for the Lord's interest than for the success of his own Christian work or ministry.

I soon discovered that Mr. Sparks was a product of a whole group of Christian servants of the early twentieth century, some of whom were associated with the Keswick convention. His life was one of learning from these many believers while constantly seeking something higher and deeper and more real of Christ. From his seeking of Christ in this environment, four emphases became the pillars of his ministry 1) a vast heavenly Christ 2) God's purpose—to gain a corporate expression of Christ through his Body 3) the heavenly church—the base from which God works on the earth and the unique vessel that God desires to build up for His testimony and 4) the cross—the unique means the Holy Spirit uses to make all the riches of Christ part of our experience. Mister Sparks also realized that any experiential establishment of these emphases in fullness is fraught with conflict and is therefore a matter of great spiritual travail.

I hope this book serves to emphasize the work that God did in Mr. Sparks throughout his long life of service. It is this work of God, through which the Holy Spirit created a particular character in this man, that produces a real pattern and provides real benefit to all the members of the Lord's Body. Of course, no servant of the Lord is perfect and, apart from the Lord Jesus, no man in whom God works can be admired in every aspect of his person. Mr. Sparks is no exception. A quote of Mr. Sparks found in volume one of *The Stewardship of the Mystery* may aptly point us to what we should look for in the story of his own life.

> The Bible abounds with men. It abounds with many other things, with doctrines, with principles; but more than anything else it abounds with men. That is God's

method, His chosen method, His primary method of making Himself known. These men who were in relationship with God, with whom God was associated, bring distinctive features into view. Not in any one man is the whole man acceptable, every feature to be praised, but in every man there are one or more features that stand out and distinguish him from all others, and abide as the conspicuous features of that man's life. Those outstanding distinctive features represent God's thought, the features which God Himself has taken pains to develop, for which God laid His hand upon such men, that throughout history they should be the expression of certain traits.[1]

God worked some conspicuous features in Mr. Sparks to give him a particular vision and exercise that was to be for the benefit of the rest of the Body of Christ. His vision became his living; his vision even became his being. What he spoke was not mere objective teaching from books and study. Rather, he spoke who he was and what he had experienced. This is consistent with his teaching that the true minister is the same as his ministry. He lived the vision, travailed for the realization of the vision, and suffered greatly for the vision God had given him. From this we can learn much from God's work in Mr. Sparks' life and person.

This book is divided into two parts. The first is the history of Mr. Sparks including his early years, his ministry, his abundant labors for the Lord, and his lonely last days. The second part is a series of summaries of 24 of Mr. Sparks' books spoken between 1926 and 1970. These summaries are intended to give the reader an overall impression of the content of Mr. Sparks' revelation and ministry. By combining both his history and ministry, my intent is that this book will provide a more complete portrait of this man and what God did through him. Of course, it is also my hope that my brief and selective summaries will draw more readers to the riches contained in Mr. Sparks' original books.

Any biographer probably looks at his work and questions whether or not the person has been portrayed adequately. As I consider this book, the biography of a spiritual man, I am acutely aware of its lack. However, I ask that this imperfect offering may inspire some to seek the Lord to receive the same vision Mr. Sparks had. Likewise, I hope that in reading his life some may be inspired by God to stand in travail, like Mr. Sparks, for God's heavenly testimony to be established on earth.

Early Years
1888 - 1926

The British Empire of the late 1800s was an empire nearing its most splendid hour. It boasted of holdings that would soon encompass one quarter of the land on the surface of the globe. In 1877 Queen Victoria was proclaimed Empress of India. The Indian sub-continent became the jewel on the crown of the Empire's holdings. Furthermore, the Queen's influence extended southeast from India to modern day Myanmar, Malaysia, Borneo, Australia and New Zealand. The Empire had interests in China and vast land holdings in North America. In the late 1800s its reign in Africa extended beyond its long held possessions in South Africa into modern day Kenya, Uganda and Northern Somalia in the West and to the resource rich lands of Nigeria in the East. Interests of the Empire affected Egypt and much of the Middle East. The sun never set over this vast empire.

At this time England became the center of the world's attention. The Empire had made it one of the richest and most powerful nations on earth. As a result, many citizens had concerns that reached far beyond the little island upon which they lived. The Empire caused them to open their eyes to a world which suddenly had become smaller and gave many citizens an active interest in events once deemed too remote to matter. The Victorian era was a time of expansion, of involvement, of great wealth and of national pride.

The late nineteenth century found London a sprawling metropolis reaping the benefits of the Empire's vast commerce. Its growing middle class had time for leisure and comfort. Gilbert and Sullivan entertained tens of thousands with musicals such as *The Pirates of Penzance* and *The Gondoliers* and the roaring nineties were about to begin. Amidst this scene, in the same year Gilbert and Sullivan wrote *The Yeoman of the Guard*, Theodore Austin-Sparks was born in London on September 30, 1888. His parents were of common means and of little reputation in the bustling city of the late 1880's. His father managed musical groups and moved in the small scale entertainment circles of the time. His mother is best remembered for her devout Christian life and her heritage of faith borne from a long line of Baptists rooted in Suffolk County farming communities. Together, they raised Theodore and his siblings in this modern England of the late 1800s.

At the same time the British Empire blossomed in possessions, commerce, and military power, many extremely devout and gifted men and women of God grew to serve the Christian community at home and abroad. The Empire did not only extend the reign of the British Crown but it also provided a way for Christian missionaries to reach the world with the message of the gospel. Coupled with the spread of missions and more than essential to their success was a deep inward work of God in the Christians "at home" in Britain. During this century, John Nelson Darby was expounding the Bible with great new light, George Mueller was caring for thousands of orphans by faith in God alone, J. Hudson Taylor was carrying out a profound work of spreading the gospel to the inland regions of China, D. L. Moody was holding a multitude of gospel meetings in England and affecting thousands of people, Robert Chapman was ministering and testifying to a life of Christian service, and C.T. Studd had given up a fortune and a place on the national Cricket team to go to China as a missionary. Great Bible teachers like Robert Govett, William Kelly, Benjamin Newton and G. H. Pember were shedding new light on the word of God. Great ministers like C. H. Spurgeon, F. B. Meyer, and G. Campbell Morgan were preaching weekly. This time period provided fertile soil for many men and women of God to grow in their Christian service. British society was surely affected by these many Christian influences. Reports of missionary activity routinely appeared in newspapers, gospel campaigns regularly beckoned citizens to listen, and movements toward a deeper inner life with God steadily influenced many believers.

Conversion and Early Years with Christ

Theodore's father was not keen on allowing his son to be exposed to the growing Christian influence. Most likely he wanted his child to grow up in the refined musicians' culture in which he himself lived. Even more he did not want his son to be affected by the thoughts and beliefs of his Christian wife. Thus he sent Theodore away to live with his relatives in Glasgow, Scotland. Theodore was to study there, in an environment free from his mother's Christian persuasion. In later years Theodore lovingly referred to his childhood home away from London and remarked how he longed to return now and again to that same place. "Now, I spent much of my childhood and my schooldays in a certain place, and somehow through all the years I've wanted to go back to that place again and again, so, from time to time I have gone back."[1]

In spite of the recollections made in his later years Theodore was for the most part lonely in Glasgow and his
school years were generally not joyful times. One Sunday
afternoon, probably in the spring of 1905, at the age of
seventeen, Theodore walked dejectedly down a Glasgow
street and came upon a group of young people preaching
the gospel in the open air. He stopped to hear them, went
home, and that night, while he was alone in his room, he
committed His life to the Lord Jesus Christ. The very
next week he found himself joining the same group of out-
door preachers. Soon he also began to add his testimony
to theirs and he thus began a life of announcing the gospel
which was to last more than sixty years.

From the very beginning of his Christian life,
Theodore was earnestly pursuing Christ and learning to
live by the inner sense of God's life within him. A friend
who knew him in his later years described him as a man
who truly knew God's life within him and did not do
things which would grieve that life[2]. In 1964 Mr. Sparks
gave a testimony of some of his first experiences of learning to live by the sense of the new life within him:

> But there is another thing that hap-
> pens when we are born again. The Holy
> Spirit Who is the Spirit of God comes into
> our new spirit. We do not hear the speak-
> ing out from heaven to us. But we know
> that God speaks in our hearts. We know
> that the Holy Spirit in our spirit tells us
> when we are wrong, and gives us the joy of
> the Lord when we are right.... I think this
> is one of the first lessons that I ever learned
> in the Christian life. I used to do certain
> things before I was born again. I did not
> see any harm in it at all. Indeed, I would
> argue with this soul of mine, 'What is

wrong with that?' I will not tell you what those things were. They are just things that all the people of this world do, and the places which they go.

Well, I used to do those things before I was born again. Then I had a very real experience of the Lord. No one said to me, 'Now you are a Christian, you may not do those things. But one day I just did one of those old things, and do you know all the joy went out of my heart. I had been able to do that for years and not be troubled about it. Now when I did it, I lost all my joy. Everything seemed to have gone wrong, and I had to go home and go into my room and get down on my knees, and ask the Lord what had happened. Why do I feel so miserable, what does this mean? And the Lord simply said, "You are bringing over the old life into the new. And I cannot have this mixture. You are a now a new creation in Christ, and the old things are passed away."

Now I say that was one of the first lessons I learned in the Christian life. This was very real then. I was born again, the Holy Spirit had come in, and He was just teaching me what the Lord was pleased with, and what the Lord was not pleased with. You can all understand that, I am sure. That is how it ought to be at the beginning of the Christian life. But it ought to be like that all the way through the Christian life.[3]

It was these kinds of lessons and this kind of earnestness that characterized Mr. Sparks' Christian life.
Later his ministry began to emphasize the utter importance of an inward revelation of the Son of God. Even at
the beginning of his Christian life, he began to know the
Son inwardly, and became well attuned to the inward
sense of what was pleasing to the Lord and what was not.

Not long after Theodore was saved, he returned to
his father and mother in London. The city was at that
time abuzz with the talk of a great gospel campaign held
by R. A. Torrey and his music leader Charles Alexander.
The campaign began in February in the great Royal Albert
Hall and was to extend until June, 1905. Torrey would
report that over 1 million people attended their nightly
gatherings and that over 15,000 people professed conversion during their stay. Theodore, freshly inspired by his
newly found Savior and encouraged by his public announcing of the gospel with the faithful band of young
people from Glasgow, enthusiastically participated in the
city wide gospel campaign. This must surely have been
an inspiring experience for a young Christian who was as
recently saved as Theodore. These campaigns were full of
impact derived mostly by prayers of thousands of people
worldwide. They relied on no gimmicks in order to draw
crowds, rather they trusted simply in the drawing power of
Christ who was lifted up on the cross and who Himself
would draw all men. Years later, in a famous gospel message, R. A. Torrey spoke about his London experience.
His description gives a vivid picture of what might have
impressed Theodore, a young, observant man in Christ.

> Nineteen centuries of Christian his-
> tory prove the drawing power of Jesus
> when He is properly presented to men. I
> have seen some wonderful verifications of
> the assertion of our text as to the marvelous

drawing power of the uplifted Christ.

In London, for two continuous months, six afternoons and evenings each week, I saw the great Royal Albert Hall filled and even jammed, and sometimes as many turned away as got in, though it would seat ten thousand people by actual count and provide standing room for two thousand more in the dome. On the opening night of these meetings a leading reporter of the city of London came to me before the service began and said, "You have rented this building for two consecutive months?" "Yes." "And you expect to fill it every day?" "Yes." "Why," he said, "no one has ever attempted to hold two weeks consecutive meetings here of any kind. Gladstone himself could not fill it for two weeks. And you really expect to fill it for two months?" I replied, "Come and see." He came and he saw.

On the last night, when the place was jammed to its utmost capacity and thousands outside clamored for admission, he came to me again, and I said, "Has it been filled?" He smiled and said, "It has." But what filled it? No show on earth could have filled it once a day for many consecutive days. The preacher was no remarkable orator. He had no gift of wit and humor, and would not have exercised it if he had. The newspapers constantly called attention to the fact that he was no orator, but the crowds came and came and came; rainy days, and fine days they crowded in or stood outside, oftentimes in a downpour of rain, in the vain hope of getting in. What drew them? The uplifted Christ preached and sung in the power of the Holy Spirit, given in answer to the daily prayers of forty thousand people scattered throughout the earth.[4]

Theodore's enthusiastic championing of the gospel campaign was met with strong disapproval at home by his father. It seems that in spite of his best efforts to isolate Theodore from his mother's Christian influence, Theodore had become an ardent follower and a desirous servant of the Lord Jesus. His father's displeasure at this turn of events proved so severe that Theodore was turned out of his house and was offered no family support from that time onward.

Thus detached from his father, Theodore returned to Glasgow to finish his school. He soon graduated from high school and, lacking sufficient means to continue his education, began to engage himself in a business in Glasgow. Unlike the England of power and luxury, early twentieth century Scotland was not a desirable country for those who sought to forge out a new life and find a good living. In fact from 1904 to 1913 600,000 Scots, or 13 percent of the population, left the country for America or other nations within the British Commonwealth. They took with them a great portion of the skills and education of the people. It was in the midst of this exodus that Theodore began in business in Glasgow. Nothing is known by this author about the business in which he engaged himself. I surmise that it was not an occupation requiring strenuous physical exertion, because Theodore never had good health. I also surmise that it was not a profession requiring a high degree of education nor one which compensated him more than a common man's salary. A few years later, when Theodore was faced with the prospect of furthering his education he was still prohibited due to lack of sufficient means.

We can guess that job and career were not the first things on Theodore's mind during this time. When he wasn't working, he applied himself diligently to seek out the things of Christ and engaged himself in many different avenues of service to the Lord. He involved himself in childrens' work and frequented the slums of the city rendering material and spiritual help to the unfortunate. Additionally, he gathered some desirous learners into his own house for Bible study. It was in this atmosphere of serving that Theodore began to preach Christ in small mission halls both in Glasgow and in the London area. As he engaged himself thus, he sensed that he might have a gift from the Lord in the area of speaking. So he began to apply himself to seek ways to further develop this gift. He lacked the means for a formal education and thus was not able to attend seminary or any Bible institute. Instead he gave himself to voraciously read the Bible and poured through many books written by spiritual men. In his later years he expresses much appreciation for the books he read by men such as A. J. Gordon, A. T. Pierson, and A. B. Simpson, from whom he received much spiritual profit. He also used his free time to visit places where great preachers spoke. He visited congregations where F. B. Meyer preached and frequented Westminster Chapel to hear G. Campbell Morgan expound the Bible. Years later he writes of his appreciation of these servants of God who helped form him in his ministry: "I was greatly inspired and helped by the life and ministry of such greatly-used servants of God."[5]

In many ways the United Kingdom at that time provided a unique environment for Christians to grow. In 1904, one year before Theodore got saved, a great revival swept through Wales and affected tens of thousands of people. In some towns, pubs and theaters closed down because everyone had become a Christian and no longer frequented these establishments. This revival marked the beginning of a whole series of movements emphasizing and focusing on the subjective experience of the Holy Spirit. Many of Theodore's teachers were greatly influenced by these deeper life experiences. David Bebbington estimates that these movements extended from 1904 to the late 1920s.[6] Undoubtedly, these influences affected Theodore's growth and outlook. Many believers considered that this move of the Spirit was helpfully delivering people from mere Bible knowledge and bringing them into the genuine, subjective experience of Christ, which is associated with that Bible knowledge. On the other hand, many believers thought these movements caused people to become overly proud, self-centered and eventually divisive or exclusive towards other believers. As Theodore matured in this setting, he had opportunity to see both extremes related to the experience of the Spirit. One extreme wandered too far from the Bible, and was based only on an "experience" of the Spirit. The other ventured too far from the Spirit to the point of excluding any subjective experience. This extreme left the believer full of book knowledge yet lifeless and powerless. It was Theodore's learning through seeing many examples that eventually brought him to the Bible and the Spirit. This revelation became a hallmark of his ministry and operation in the future years. For eight years Theodore continued earnestly serving the Lord in Glasgow and learning from others who had gone before him and who were also growing and serving in this unique environment.

Congregational Minister

Theodore's devotion to the Lord and growth in service was recognized in 1912, when at the age of twenty five he was asked to pastor a congregational church in

Stoke Newington, a modest neighborhood of London, located about three miles north of the city center. He was invited to the pastorate when the congregation was at a low ebb and was to bring the congregation forward in life and vitality through his service. Many years later he related how the first sermon he ever preached was on Acts 26:17b-18 "to whom I send you, to open their eyes, to turn them from darkness to light and from the authority of Satan to God, that they may receive forgiveness of sins and an inheritance among those who have been sanctified by faith in Me."[7] Mr. Sparks began his ministering in this congregation with the desire that the Lord would raise up men who have spiritual sight and who have a commission and anointing from the Lord. Fifty-seven years later, when he related this incident, he noted that the initial desire that he spoke out in his first sermon never waned, but governed his whole life of ministry.

It was at this time that Mr. Sparks probably began learning from the great Bible teacher of the time, G. Campbell Morgan. Friends who knew Mr. Sparks personally recall him speaking about the training he received under G. Campbell Morgan, who was pastor of Westminster Congregational Chapel from 1905 until 1916. In the 1960 book *Our Warfare*, Mr. Sparks himself testifies of his early years, "For some years I was closely associated with Dr. Campbell Morgan, as one of the members of his Bible Teachers' Association, the whole method of which was the analytical teaching of the Bible."[8] Campbell Morgan labeled himself as a Bible teacher and defined his role as that of a person whose sole intention was to teach people exactly what the Bible said. Morgan also desired to lead others into this same art and to train them to teach as he taught. Campbell Morgan formed a Bible teaching society, held yearly conferences, published a bi-monthly periodical, and offered correspondence courses to train men and women how to teach the Bible. It is very likely that

Mr. Sparks put himself wholly into this endeavor and gained a deep appreciation of the word of God from his tenure under G. Campbell Morgan. Campbell Morgan had a unique style of teaching the word by using a chalk board to summarize great sections of the word of God for his congregation. In his bi-monthly periodical, he even made chalk boards available for sale to his students for such a purpose. It is interesting to note that Mr. Sparks describes one of his own Bible teaching sessions as one covering great portions of the Bible and using a chalk board. Much later, after Mr. Sparks left the congregation at Stoke Newington, he mentions that his time there left him "well-instructed and firmly founded on the ever-enduring truths of the gospel of Jesus Christ."[9] This was largely due to his contact with Campbell Morgan as a young pastor.

Theodore put himself wholeheartedly into his service to the Lord and later described himself as "stretched out to the full for God's best." He not only earnestly served his congregation through his preaching, teaching and evangelistic enterprises but he also engaged himself in much broader fields. For example, he describes one such activity where he collaborated with other believers for a tribute to the missionary David Livingstone. "I expect most of you have heard of the great missionary David Livingstone, and some years ago I was associated with a great movement for the celebration of the centenary of his birth. [This would be 1913] You know, for nearly a whole year we were busy, almost night and day, making the arrangements. We took the greatest hall in London, got the archbishop of Canterbury to promise to preside, we had a special oratorio composed, and had special biographies of David Livingstone written. My word, we had to work hard."[10]

While Mr. Sparks was involved in these various activities among the Christians in Britain, political events oversees were shaping themselves in preparation for a conflict the size of which the world had never seen before. On August 4, 1914 Britain declared war on Germany and entered into "the Great War" which was to engulf the world for the next four years. The Christian community in Britain felt a grave responsibility to minister at this crucial hour both to the people on the home front and to the troops abroad. Theodore began traveling to minister to the troops stationed abroad. Later he related a small story which gives a taste of his work with the troops. "In the First World War, I was out in the Mediterranean with the troops, and on Sunday nights we had a great gathering of soldiers for a service. There were twelve hundred men who had come back wounded or sick. We used to say: 'Now, boys, what shall we sing?' Do you know what they chose every time as the first hymn? 'When the Roll is called up yonder I'll be there'!"[11] This war was to profoundly affect the British Empire and would eventually claim the lives of more than 900,000 British subjects. For decades afterwards Sparks referred to the war in his spoken and written messages, using it as an example of the tumultuous waves of the political, national and military landscape in contrast to the exalted Christ who walks peacefully amidst the turmoil. The war ended November 11, 1918 leaving Britain to recover and mourn the loss of almost an entire generation of young men.

During the war, in 1915, Mr. Sparks married Florence Rowland while he was pastor at Stoke Newington. Florence was the daughter of godly parents and became Theodore's life-long companion and support. She was a quiet woman who was reported to be content being an ordinary member of the congregations in which her husband played such prominent roles. She was known to have a great interest in many of the Lord's servants who came in contact with Theodore; she kept up an encouraging and grace-filled correspondence with many. She was to become the mother of four children and a trusted companion to Theodore all throughout his life. Most of all in her later life she was known for her intercession. She prayed every day for her children and later for her grandchildren. Her prayers also roamed around the whole world in her hidden, but powerful, ministry of intercession on behalf of the Lord's interests.

Honor Oak Baptist

After nearly ten years of faithful service, both at his home congregation and to the broader Christian community, Theodore left Stoke Newington Congregational church to become pastor of Honor Oak Baptist church, located in an "undistinguished" South-East London neighborhood. I have few details about why the move transpired and can merely guess that it was a move made after much careful searching for God's leading and will. Theodore seldom did things lightly and would many times search out matters before the Lord for many months before acting upon them. After his move, an even more intense desire arose within him for reality in his Christian service. This desire caused him to seek the Lord even more desperately than before. The Lord used this move to put Mr. Sparks in a position where he would become an open vessel to God. Eventually he would testify that he was ministering under "an open heaven," where his speaking found boundless expression from the heavenly source of revelation shown to him.

At Honor Oak Baptist, Mr. Sparks began anew his industrious labor on behalf of his congregation and became even more involved in his service to the greater Christian community. When he arrived , the congregation demonstrated little genuine seeking after God and, according to some, was more like a social club than a group of Christ-seekers. It had groups of committed faithful who applied themselves to arranging and continuing different types of social activities for both children and adults. Mr. Sparks' labor would spiritually enliven many of these attendants. Additionally, after arriving and beginning his regular and able ministry of the word, people from further reaches of the city began to be drawn to Honor Oak Baptist. At the same time, Mr. Sparks started to travel more widely in Britain, speaking to different congregations. More Christian conventions sent invitations for him to speak at their gatherings. Mr. Sparks was quickly becoming well known among Christians as an eloquent, powerful and able minister of the word.

Outwardly Mr. Sparks' move to Honor Oak Baptist seemed like a step toward a successful career as a minister, but Theodore was never a person who was satisfied with mere outward "successes." In fact in his later years he would testify about his outward successes as a young Christian and contrast them with the utter necessity of the inward experience of "when it pleased God to reveal His Son in me." He was a person who sought reality in his Christian experience and was not interested in mere activity, popularity, or 'success.' He later framed it by saying that any Christian must have a deep personal history with God and can only gain this through crises in which a believer apprehends Christ and realizes that only Christ is sufficient. He writes,

> There is a very big difference between giving out the truth concerning the Lord Jesus—even in large measure, in great fullness, truth which cannot be denied because it is the truth—and that strange, deep, indispensable element that we are that truth, that that truth itself takes its power, its strength from the fact that we are those who are a living expression of it; who have

gone through the depths, been tested, been
tried, been taken from place to place, been
subjected to experiences of intense severity, and in the fires have learned Christ, and
are therefore themselves the embodiment
of the knowledge of Christ.[12]

It was this kind of yearning in Theodore that
caused him to seek the Lord more desperately as his popularity began to increase, as more people became attracted
to Honor Oak Baptist because of his preaching, and as
more speaking invitations came to him. He was not content with giving good Bible messages and drawing large
crowds, rather he sought Christ for the reality of what he
spoke.

It was at this point that the Lord brought Theodore
to a milestone in his experience of Christ and in his service toward God. Theodore wrote about this experience
in an editorial in 1946. There he related,

Years ago I was unquestionably stretched
out to the full for God's best (as I trust I am
now), and there was no doubt whatever as
to my devotion to the Lord. I was right in
the full tide of every kind of evangelical
activity, and especially in conventions everywhere for the deepening of spiritual life.
I was a member of many Missionary
Boards and Committees, and was greatly in
demand because it was believed that I was
a man with a message. This is putting into
very few words an immense amount of
truly devoted activity and concern for the
Lord's interests. Being a man of prayer, I
was open to the Lord for all His will, I believed. But there was a certain realm of

things against which I was deeply prejudiced. It was really the very essence of the
original "Keswick" teaching, but I would
not have it at any price. I fought it and
those who taught it. To make a long story
short, the Lord took me seriously in hand
along another line, and brought me into
great spiritual distress. The very thing that
proved my emancipation was that which I
would not formerly have touched for anything. That proved the key to a fuller life
and a worldwide ministry. I came to see
that my judgment had been wholly wrong,
and that I was blinded by prejudice. I believed that I was honest and right, and
seemed to have evidence of it; but, no, I
was in my ignorance shutting out something which was of great value to the Lord
and to myself. Thank God for the grace to
be perfectly honest when the fact of prejudice was brought home to my heart.... No
man is infallible, and no one has yet
"apprehended" nor is "yet perfect." Many
godly men have had to adjust in the presence of fuller light given when a sense of
need made such necessary.[13]

Here Theodore describes himself being led by the
Lord into great spiritual distress in order that he would
become open to experiencing something much more of
Christ. The "Keswick" teaching that Mr. Sparks referred
to in this excerpt is a teaching of a deeper, inner life with
Christ. This teaching, heralded at a yearly convention in
Keswick, England, was intended for the deepening of the
believers' spiritual life. Hannah Whitehall Smith, who
wrote, *The Christian's Secret to a Happy Life*, was instru-

mental in beginning this gathering in order to focus the
believers on the need of consecration to God as the opening step for experiencing deeper aspects of Christ. It was
a message not for initial salvation but for those who have
already been saved to grow and advance in their Christian
walk. Such advancement only comes through knowing
Christ and the first stage of knowing Christ is to consecrate yourself totally to Him. Robert Delnay, ThD, describes characteristics of this movement, "What then, at
its best, did the movement stand for? For daily fellowship
with Christ and being taken up with Him, for human de-
pravity and the dangers in the old nature, for the walk in
the Spirit, for the demands of the cross in total sacrifice,
for daily quiet time in Bible reading and prayer, for immediate confession of known sin, and for leaving guilt at the
foot of the cross. Much of the preaching had to do with
death to self, renouncing the world, separating to Christ,
confessing Him faithfully, promoting foreign missions,
and living by faith."[14]

Although it sounds simple, the teaching at Keswick was not without controversy. And in the above excerpt Mr. Sparks says that he himself was an opponent of
Keswick before the Lord brought him to the point of spiritual distress. Opponents claimed that Keswick's Christian
experience was too subjective, that its teachings led believers to look for a "sinless perfection" in their living (a
claim that is difficult to believe because of Keswick's emphasis on the study of the word), and that the movement
led to an overemphasis on personal experience that resulted in a hyper-focus on the self and spiritual pride in
many of its followers. Opponents also claimed that the
movement, because of its emphases on personal experience, was too liberal with its interpretations of Scripture
and thus had the possibility of straying far from the sound
doctrines derived over centuries from God's word.

Theodore's thirst for a deeper reality of Christ and

his true heart hunger would not let him remain in the opposition camp. His resistance to Keswick may have been the influence of some Bible teachers that Theodore had learned so much from and that he had grown to rightly respect and admire. However, when he was brought to this deep spiritual distress, he was led by the Lord to question his every foundation. Some say the distress was occasioned by a severe sickness, which would not be uncommon for Theodore, whose health was never vigorous. Some say the crisis was precipitated by his meeting with F.B. Meyer, a man in whom Theodore saw a Christian living with a weight and a reality which he did not see in others. Whatever the case, Theodore's eyes were opened, God's light came in and he adjusted his whole Christian outlook according to the light he received from God. It was at this point that Theodore began to speak more fully about the cross of Christ and the necessity of the subjective experience of the cross for believers to advance.

It is said that after Mr. Sparks' crisis experience, which we place in 1923 or earlier, many faithful brothers and sisters at Honor Oak Baptist began to have a genuine turn to Christ. Yes, they were saved before this, but to them the Christian life held little depth and commanded little reason for heartfelt commitment. But when the Lord brought Theodore through this experience, others were affected by his freshness, newness and new-found consecration. Of course, not all at Honor Oak Baptist were keen on these new developments. That is why after a number of years of change, 1925 was described as a "year of crises" among the congregation. Many social, recreational or merely educational activities of the church were ceased in the wake of a true spiritual character that was settling in amongst the congregation. Even the Sunday school, which formerly was merely a popular educational institution, was altered to the extent that there was a true "soul-saving, Christ manifesting work" among the young

people. Later Mr. Sparks testified of the support and supply he received from the earnest prayer groups who began
assembling at Honor Oak during this time.

During these times of "Christ manifesting" at
Honor Oak Baptist, Theodore began to give messages in
association with the overcomer ministry of Jessie Penn-
Lewis. His first message was given in a conference in
Swanwick in 1923. His association with Jessie Penn-
Lewis is said to have been the cause for which many
Christians of position in the British Christian community
broke off their relationship with him. He was now ventur-
ing into the "Keswick" experience which he himself once
opposed. Now he found himself on the other side. However, as so very many times stated in his life, he took all
the rejection from the Lord's hand, being heartened by the
experience of the Lord Himself leading him this way.

His association with Jessie Penn-Lewis deepened
as he began to share at more of the overcomer conferences
and travel more widely. It has been said that Jessie Penn-
Lewis viewed Mr. Sparks as the successor for her work
and that she placed great trust and hopes in him. In 1925
she wrote in an editorial in her publication *The Overcomer:*

> There is a movement too, in connection
> with the "Overcomer Testimony" in Brit-
> ain. Our readers will have read with appre-
> ciation the notes we have given in The
> *Overcomer* of the addresses delivered by
> the Rev. T. Austin-Sparks at various con-
> ferences. His words at Swanwick last year
> will not soon be forgotten. They will
> therefore thank God with us that Mr. Aus-
> tin-Sparks has agreed to become
> "International Secretary" of the Overcomer
> Testimony to the Church of Christ. This is

truly an answer to prayer, because for years we have been in correspondence with ministers and workers in other lands, who have been earnestly asking if there was no way in which they could be "linked up" with us in our witness to the full-orbed message of the Cross. But this has never before been possible, nor have we been given any clear indication of the Lord's mind in the matter until now....I am thankful therefore, to have the fellowship of Mr. Austin-Sparks in this ministry to the people of God, whilst he continues, as heretofore, the Pastor of his own Church. For the information of my Ministerial readers in other lands, I will just say that after Mr. Austin-Sparks returns from America we shall be prepared to link up Ministers in other parts of the world, in an "International Ministers' Prayer Bond," with a circular letter written by Mr. Austin-Sparks, who also hopes to correspond with those who join it, for the purpose of consultation and prayer in any serious "supernatural" situations which may occur in their ministry. He will also be available for consultation by ministers and workers who may be desirous of holding conferences on the message of the Cross throughout Great Britain and elsewhere. For *consultation and prayer*, be it noted, and not for the planning of machinery.[15]

Jesse Penn-Lewis (1861-1927) ministered to God's people a message of a deeper life in Christ and of a subjective experience of the cross of Christ. She coauthored a book, *War on the Saints*, with Evan Roberts, a brother instrumental in the Welsh revival. This book was to become a handbook for spiritual warfare. In her later years she began publication of *The Overcomer* magazine and began to minister to all the members of the Body the deeper message of the cross. Mr. Sparks' messages at this time strongly emphasized the experience of "Christ and Him crucified" and the central position of the cross of Christ for God's entire plan. His involvement with Jesse Penn-Lewis exposed him to a far greater number of God's people and led him to travel to America for the first time.

In the summer of 1925 Mr. Sparks went to America and spoke at a conference associated with the work of Jesse Penn-Lewis in Keswick Grove, New Jersey. He also used the time to seek out various Bible teachers from whom he received help and to visit small gatherings of believers hungry for the message of the cross. The visit was a broadening experience for Theodore. He relates one story. "When in Boston in 1925 (my first visit to that country) I made a point of visiting the church (Clarendon) where Dr. Gordon fulfilled his main life work. I was deeply disappointed at finding nothing that spoke of my dear spiritual benefactor, but I pursued him in his books, which I found in Philadelphia."[16] Although he was not able to find any remnant of the work of Dr. A. J. Gordon, this story shows that he was certainly seeking after fellowship from Christians who had gone before him and helped him greatly. Mister Sparks also visited F. N. Douty who wrote a letter of thanks for his visit and composed a hymn on our identification with Christ with the first line "One with Thee Thou Son eternal." While near Philadelphia, Mr. Sparks visited a small company of the Lord's children. They wrote a letter of thanks after his return to England reporting that "We have a small group standing in the full message of Calvary, and really accomplishing things right now. Things are still developing far beyond my hopes. Yes, it works, it works." His main purpose of his visit was to speak at the Victorious Life Conference, in Keswick Grove, New Jersey. Here he continued in his "giving forth the message of the cross." Of this visit and of his well received message Jesse Penn-Lewis wrote

> From many correspondents in the U.S.A. also, we have heard of the signal witness of God to the Rev. Austin-Sparks' brief visit to the States. An Editor writes, "I believe his message is the greatest individual message of the Age, with which God is meeting Fosdick's anti-Christianity..." And these brethren are but two out of other witnesses to Calvary whom the Lord has been using in America. Let us give thanks, and pray that many others may be called of God, and thrust out to every land in this hour of deepest need.[17]

Upon returning from America, Theodore's duties beyond the confines of Honor Oak Baptist grew. He began to respond to invitations from other countries to minister on the fuller message of the cross. For example, he visited France to speak at a Dieulefit (meaning "God is Able") convention. A letter from a convention participant well describes his visit and the hungry reception of his ministry.

> ...if ever the visit of a servant of God was rightly timed and a ministry undertaken in the power of the Holy Spirit it was his to Dieulefit Convention.
>   The divine endowment which poured through his lips broke down before our eyes the strongholds, 'cast down imagi-

nations, and every high thing exalting itself against the knowledge of God, and brought into captivity every thought to the obedience of Christ.'

During my last seventeen years' experience as a missionary in France, I have not seen and had well nigh lost hope of ever seeing, anything resembling the victory won over what I may be permitted to name 'the French theological mentality.' Modernism, too, was shattered like Dagon before the Ark, broken without hands, and turned into a ridiculous stump.

There were fifty Pastors present, and a strong contingent of students. They simply surged around Mr. Sparks and clamored for further light after each of the regular Convention addresses, and passing out of the Reformed Church, we went over to the Methodist Chapel for two hours extra each day. The seven addresses are to be published, together with those delivered by the Conveners, and this will make up the report, so to speak, of the French Keswick[18]

As these and other travels engaged Mr. Sparks, the Lord was working among the believers at Honor Oak to support him and to stand with him for a ministry that was not only for the congregation itself but for a worldwide reach to all the members of the body. First of all, the Lord brought a co-pastor, Rev. T. Madoc Jeffreys to Honor Oak. Brother Jeffreys was to become a close companion and co-worker with Mr. Sparks throughout the next several years of drastic change and crises in Sparks' life and ministry. Concerning Jeffreys' becoming co-pastor, the church secretary at Honor Oak writes "The events leading up to this happy consummation have been so entirely independent of human arranging that there is no room to doubt that the Lord Himself, for His own purposes, has brought about this union."[19] Their co-working arrangement involved Mr. Jeffreys in the pastoral work mainly at the 'base' of Honor Oak Baptist while Mr. Sparks would be freer to sound the message of the cross in distant regions. In the next few years many joint conventions were given by these two brothers and both of their messages sounded a similar, deep, experiential tone to bring the hearers to the depths of the experience of Christ through His cross. In their co-laboring together, they had more than a business relationship. They entered into a spiritual oneness such that they testified in a joint "ministers' letter" that, "In the close personal fellowship of our joint ministry, if you will permit the reference, we are proving the essential "oneness" of our testimony and life, and how true it is that if one member suffer, all suffer with that one and if one rejoice, or exult in life, and ministry, all benefit."[20]

Preparing a Company for Ministry to the World

At the same time that Mr. Jeffreys began to serve at Honor Oak Baptist, the Lord was doing a marvelous, though less manifest, preparation work among the congregation. The church secretary writes concerning God's move among the members at that time. "It is clear that one of these purposes is concerned with the wider ministry to which Mr. Sparks is constantly being called, and we are glad to note a more intelligent vision, and a corresponding deeper interest, in relation to this larger work on the part of the rank and file of our church. This is especially manifest in our prayer fellowship. Our prayer gatherings are not only proving the possibility of real accomplishment for the Kingdom, but are moreover seasons of joyful fellowship in which many friends who are not upon our local membership-roll are joining with us."[21]   The Lord was to greatly use such prayer fellowship in the coming year to further prepare those in the congregation for a worldwide ministry and view and as a support and vital strength in fellowship for both Mr. Sparks and Brother Jeffreys.

While at Honor Oak Baptist, Mr. Sparks began a monthly publication which contained church news as well as messages given to the congregation.   In January of 1926 he redesigned the paper and gave it the new title: *A Witness and a Testimony*.   Mister Sparks may not have realized at the time that "this little paper" was to be faithfully published by him for the next 49 years without even a pause during the Second World War when the buildings housing the printing enterprise were destroyed by the Germans.   Although its distribution would never be large, in the years to come subscribers were to be found in nearly every country on earth.   The paper was to become a means to feed many hungry seekers of God's full gospel and was intended as an instrument to encourage God's children to attain "unto the full grown man, unto the measure of the stature of the fullness of Christ."   Little did Mr. Sparks realize that in his future dark and trying seasons, "this little paper" would at times be the only outlet for his ministry to reach God's children.   But for now the journal was billed as "an expression of the out-working of Calvary's Victory in the life of the church at Honor Oak."[22]   It was edited by T. Madoc Jeffreys and consisted of messages given by Sparks and Jeffreys as well as church news, etc. The paper had no subscription fee and was supported by gifts and contributions from those who rendered benefit from its message.   Its distribution soon became broader than those in the fellowship at Honor Oak Baptist; its deeper message being warmly received by those in various Christian circles both in Britain and in more distant lands.

The messages in *A Witness and a Testimony* were almost verbatim transcriptions of the spoken words of Sparks and Jeffreys. Mister Sparks felt that the value in messages was mainly related to the impact received from the hearers and not merely in the content they conveyed. For impact and impression, a speaker will often adjust to the audience, repeat points in a slightly modified form, or illustrate in order to drive home his message in a way that produces something of the Spirit's work in the audience. In order to preserve this sense, Mr. Sparks did not want the messages appearing in *A Witness and a Testimony* to be substantially edited away from their spoken form. Positively this preserved their impact and buoyancy. However, the presentation often sacrificed readability and, in future years, messages were often misunderstood due to a lack of sufficient context that would be provided by a good editor. To those hungry for a deeper walk with God and with the believers around them this little paper became a source of food and nourishment. To those suspicious of Mr. Sparks' motives (especially in the future years) excerpts of the spoken messages were used out of context as weapons against the furtherance of his ministry.

In addition to distributing this journal to many outside the fellowship of Honor Oak Baptist, in early1926 Mr. Sparks continued to minister to believers both outside of London and in other parts of the city. The growing receptivity of many believers to his message again brought up that seeking in Mr. Sparks for a deeper inward reality, not merely for more outward "success." In February of 1926 Mr. Sparks gave a message in Highbury-Quadrant Church, a North London neighborhood. This same group had a great season of blessing under the ministry of G. Campbell Morgan and subsequently under Dr. Douglas Adams. Dr. Adams fell sick and Mr. Sparks was asked to help with the congregation and begin courses of address every Friday in this North-London church. In 1964 he described his experience in Highbury Quadrant, where he established a Bible teaching course similar to what G. Campbell Morgan led his students to practice. His story relates more than merely what he did in Highbury Quadrant. It also relates what God was doing in Him at this time to lead him to an even deeper inward reality.

For many years, I was what was called a minister in the denominations. I was a minister of two denominations at the same time. So I had the big religious buildings. And I wore a clerical collar and attire, and I was in that whole system of organized Christianity. I had a big pulpit. And I preached sermons, and I was paid to do it. Well, I was very earnest. I really believed that I belonged to the Lord. My heart was reaching out to the Lord.

But the time came, when the Lord showed me Jesus Christ. He began to reveal His Son in me. You see, I knew the Bible. I was teaching the Bible everywhere. When I went to a big church in the North of London, they had no Bible teaching meeting. They had only a very small prayer meeting. But I decided that we would have, what we called, a Bible school. So I got a big blackboard made, a blackboard as big as this whole platform. I decided that I would give Bible lectures. So I started going right through the Bible. I went from Genesis to Revelation. The result was that that place was crowded with people for the Bible lecture. I say that to show you that I did know something about the Bible.

The day came when I saw the Lord Jesus, and all these other things were like nonsense. All this church business was like little children playing at going to church. All this dressing up in clerical clothes, oh, how silly it was. I really had not seen the Bible. I had it all in my head, but really the Bible was a closed book. When the Lord showed me His Son, all these other things went. It was like nonsense to me, I saw that the Lord Jesus is the Church, not these things. I saw that the Lord Jesus is everything in the Bible. The Bible is not a book, the Bible is Christ. I saw the Bible in Genesis, I mean, I saw Christ in Genesis. All through the Bible I saw Christ. It made everything else so foolish. It simply turned me inside out and upside down. All those other things had to be left behind. I saw the Lord Jesus. I do not mean I saw Him with these natural eyes. But what Paul meant when he said, "It pleased God to reveal His Son in me." That is what happened in my case.

And a new thing began from that time. A new ministry began, a new work of God began. And I am here today on the other side of the world because of that.[23]

Mr. Sparks was described by many who knew him as a person always seeking for a deeper and richer reality in his Christian life. In this instance, he was not satisfied with his many outward successes, with his expanding congregation at Honor Oak Baptist, with his publication that was growing and reaching many, with his position in the Overcomer testimony of Jesse Penn-Lewis. He was a person seeking not merely to give messages, to draw large crowds, or to win accolades of many admirers. Mister Sparks sought to gain the reality of what he spoke, whatever the cost. He sought the experience of God being pleased to reveal His Son in him and not merely the full knowledge of the Bible and the rich truths in God's word. Mister Sparks was a man continually seeking growth in Christ and reality in His Christian experience.

Before we look at the developments taking place at Honor Oak Baptist, we must be reminded of the inward work that God was doing in Mr. Sparks, in Mr. Jeffreys and in a good number of the members of the congregation. God was working to reveal His Son in Mr. Sparks to give him a fuller experience of all the truths he was speaking. At the same time God was working in a large portion of the congregation to prepare them to take a step of faith for something that God would do through them that they could uphold a testimony of God's full thought to the entire Body of Christ. It is important to keep these inward positive works of God in full focus and then see how the outward circumstances of Honor Oak Baptist occurred at the same time. If one focuses too much on the outward happenings, then he may view Sparks' actions as a reaction to outward pressures and not as a response to an inward urging. For the rest of Mr. Sparks' life, the crisis that was about to happen made a deep and profound effect on him. He would rest on the fact that it was the product of God taking him through deep and desperate experiences where he realized that only Christ is able and only Christ is sufficient. He would also be more than careful to emphasize that he did not desire believers merely to repeat his outward actions. Rather, he very much desired believers to follow his example in having an inward response to God's revelation within.

While God was working within, there were several steps taking place among the congregation at Honor Oak Baptist that signaled that the Lord was leading Brother Sparks and Brother Jeffreys to come out of association with the Baptist system. Mister Sparks had a custom of praying every Tuesday at lunchtime with two of his colleagues, George Paterson and George Taylor.[24] This custom had established quite a spiritual base of fellowship between Mr. Sparks and his close colleagues at Honor Oak Baptist. There is a story that Mr. Sparks was praying concerning the matter of coming out of the Baptist association and was greatly seeking the Lord about it. In prayer he felt led by the Lord to go to a certain place and there he found two deacons of the Honor Oak Baptist congregation, George Patterson and brother Oliphant. They had been praying similarly concerning the denominational relationship of Honor Oak Baptist and had been led to go to this very same place. Their meeting and subsequent fellowship was a great encouragement to all to begin stepping out in faith, in response to the Lord's leading within.

The first small sign of this stirring is seen in the March 1926 edition of *A Witness and a Testimony*, where Mr. Jeffreys and Mr. Sparks' "ministers' letter" is addressed from "Honor Oak Free Church" and not from "Honor Oak Church." In the same issue they report that the church has embarked on a new financial basis of faith and that, unlike the former Baptist Union fund raising practices, there will be no more "hand to hand" collection of offering. The church notes record, "after March 31st, all gifts for the pastorate, current expenses of the church, and missionary service, respectively, will be placed in receptacles provided for the purpose in the vestibule of the church, with no obligation upon any, and no check of name or number, but as before the Lord. What God hath wrought! To Him be the praise!"[25]

In the next edition of *A Witness and a Testimony*,

published in early April, it is made known that the entire congregation was asked to consider the situation concerning their relationship with the Baptist Union. The church secretary writes, "The church was asked to prayerfully consider during the coming month its relationship with denominational organizations. The deacons, with the pastors, are of one mind and heart in realizing the inconsistency of our present position. We stand as members of a fellowship which is of One Body by One Spirit, and our present attachment with the denomination is almost entirely that of a nominal character. We feel the time has come when the position has to be faced honestly and upon the basis of our testimony."[26] Later that month, after a month of prayerful consideration, the Christians at Honor Oak decided to remove all association with their Baptist denomination. The church notes describe the meeting as "the church without a single expression of dissent decided that the time had come to go forward with the Lord as an assembly of His people without any label or association that would fetter or compromise our 'Witness and Testimony.'"[27] Now that the decision was made, it was not yet clear what to do about it or where to go from there. It was as if the Lord were leading them in faith and for now had only revealed one step of many that He would eventually lead them through.

In June of 1926 the inevitable question of leaving the current premises arose. The church secretary writes, "As a result of our decision to be a free assembly of the Lord's children gathering together unto His Name, and in fellowship with all other members of the One Body, His Church, in all the world, we have been brought face to face with certain eventualities. Our right to retain the church premises is being challenged."[28] At this same time it became known to the brothers that a former school complex became available not far from their current premises. In a sign of the Lord's future financial supply to the brothers, a brother who was not aware of any current needs of the assembly offered one pound toward the purchase of a hostel! This brother felt that his pound would be the first of £1000 that the Lord would supply. However, the funds which came in up to this point did not prove sufficient to lease the nearby property. And somehow, although the property was for sale, the transfer of title was bound up in legal mire.

In order to facilitate all the needed transactions at this time and to face the many crises, Mr. Sparks cancelled all his distant speaking engagements during these months. This way he could be home to stand with the congregation as the Lord moved inwardly and outwardly through him, Mr. Jeffreys and many others in the assembly. Throughout this time, the spiritual life at the Honor Oak assembly was considerably enriched. The church secretary writes "The services seem to have had an accession of life. The prayer-gatherings have been thronged, and the praying has been more markedly under the direction of the Spirit."[29] In the August conference at Honor Oak Baptist, a marked remnant of denominational significance impressed the congregation with exactly what they were leaving. The September report of the August gathering describes how the conference and prayer were open to all regenerated members of the Body of Christ. These gatherings were joyous and bountiful occasions. Then, after the prayer in oneness, a "church meeting" was held, at which time only those who were "members" of Honor Oak Baptist were permitted to remain. The stinging scene only made the congregation long more strongly for the day when their fellowship could truly be open to all children of God.

At the meeting, the deacons discussed their past months of prayer to God and correspondence with the Baptist Union. It seemed that there was no hope of bringing the current fellowship into a fuller relation to all the members of the Body.   Furthermore, they felt that the Lord was leading them out to stand for His ministry which was to be received by all Christians, of all backgrounds and from all places around the world. They felt that this was the position the Lord was calling them to fulfill. Based on their sense from the Lord, they decided to take a step of faith and determined to vacate their current premises in the near future, even though the Lord had not yet made another facility available for them. They decided to go out "not knowing at the moment whither we go; but amply assured that the Lord will provide us with a spiritual home."[30] At the September church meeting, held with the pastors absent, the congregation decided on a date to vacate the premises. They would leave after the upcoming November Conference, even though as of yet no facilities had been opened up for them by the Lord.

Becoming a Sign to this Generation

After this step of faith, the Lord again met their need, just like He met Joshua's need and stopped the river Jordan *after* the priests stepped to put their foot in the water. Funds came in from several anonymous donors adding up to around £900. At the same time, the premises of the former Forest Hills School, which the congregation had been seeking to buy as their "hostel" and which had, up to that point, been tied up in legal straits, suddenly was free and available for purchase. This former school had a hostel facility and a meeting room with conference capacity for 150 to 200 attendees. The intention upon moving there was to use the current facility as hostel and base and to immediately begin construction of a 500 seat conference meeting facility. The rest of the buildings would be used as support and hospitality for the assembly life. The total cost for this endeavor was estimated to be about £5000. As of November 1926, the Lord had provided nearly £1500 towards the cost of the new premises. A brief remark in *A Witness and a Testimony* notes that these gifts were given by people who did not know of the need of the assembly and were from an entirely different source than what the brothers had imagined. The brothers at Honor Oak had not spoken to these people and were quite sure that they had not even read a report of the current financial needs of the assembly. This was a strong testimony that the resources were in the Lord's control and He had the responsibility to meet them and also had full control over the timing in which they were released.

As we have been seeing, the Lord commissioned brothers Sparks and Jeffreys along with the deacons and many of the congregation to leave their denomination and set out to stand as a ministry to the entire Body of Christ. However, the exact nature of what they were standing for was not easy to convey to Christians and non-Christians alike. In fact, their move immediately caused local newspapers to seek them out in order to cover any story of division or discontent within the church. This was surely never the intention of the congregation. In the future, Mr. Sparks never emphasized the negative situation he was coming out of and never wrote negatively about any person in the denomination with whom he had personality problems. Rather, time and time again, he emphasized the positive "thing" the Lord was leading him and his congregation to become. He realized that the Lord would call out a few to stand according to His desire for the sake of the whole. For this reason, Sparks and Jeffreys sought to define what they were becoming and to diffuse any thoughts that they wanted to become a new denomination or wanted to start a movement of leaving denominations. To leave denominations without the inward stirring of the Spirit of God, who alone can call a person into something positive, serves no purpose in God's arrangement. However, if God does call and one misses His calling then that person bears responsibility before the Lord. Thus, Sparks and Jeffreys published five points that describe what they were not intending to become by establishing themselves apart from the Baptist Union. We will list these below: "1. We are not a new sect. 2. We do not seek to de-limit the Body of Christ; that is to say, we do not consider that our fellowship, or the standard of our fellowship, de-limits the church, the Body of Christ, as distinct from all other members of that Body in the world. It may seem obviously unnecessary to state this; but there have been misrepresentations along this line, foolish as it may seem. 3. Therefore we are not against other forms of Christian expression and ministry. We believe that 'Grace is with all them that love the Lord Jesus Christ in sincerity.' 4. But we are not considering ourselves a 'church' in the modern acceptance of the term, with a closed membership roll. We hold ourselves free to be in fellowship with all the children of God who may come to us. 5. We are certainly not an organization, driven by machinery along hard and fast lines, or under the domination of two or three individuals. We recognize that organization will be necessary to discharge our duties and functions as a fellowship of believers; but this, with all leadership and guidance, must come out of our corporate prayer-life, and thus be free to be continually ordered by the Spirit."[31] Sparks and Jeffreys continued to define positively what they seek to become. "we desire to be a free fellowship in God, the Holy Ghost, for all believers who have the witness within themselves, and whom we discern as such, that they are the children of God through faith in Jesus as the Christ, and Him crucified....We have a conviction that the Lord is giving to us a ministry to all such true believers, who may be led to us, or we to them, and this for the perfecting of the saints, and unto the building-up of the Body of Christ, in these final days....We seek no prominence, no publicity. We have no world-ambition to be a 'movement' of any kind or degree."[31]

With the Lord calling them to be such a fellowship inclusive of all the members in the Body, much consideration was given to the name of their fellowship. It was finally decided on "Honor Oak Christian Fellowship Center." "Honor Oak" was chosen to denote the locality in which the Lord stirred in them to gather and to endeavor in such a ministry of grace. "Christian Fellowship" was agreed upon to denote the basis of their fellowship being the Lord Jesus Christ Himself and the fellowship which was created by Him through the Spirit indwelling all the believers. "Center" denotes a spiritual ministry in prayer, and the source from which many could be sent out into the "field of the world" to help meet the needs of the entire Body of Christ.[32]

On November 29, 1926 the assembly at Honor Oak Baptist church held their last meeting in the denominational premises. It was a meeting for prayer and a time of great crises for the ministers and the congregation. Here is a copy of the address given at that time by Mr. Sparks.

"Say ye, I am your sign"
Ezekiel 12:11.

The mental conception of consecration has come to mean to be blessed and to be made a blessing. That is not a true conception if you just left there. These passages which we have read contain a proposition which is the central and basic principle of consecration to the Lord, of being given to the Lord. And what is it? That He might make us a sign. They contain this law, which we have often pointed out, that God in His eternal purpose determines that the method of His realization should be an

incarnation of Himself, that is, a manifestation of Himself in the flesh; and that He
should do something in that incarnation
which would be a sign to the universe, that
should signify something of the infinite
Wisdom, Power, and Sovereignty of
God—that He should take hold of the form
of a man, and in that form do things and
say : "Look at that and learn." By what He
does in such an instrument, He is making
that instrument a sign and signification not
only to man, but to angels of the two hier-
archies, the divine and the satanic. As ex-
ampled in Job, that He might do a thing
that the whole host of angels and demons
should look at and learn, and be made
wise; so that in every realm amongst men
and in the heavenlies, the lower and the
super heavenlies, God should be able to do
a thing in those who are His, which might
be the means of instruction, making aware,
informing and demonstrating.

Moses was a sign to the Children of
Israel. He disobeyed God and God had at
once to act, and because Moses stood in
such a prominent position before the people, his disobedience was publicly pun-
ished. In that judgment he became a sign
to the Israelites, lest they should come to
regard lightly the sin of disobedience. And
with us, there will often have to be a public
demonstration and judgment of the flesh
for the warning of others, as well as the
vindication of the truth in its living outworking. Moses was God's sign. It costs
to be God's sign. Are we willing? How

great the cost to Moses!—but—the afterward!

I believe the Lord in these days is
seeking to gather out a people, and to
gather in a people—few they will certainly
be, and one does not say that the Lord can
do this with all who are His—who shall be
His sign to the spiritual house of Israel.
Their testimony may not be a testimony
that the house of Israel is utterly wrong; but
their testimony will be that there is a higher
and deeper life in God to which he would
call them. One feels this borne in upon one
so much in these days, and you will understand the signification of this, that when the
Lord calls a people, a small company it
may be, when He puts His hand upon one
here and one there, adds them one by one
to a small company of those who are to be
a special sign to His household, He deals
with them in different ways altogether from
those which He follows with other people,
and He says: "I will do a new thing."

Now it is no use your making comparisons with others. They may, in their
way, have a certain seal and blessing of
God upon them; but it does not mean that
the way the Lord is leading you is a wrong
way; and you dare not argue according to
the ways the other people go. This is the
way of the Lord for you. Do not stay to
make comparisons. We stumble at that so
often, we who have given ourselves wholly
to God, and then have these exceptional
and trying experiences to come up
against—the full impact of the wrath of the

enemy. We look around to others who have an easier time, because they are not going the way we are going. Immediately we do that, the bottom begins to fall out of the whole thing. The point is, the Lord has His wheel within a wheel, His instrument with which He desires to make a special sign to His people, of His Wisdom, His Power, His Grace, His Methods, His Purpose, so that He can reveal Himself through them to others. Do not have, for one moment, the thought of anyone being on a pedestal, and being in solitary isolation, of special account to the Lord. It simply means that we go deeper down to death, and in humiliation before the world, than anyone else. And because the Lord takes us deeper, He is able to reveal something higher.

To speak now as we are closing the days of our sojourn on the older lines, and with certain of the older associations—God is leading us out into a way which is unusual, which is, if you like, peculiar; and doing a thing which we know not of as having been done anywhere else. As He leads us in a fellowship, I believe it is in order that in doing this thing, with all its cost, with all its pain, with all its need of the slaying of every bit of the flesh, pride and arrogance, and its desire for the approval of men, and all that kind of thing—I believe that in His new way He is seeking to have such to go with Him, in order that He may make them a Sign, as something spiritual, and something spiritually powerful; not that men can applaud, not that men may approve, but which perhaps will be like the impact of God from the throne of God upon the throne of Satan, in these closing days. That is the burden of the Word of the Lord: "Son of man, I have made you a Sign"; "Say unto them, I am your sign."

I take it that we who are gathered in this place tonight are all the Lord's people. Nearly all of us are in this fellowship of the Spirit, having abandoned ourselves to go with the Lord all the way. It seems to me that this moment is a moment when we should face the implication of this word; as to whether we are going the popular way, or whether we are going the unpopular way; as to whether we are going to be the Lord's Sign. When Paul uttered these words: "God has made us last of all a spectacle," he was taking account of the holidays of the Romans, when they gathered for a day's sport; when all the other things had been got through, the last thing was the turning into the arena of criminals who were made sport of the crowd this holiday, for people to laugh at, jeer at, ridicule, make fun of; and Paul says: "Last of all we are made a spectacle"—the world laughs, just as the world laughed at Nehemiah in the building of the walls of Jerusalem.

"God has made us a spectacle." Are we ready to be made a "Sign"? The thing which the world laughs at? The cross of the Lord Jesus has proved ever and always to have been the superlative wisdom and power of God. For the time being the sharing of the cross is the real test. The Master endured the cross, and despised the shame, in order to be made a Sign. Was there ever a Sign more glorious and mighty than that cross?

So our Master came to the end, and said: "For their sakes I consecrate Myself, for their sakes I give Myself unto the full consecration; and that consecration is the cross and I am willing to be made a spectacle to men, demons and angels, for their sakes." The Lord wants us to be Signs. One says this with bated breath, knowing little what it means, but knowing also that His Grace is sufficient. Beloved, He is just seeking to gather a company of people together with whom He can make a Sign, not only of suffering and affliction, but of Power and Glory, to show to others His wisdom, His Might, His Sovereignty, His Grace. Will you say on those terms, on that ground: "I am the Lord's? At Thy feet I fall; to suffer, live or die, for my Lord crucified"? This is what it means to be His witnesses. "Ye are My witnesses"—it does not mean going out and talking, it means the Lord working in our lives, and others looking on, and saying, "That is the mind of God; that is the Way of God; that is the Will of God." And as He does it, so demons learn what God is, the Glory of God, the Sovereignty of God; angels bow because of His doings in the church, and glorify Him on our behalf.

May He lead us to give our assent

and consent in a new, fresh act of abandon-
ment and consecration individually, and as
a people for these coming days.[33]

Mr. Sparks and Mr. Jeffreys were not alone in developing the vision they saw for a fellowship to all the
members of the Lord's Body. They were with many others from the congregation. While the Lord was stirring in
Mr. Sparks and Mr. Jeffreys, just as importantly the Lord
was working in the deacons and the members of the assembly at Honor Oak. The importance of the assembly to
support the function of these ministers cannot be over-
emphasized; as Sparks himself said, the Lord wanted them
all to be a Sign of what He was doing in them. He did not
want merely a few men writing books and talking about
their ideas, no matter how Biblical such ideas may be. A
sign could not simply be one or two people. It had to be a
company, because this was the commitment that the Lord
showed to the assembly at Honor Oak. They all were to
be a testimony to the Body of a deeper life in Christ,
therefore they had to have the setting in which they could
be this testimony. Herein lies the difference between so
many ministers setting out for the advancement of their
ministry and Mr. Sparks who set out to become a sign
with his assembly of the Body of Christ, for the Body of
Christ. In 1933 Sparks summarizes this view in an editorial in the January edition of *A Witness and a Testimony*.

We feel that the Lord has given us a
ministry to all His people, and that this
ministry has something—at least—to do
with the recovering of His full testimony at
the end-time. We feel that the Lord's way
is preeminently with the assembly as the
local representation and expression of the
whole "Body." We cannot and do not deny

that the Lord has blessed and used other means: missions, societies, etc., and we rejoice in everything which means something for Him. But we see that the New Testament way was in the assembly—ordered according to God's pattern—as the training school, testing ground, and channel or instrument of sending forth to the nations to gather out of them the "people for His name." This constituting of such assemblies is the work of the Holy Spirit and not ours. Therefore no initiative with a scheme is taken by us. Everything must be marked by that life and spontaneity which characterizes the Holy Spirit's movements.[34]

After these stirring words defining their vision before the Lord, the Lord led the congregation to their new premises on Honor Oak road. They had decided to vacate the premises known as Honor Oak Baptist Church on November 30, which was the date of the prayer meeting when Mr. Sparks ministered this word. On December 1, a Wednesday, the congregation along with the deacons and T. Madoc Jeffreys went "up the hill," about a ten minutes walk, to the new facility and gathered in their first meeting for prayer and thanksgiving to the Lord. Three days before this, some industrious members began working to ready the facility for gathering and use. They did an admirable job and many of the participants felt at home in their new premises on that Wednesday evening. Mr. Sparks was absent from this joyous occasion due to a speaking engagement in Falmouth and could only participate in spirit and via telegram.

This was surely a time of crisis for Mr. Sparks and a time when the Lord's revelation and stirring that had been brewing in him for the past four or so years manifested itself in action and movement. He, along with Jeffreys, the deacons and the assembly at Honor Oak, took a bold move to disassociate themselves from the Baptist Union and to stand as a sign to the whole Body of Christ. During this transition, Mr. Sparks also was very much before the Lord concerning his relationship to Jessie Penn-Lewis' Overcomer Testimony. From 1925 Sparks was an international secretary for the testimony and was involved in much correspondence with believers worldwide in order to assist them in their ministry and application concerning the message of the cross. In November or December of 1926 Sparks felt led by the Lord to remove himself from the Overcomer Testimony. A short note appears in the January 1927 issue of Jessie Penn-Lewis' magazine, *The Overcomer*.

> For now the Rev. T. Austin-Sparks has made known to us that he had been given the definite leading of God that he should withdraw from all active association with the Overcomer Testimony. Our brother writes that, after much prayer, and "testing the matter in all directions," with "increasing conviction" he had become "convinced that it was the Lord's doing." Since writing this, the course Mr. Sparks has taken in his pastoral work indicates that he is being led out into an independent ministry.
> Thankful for the memory of unbroken cordial relations with our brother since his first attendance at our Swanwick Conference in 1923, we may confidently hope that as the Lord's servant has declared his unalterable purpose to preach the Cross in

all its fullness, his decision will work out to the furtherance of the gospel.[35]

Later, in July 1927, due to many questions raised by some who wondered why Mr. Sparks withdrew from the Overcomer Testimony, this word of explanation appeared in *The Overcomer*.

> In reply to enquiries, it seems necessary to remind our readers of a paragraph in my letter for January, 1927, in which I said that our brother, Rev. T. Austin-Sparks, had felt led to withdraw from all active association with the Overcomer Testimony. Subsequent developments in connection with his pastoral work indicated that he was being led into an independent ministry.
>
> In this connection it will be of interest to many to learn that, in addition to carrying out of the other burdens which they feel laid upon them, our brethren lay stress upon the necessity of baptism by immersion as an outward expression of the truth of identification with Christ in death and resurrection, and upon the laying-on of hands. Our readers will see that this line of external action could not have been carried out as part of the "Overcomer Testimony."[36]

Mr. Sparks' stand to respond to the Lord's inward leading forced the breaking of many ties that previously had been centerpieces of his service to the Lord. Honor Oak Baptist and the Overcomer Testimony had both opened new doors for Mr. Sparks' ministry to go out.

However, now the Lord led him to cut these ties and trust the Lord Himself. Now Mr. Sparks and the company at Honor Oak had cut many old ties to step onto new ground. They were in a fresh environment to follow the new course the Lord laid before them. This was the fruit of many years of inward work and preparation that the Lord had done in Mr. Sparks, Mr. Jeffreys and in many members of the congregation.

On December third, the assembly held its first conference in the new center. The subject of the conference was "The Cross and the Eternal Glory of God" and included messages on "The Glory before times eternal", "The Glory Incarnate....The Father glorified in the Son", "The Glory—post incarnate....The Son glorified in the Father", "The Glory, the abiding manifestation....The Son glorified in the Church, by the Spirit", and finally "The Glory, unto the ages of the ages, the manifestation of the Son of God in and with the sons of God." It was noted in the December issue of *A Witness and a Testimony* that "The whole subject seemed to come to us as a prophetic vision of the truth the Lord will reveal, and lead us into experimentally, during these next months or years."[37]

With a firm conviction of God's leading and with a long time to allow Him to adjust them, Mr. Sparks and the congregation at Honor Oak Baptist set out even though they did not know where they were going. Soon conferences and fellowships would be attended by more believers from different Christian backgrounds and from different countries. Missionaries also had some connection to this assembly through the publications and the help they received from the ministering. A growing number of laborers from the many mission fields abroad began to visit to be refreshed and supplied by a deeper message of God's work. However, those who received help, including missionaries and other workers, never became a large group; that was not the intention of the assembly, nor was the message of the cross and its price changed to attract the masses. At that time the little paper, *A Witness and a Testimony* had a circulation of about one thousand. Six hundred copies of each issue were mailed to addresses in England and abroad; four hundred were distributed locally. The funds to support the printing and mailing of the magazine as well as the extensive new conference and fellowship facilities had been faithfully supplied up to this time by the Lord's stirring in some to give freewill offerings.

Although the scale of this entire enterprise was small, its value was high because it was something of the Lord. Its participants were characterized by earnestness, consecration and a purity in seeking to become what God desired and not what men admired. In the future, the Lord was to lead this faithful band through many fiery trials. Opposition from many Christian groups began almost immediately upon leaving the Honor Oak Baptist premises and continued until after Mr. Sparks' death in 1971. A war was to devastate their new premises. Internal problems were to afflict them. However, when God does something, He proves that what He does is in resurrection by sending it through deep and fiery trials of death. What emerges is truly of God, because He is the resurrection. In this light, the forthcoming ordeals were merely the Lord's gentle dealing with the assembly, because they voiced their desire for something deeper. And they acted on it. They offered themselves to God to become a Sign to angels, to demons, to unbelievers and to all the members of the Lord's Body. God's dealings with them proved their stand in Him time and time again.

A Sign to the World and a Ministry for All
1926-1939

The little band that left Honor Oak Baptist began their journey by faith, because none fully knew where the Lord was leading them, nor the full orbed pattern of what He desired them to become. What was clear at the outset was that the congregation felt at home in their new position and especially enjoyed a freedom to have open and inclusive fellowship with all members of the Body. The congregation was richly enjoying a very real presence of the Lord in their gatherings. In the description given by the secretary much praise is given for the earnest and anointed prayer and for the rich presence of the Lord, even when not trying to realize His presence. This is Immanuel, they declared, God with us. Their first conference included their first "open" bread breaking meeting. The atmosphere was encouraging, full of the Lord's presence, and full of joy. The ministering was rich, profound and relevant. The messages, whose subjects touched on the theme "The Cross and the Eternal Glory of God," were apprehended by the congregation as a living portrayal of what the Lord would bring them through experientially in the coming months and years. It was surely a time of joy, of release, and of eager anticipation for the Lord's next move.

Soon after this splendid beginning, during the first month the company was in their new premises, Mr. Sparks became seriously ill to the point that doctors wondered if he would live. His health had not been good in the recent past and now it took a turn for the worse. The congregation prayed earnestly for him to be healed, but it was not the Lord's will to perform a miracle. So finally he had to undergo a serious operation and entered the beginning stages of a long recovery.

This was the first of many instances that the company at Honor Oak would be in prayer for Mr. Sparks' health. In fact, he would not be fully cured of his ailment until about 1950, when a more advanced surgical procedure could be performed to finally alleviate his suffering. This problem was to greatly limit his physical capacity. Often he would get up from his sick bed to give a message and then return to bed after he was finished.

His chronic ailment was viewed by many as a means by which God caused him to delve deeper in his spiritual walk and through which God was able to work a purer, richer and more profound ministry in Mr. Sparks. Such an experience agrees well with Mr. Sparks' own teaching that a disciple in the school of Christ learns more by suffering than by studying. Learning to cope and serve with his ailment was a living out of his teaching. So it was that with each inflammation of his condition there was something the Lord was working into Mr. Sparks and into the little band at Honor Oak. Often there were things learned and light shed on specific situations during these times of illness. Other times it was a suffering for the Body's sake and for the sake of making the testimony clearer.

This first case of Mr. Sparks' sickness served, among other things, to dispel one rumor that had begun to propagate concerning the Honor Oak Christian Fellowship Center. The rumor stated that the new group was a faith healing sect. Mr. Sparks' sickness and subsequent operation gave the Center an opportunity to make clearer its testimony. They wrote that they did believe in the ability of the Lord to physically heal and to give life to these mortal bodies through His indwelling Spirit. This is by far the highest and first appeal of any Christian. However, not all illnesses are allowed for the glory of God. Furthermore, a misconception that all are to be healed in this way may give ground for a passive attitude and for the devises of the enemy to damage us. Thus, their attitude was one of first seeking the Lord for healing, but also taking into account the Lord's sovereign will in each situation. In this particular situation, it was not the Lord's will to miraculously heal Mr. Sparks, so he underwent an operation and entered the tedious process of recovering.

Mr. Sparks' operation and recovery were subjects of much prayer during the early months of the fellowship at Honor Oak. The brothers testified of much struggling and subsequent blessing during their petition for Mr. Sparks. By January his condition stabilized and he was on a long road to recovery. He stated in a letter of thanks for the prayer and support of his friends that many doctors and nurses told him "It is a miracle you are alive." This was the way the Lord used all means, including prayer and medical, to heal Mr. Sparks.

While Mr. Sparks was recovering, the January conference was given by a guest speaker from the Kurku and Central Indian Hill Mission, Mr. A. S. Crowe. His message on "The Secret of Fruitfulness," published in *A Witness and a Testimony*, is an encouraging inspiration based on the picture of the temple portrayed in Ezekiel 47.

Assembly Order by the Spirit

Upon leaving the premises of the Honor Oak Baptist Church, the fellowship also left many other things. They discarded their membership list and all the organizational structure that supported the working of the congregation. They also left any thought of becoming a similar organization, with strict guidelines and operational structures. However, they realized that in order to get things done within the fellowship, there needed to be some organization. The difference, though, would be that such organization would have its source in the corporate prayer-life of the fellowship and that it would have the freedom to be "continually ordered by the Spirit." It was this desire that began to work itself out at Honor Oak in January. It might have been according to the sovereign hand of the Lord to have Mr. Sparks recovering at home during this time. Because he was not traveling, he could see the beginning stages of the development of the day to day workings of the fellowship.

The first such manifestation is that most of the practical affairs were being handled spontaneously by many brothers and sisters among them who shared the same vision the fellowship had in its leaving and establishing itself upon the present basis. In addition to these offerings for service, a board of trustees was selected to "ensure the continuity of the ministry and testimony of the fellowship in this locality."[1] These included Brothers Paterson, Bond, Taylor and Alexander, whose names appear on the lease for the facility at Honor Oak, along with the names of Austin-Sparks and Madoc Jeffreys. Furthermore, there was a manifest, prayerful waiting on the Lord that out of the many willing offerings among the brothers and sisters, the Lord would raise up "aids, helps, governments and administrations" necessary for the discharge of the various duties of the fellowship and ministry.

Another aspect of the fellowship at Honor Oak that was developing at this time was a hostel facility. This boarding house was to be cared for by two sisters, Mrs. Brand and Lady Ogle, both from America. T. Madoc Jeffreys states that its purpose was to "provide a spiritual home, upon a moderate scale of charge reduced to the lowest minimum, for such of the Lord's servants at home and abroad as feel their need of our fellowship and ministry for the quickening of faith and the renewing of spiritual strength."[2] The hostel was also to be a house of prayer, where an environment could be provided for those partaking in prayer service to seek out the prayers of the Spirit. This also would continue a universal prayer fellowship including and cooperating with all the members of the Body for the dire needs of God's people all over the world. Such a need was felt even more pressing as requests for prayers were coming to the Center from brothers and sisters in many different countries.

The first four months of 1927 were filled with efforts at bringing the new premises up to full operation. During the entire time, Mr. Sparks was recovering from his sickness. His recovery was made much more joyful by the birth of his first son in February of 1927. He and his family eventually retired to a house in the country for one month in order to speed his recovery. During this time A.S. Crowe and T. Madoc Jeffreys continued to minister at the monthly conferences. Mr. Sparks recovered his strength to release messages at that year's Easter Conference. The subject of the time was the "Cross and the Pattern in the Heavenlies."

These words were strongly used by the Spirit that weekend to work in specific ways in four brothers, confirming in them what the Holy Spirit had been speaking in them for a significant time. As the brothers and sisters in the fellowship labored to ready Honor Oak Center for the influx of people, the Lord was working by the Spirit in some of the attendants to continue His readying of His Body according to the "pattern in the heavenlies."

The first to be thus moved was Brother George Paterson. Brother Paterson was a "general secretary" of the Fellowship Center and was greatly involved in the administrative affairs. He had a good paying, full time government position and had been giving the lion's share of his free time to attend to the affairs of the Center. In this Easter conference, George felt a call from the Lord to drop his job to devote himself full time to his duties with the Center. As for his material needs, he would have to cast himself upon God for His provision. George felt that he could make such a step in faith if indeed the Lord was calling and if indeed this was the hour of his calling. The Spirit's work in him was confirmed during the conference and thus he began his life-long full time service to the Lord at Honor Oak Center. He was to become an integral part of those standing with Mr. Sparks in the years to come for the furtherance and release of the ministry of the word.

Three others were moved by the Lord to give themselves to serve the Lord full time at the Honor Oak Christian Fellowship Center. These would be the first three to fulfill another aspect of Christian pursuing that was developing at the center—training. These men did not respond in this way because of an announcement or any attempt to gain a registration list of trainees. These men were "independently and without word from us, led to come out into a free ministry of the Spirit as in the 'House of God.'" As soon as these brothers made known their decision to give themselves thus to the Lord for training, the fellowship at Honor Oak immediately began a long awaited training program. The hostel facilities that the Lord had prepared thus far were used to house these brothers. The intent of the training was made clear by Mr. Jeffreys in the May 1927 Issue of *A Witness and a Testi-*

mony. He writes, "We wish to make it plain, however, that by 'Training' we do not propose the usual curricula of seminaries and colleges, but rather that intensive fellowship in prayer, and over the word of God, by which the revelation and equipment of the Holy Spirit shall be given, and that then those who share such fellowship with us shall go out as the Lord directs, preaching the gospel, returning here as to their 'base' if need be."[3]

Such a training endeavor had been on the heart of Mr. Sparks and Mr. Jeffreys for quite some time. Even while the assembly was occupying Honor Oak Baptist, they wrote of a longing for a way to have such training. In the April 1926 issue of *A Witness and a Testimony*, they wrote, "we are no further with any practical outworking of the vision of a training center except the Lord seems to be impressing us with the necessity for 'the works of faith.'"[4] Then in January of 1927, after more waiting on the Lord concerning this matter, this notice appears concerning a training center, "We do not specify here any details of our prospective course. We must obtain all such matter from the Lord, but all who are interested in the 'department,' if it may be so termed, of our Fellowship and Ministry are requested to write"[5] Over the course of many months, instead of acting immediately to arrange or advertise, they simply sought the Lord for how He would further open the door. Finally, at this Easter conference the Lord moved in three to give themselves for the training. This move served to commence the first practical training at the Honor Oak Fellowship Center.

Training at the Honor Oak Christian Fellowship Center

It is useful to dwell on exactly what kind of training Mr. Sparks visualized for these young men, because it seems that it was not the usual kind. It did not involve the typical curricula of a seminary, but rather it involved "intensive fellowship in prayer, over the word of God, by which the revelation and equipment of the Holy Spirit shall be given." Mr. Sparks, in 1952, expounded much more fully on his views for the training of those who desired to give themselves to the Lord in a more specific way. His comments in 1952 are the fruit of the seeds he mentioned here in 1927. He still emphasized the importance of being in the word in a living way, which can bring forth revelation, but his understanding had grown to stress the importance of a close relationship with the local church, those with whom you assemble, during the training process of the worker. In "The Service of God" Mr. Sparks writes,

> The training must be at once Biblical and practical. It is essential first of all that they have a strong, sound grounding in the knowledge of the Scriptures. For every obvious reason this is so. But when we have given this matter all the place that it must have, it is necessary to remind ourselves too that the letter of the Word is not enough. Lectures on the Bible and analyses of its books will never, by themselves, make a true servant of Christ. The need is for the word of God to be spiritually taught and apprehended. That which lies behind the letter as to the divine mind and intention must be seen and responded to. The teaching and study of the Scriptures must have immediate spiritual effect in the life of those taught. The word of God will profit us only in so far as it brings Christ to us in Spiritual power.
>
> Furthermore there must be a practical life running side-by-side with the study

of the Scriptures.   This practical side should have three aspects at least.

First there must be a life alongside other Christians, as in a spiritual family, so that all the lessons of forbearance, patience, and cooperation are learned....Secondly there must be practical everyday work of that kind for which the different ages and sexes are fitted.   It is so important that spiritual things, and what is called "Christian work," should be kept in close relationship with real life and its ordinary tasks....Thirdly, in our training the practical and spiritual lessons learned must be given expression, and the best and most directly fruitful setting for this is in the local church.   The training of workers should be in close relationship with the church's life as constituted on the true organic basis of the Body of Christ.   No mere preaching place, or venue for holding and attending meetings, will meet the need, but rather a fellowship of believers where there is true corporate life and mutuality in building one another up.[6]

Mr. Sparks' training was different from what the typical seminary or college would undertake, because he desired the people who would pass through such a training to have a very special element put into them.   He did not desire to see pastors, ministers, missionaries raised up who would know how to do a work for God.   Rather he saw that the person who is working with God is much more important than the work that the person does.   He describes the servant of God in this way.

If the work of God is essentially spiritual, then it demands spiritual people for its doing, and the measure of their spirituality, their godliness, will determine the measure of their value to the Lord. Because this is so, in God's mind the servant is more than the work. If we are going to come truly into the hands of God for His purpose, then we shall be dealt with by Him in such a way as to continually increase our spiritual measure. It is not our interest in Christian work, our enthusiasms, ambitions, energies or abilities, nor our academic qualifications—nor indeed anything that we are in ourselves, but simply our spiritual life in God that provides the basis for the beginning as well as for the growth of our service to him.

Even the work of God itself, when we are engaged in it, is used by Him to increase our spiritual measure. Any Christian work which does not have the effect of adding to the measure of Christ in the worker is either not true divine service, or worse: it is itself working to our condemnation and injury.[7]

Mr. Sparks wanted a training atmosphere that would produce spiritual servants who would have true value in the Lord's eyes. His training did not focus on teaching them to do things or to interpret the Bible in certain ways. Rather, he cared much more for the person over the work. He wanted his trainees to become servants who knew God, sought the increase of God within themselves and who could thus go forth and teach others the same. Many young men and women who stayed with the

fellowship at Honor Oak for a period of training were
raised up to go forth as missionaries and as speakers to
spread the deeper truths of the message of the cross
among hungry Christians.

The length of training in this way was not long,
only one month to six weeks. It was intended for those
who already had a good degree of discipline in using their
time efficiently and in remaining productive even in the
midst of an unstructured schedule. The time was mostly
used to give themselves to the word and to prayer and to
be in all the gatherings at the Center. Two brothers who
were called during the Easter conference to participate in
the training, Gresham Speedy and Victor Thomas, were
examples of the results of such training. They began to
minister in places outside of Honor Oak in the summer
and by September were used by the Lord to fulfill a crucial leading of the Lord in a nearby fellowship. They
spent six weeks in the "Aberdare Christian Fellowship
Center," a fellowship that formed independently from, but
surprisingly similar to the fellowship at Honor Oak.
These brothers at Aberdare felt an urging from the Lord to
step out in faith and use every day for gospel preaching,
teaching and prayer in their Center. They had a real burden to reach the many unemployed people around them
and were pressed by the Lord to carry this out morning,
afternoon and evening. When Gresham and Victor visited
them, it seemed to be a fit designed by the Lord. These
brothers were able to minister and to meet the need of
many gatherings and out-reachings conducted at the Center. Many testified of the benefits they received.[8]

Spiritual Food Producing Spiritual Works

As the Holy Spirit was using conference times to
strongly confirm His move in some members of the fellowship and others who attended from outside, the de-

mand for *A Witness and a Testimony* increased. In May of 1927 the number of copies doubled from its January levels to become 2000 copies per issue.[9] Additionally, the size of the journal was increased to sixteen pages to disseminate more of the rich ministering that was being released at Honor Oak. All the costs of the paper thus far were more than covered by the free-will offerings of the readers. This gave the brothers strong encouragement that the Lord was supplying their need and that He also would supply the additional costs of a larger paper with an increased distribution.

During this time, the frequency of conferences at Honor Oak was increased to once per week. The fellowship would gather at about 3:00 PM on Saturdays for a word of ministry, and then they would have a break from about 4:00 to 7:30 to walk the grounds and to spend a moment with the Lord. They would gather again at 7:30 for more ministry and then conclude the conference on Sunday morning. These weekly gatherings were punctuated with longer monthly conferences held at the beginning of each month and with even longer gatherings during the holidays, like Easter and the national Bank Holiday in August. The frequent gatherings and rich ministry caused there to be abundant spiritual food among the fellowship at Honor Oak. A notable conference in August of 1927 was entitled, "The Centrality and Universality of the Cross." Mr. Sparks, who fell ill in the weeks before this time of ministry, received a clear word from the Lord during his confinement and released this series of messages on the cross. These messages, amended by Sparks in the early 1940s, outlined something of the essence of His entire lifetime of ministry. The conferences were also noted for the spontaneous testifying by the attendees of the work that the Spirit was doing in them through the release of the word. Feeding on the word released in these gatherings proved to be a source of healing for many weary Christian workers and a source of spiritual energy for the brothers and sisters in the fellowship.

One result of such a rich supply was a general feeling among the brothers and sisters to go forth into the world and spread the riches which they have enjoyed. The Lord had been preparing and equipping young people and others in the fellowship to go forth and speak the message of the cross and of the building up of the body. T. Madoc Jeffreys writes, "It would appear that the clamant need for an increased number of such as can give out the full message of the Cross as the testimony of the Body of Christ from the standpoint of a personal experience of its power is going to be met in some measure from within our fellowship."[10] It was in the hearts of Mr. Sparks and Mr. Jeffreys to establish more centers of ministry to be frequented by these young brothers, prepared by the Lord through the feeding at Honor Oak. Thus the Lord could more widely release and advance the message of the building up of the Body of Christ to the greater Christian community. Mr. Sparks and Mr. Jeffreys both felt that this was a crying need of many Christians in the Body of Christ and that this need could not be met by the churches in their present condition. A stumbling block to such a "move" by the fellowship at Honor Oak was the danger that this would be viewed as a way to create another denomination out of the fellowship at Honor Oak. They struggled against this thought and wrote of a desire for a "free" fellowship with no motives of developing another sect. Jeffreys writes, "But this work needs to be free, without suspicion of any attempt to organize a new denomination (the Lord forbid!) and so each step must be taken along a way opened by the Spirit of God, and in His wisdom."[11] The distant conferences and speaking engagements which had been held thus far by the brothers (Paterson and Alexander) at Honor Oak were attended by those from many different denominations. The common-

ality of those from so many different backgrounds was
that they all sought the release of the living word of God
and a deeper, fuller message for the building up of the
Body of Christ.

At the same time, the Lord began to lead, by the
working of His Spirit, more servants to the fellowship at
Honor Oak. In July of 1927 brother Oliphant, who was to
become a vital and functioning participant in the ministry
and testimony at Honor Oak, felt led by the Lord to begin
to bear the testimony with the other brothers there. A
brief description notes that the Lord had been leading this
brother "to a recognition of the unity and corporate character of the church of Christ, and to an obedience of testimony to the truth of identification with Christ in all its
scriptural range."[12] The brothers wrote of him, "We understand he has now decided that he must be free in the
ministry of the Spirit to serve the whole Body of Christ."[12]
It was this testimony that those at Honor Oak sought to
hold and it was this way of faith that many workers
dropped their positions to join and support.

The Death of Jesse Penn-Lewis

In August of 1927, Jessie Penn-Lewis was called
home to be with the Lord. A note of appreciation for her
ministry and expression of a great debt owed due to her
faithfulness appears in *A Witness and a Testimony*. Jeffreys writes what her ministry meant to him and to the fellowship at Honor Oak and also how he viewed the current
testimony that the fellowship was bearing in relation to
the contributions of Jessie Penn-Lewis.

> The church of God owes an incal-
> culable debt to this valiant and unfaltering
> pioneer of a truth that has been but slowly
> grasped by the children of God, but which

is nevertheless the basis of all victorious life and service. We refer, of course, to the truth of the Identification of the believer with Christ, through His Cross, both in His death to sin and His Life unto God....

As is well known now the Lord has led us in this "Fellowship" to emphasize not only the personal identification of the believer with our Lord in death and life as a matter of personal salvation, but to the fact that this identification brings the believer into a Life that is corporate in nature and functioning, namely, into the Body of Christ. We have been obliged to go forward in all that this revelation means to us by definite testimony. But we have never ceased to appreciate the foundational character of our sister's great ministry, the testimony to Jesus as the Christ, and *Him* crucified as *the* message of the gospel.[13]

Mr. Sparks also writes a note on a more personal side concerning Jessie Penn-Lewis, who was his close co-worker for many years. He writes

As we go to press the news reaches us that our sister, Mrs. Penn-Lewis, has passed from the battle to join the great cloud of witnesses. We have had very blessed fellowship with our sister both personally, privately, and in ministry, and learned to know her on a side which is not discerned by a great many who did not touch her so intimately.

We deliberately chose to share with her the prejudice from which she suffered for the sake of her message, which message—'The Message of the Cross'—was and is that in which we stand.

We deeply regret that for other reasons this personal fellowship was interrupted, but we have not ceased to bear her up before the Lord for succor and protection.

Few needed covering more than she, for few have assailed the enemy more bitterly and relentlessly, and few were more in danger to his fury. The strength and aggressiveness of her nature made it difficult for her to keep under the cover which the Lord sought to give her in her servants, and one feels that she was often the more harassed because of this.

Our sister fought a good fight, she has suffered much, but there is a great multitude that will rise to call her "Blessed." God takes His servants, but carries on His work; and all work that is out from Him is immortal.

We should like to write more, but time does not permit us now. We shall meet our sister again, and the mists will then have rolled away.[13]

A Corporate Ministry and Testimony

Not long after the September conference of 1927 Mr. Sparks again fell very ill and again needed an operation and a long period of recovery. All of his speaking engagements were filled by T. Madoc Jeffreys, including the "French Keswick" convention held annually in Dieulefit. Mr. Sparks had given messages there two years past and a good number of his pamphlets had since been translated into French and were rendering help to the people there. The Lord greatly blessed the gathering and the ministry of Mr. Jeffreys.

Other brothers also took up more of a share of the burden of spreading the message of the cross to other members of the Lord's Body. Brother Paterson and brother Oliphant held many speaking engagements and, together, conducted a series of meetings in Newcastle in November. At the same time, the young brothers who had been raised up through the training, Victor Thomas and Gresham Speedy, were continuing a rich ministry with the brothers and sisters at Aberdare.

Mr. Jeffreys' ministry at this time was extremely rich to meet the need. The November conference, under the theme "The Cross, and God, the Holy Ghost" emphasized the necessity of a personal knowledge of God Himself. Some quotes reveal the flavor of his speaking. "Doctrine becomes mental dogma apart from the divine *Content*." For this we enjoy the presence of the Father as God, the Son as God and the Spirit as the Spirit of both the Father and the Son. "The Holy Spirit is none other than God Himself, coming both as the Father and as the Son, to dwell in and with those who are begotten of Him through Calvary's travail."[14] In another gathering at Waunllwyd, Ebbw Vale, the Lord gave Jeffreys a series of messages to meet the need of a congregation of the believers who had been exposed to many experiences of "supernaturalism" and a feeling of "enchantment" due to a so-called simulation of Pentecost. These messages touched on the necessity to divide our soul from our spirit. Their subject was "the psychology of salvation." Jeffreys writes, "The Lord gave us a series of messages upon 'the psychology of salvation,' in which the nature of man in his tripartite being of body, soul, spirit in the old creation, spirit, soul, body in the new creation were defined, and the operation of the Cross as the power of salvation revealed."[15]

The ministry by the younger brothers and by Mr. Jeffreys was surely a consolation to Mr. Sparks in his sickness and recovery. The Lord seemed to be taking the Body testimony that was so much a subject of revelation at Honor Oak to raise up gifted members from the midst of the assembly to meet the further need of His Body. In a letter of thanks to the brothers and sisters for the care rendered during Sparks' illness he writes, "One would like just to recognize here the wonderful way in which the Lord has strengthened our brother, Mr. Jeffreys, for the increased burden of ministry during these many months. It has indeed been wonderful in our eyes, and one of the compensations of suffering has been the way in which other of the brethren have been anointed for ministry."[16]

In the same issue of *A Witness and a Testimony* Sparks clarifies further the nature of the testimony that was being borne by those at Honor Oak. His writing at this point was an attempt to make clear the stand of exactly what those at Honor Oak were expressing. After one year of experience of bearing such a testimony, many Christians misunderstood what was going on. Some Christians wanted to "join" what was going on at Honor Oak and other groups and missions wanted to establish a "connection" to them in order to carry out a certain service or mission. Mr. Sparks made it clear that there was nothing to "join" and that neither was there any "connection" which could be made. The fellowship was nothing more than the fellowship between all Christians created by virtue of Christ's redeeming work on Calvary. It was not exclusive, it was not detached, it was not a new sect, it was not a new denomination, and it was not a new movement. "The 'Fellowship' does not imply or suggest anything more than that basic and progressive oneness of all the Lord's people as members of His spiritual and heavenly Body: a oneness which is created by the Holy Spirit—not man—even the oneness of life as of an organism and not an organization, and which is only realized or maintained by progressive unveiling of Christ. There is obedience and a continuous application of the cross to all that hinders spiritual growth."[17]

Other Christians believed that the fellowship at Honor Oak constituted a new sect because of two practices found among the brethren there: believer's baptism and the laying on of hands. This misconception shows how much practices can divide and separate the Body of Christ. To this misunderstanding Sparks first addresses what these things mean. Baptism was the practical testimony of the believer's identification with Christ and the laying on of hands was the practical testimony of the one anointing that was upon the whole Body of Christ. However, what made these things not divisive was that, to the believers at Honor Oak, these practices were not ordinances, rites, or sacraments. They were simply practical testimonies of the truths. The practices were not in any way meant to divide their fellowship; "they are no part of a constituted system by which we mechanically include or exclude any of the Lord's children."[18] They were not to become points of insistence and of imposition upon other believers. They were only to be taken up by believers who felt an inward compulsion by the Spirit to so do. It was in this way, i.e. by not insisting, that the believers at Honor Oak sought to preserve their fellowship with all the members of the Body. Thus, they could remain faithful to their calling to speak out a mature word for the building up of the Body of Christ.

There was something unique about the testimony that was borne by the believers at Honor Oak. What was unique about their position was that they felt called by the

Lord to bear a specific testimony in this age. Concerning this testimony Sparks writes,

> It will be accepted and acknowledged by all that from time to time God does raise up an instrument and prepare for Himself a voice by which he would give special emphasis and call special attention to truth that is basic and vital to the realization of His eternal purpose in Christ; Truth which has been lost sight of and for want of which there is not only a spiritual paralysis, ineffectiveness, and arrest at a certain point, but also the giving of the advantage to a mal-development and a false system which does not issue in the fulfillment of the purpose of the ages.
>
> We believe that the Lord has raised up such a voice in this testimony by which He would call His people back to or on into His own full meaning of the Cross of the Lord Jesus, and of His own real conception of and intention concerning the Church— the Body of Christ."[19]

After a year of occupying the premises at Honor Oak, these were the points that Mr. Sparks felt would address the confusion among Christians concerning their testimony and to positively put forward exactly what the fellowship was testifying. It was a ministry to the entire Body, and it was the highest desire of the members to not frustrate that ministry by any act or appearance of divisiveness or exclusiveness. In fact, while they were laboring for the commitment given to them by the Lord they were also supporting other Christian endeavors, both through prayer and through the involvement of those from the fellowship. They frequently mention other ministries which they held in prayer and they also sent many young people to Bible Schools for further training in the ministry. Concerning this Jeffreys writes "Our ministry is in and thus to the whole Body of Christ, and while we hold to the specific testimonies He has given, we would not be cut off from any of His redeemed people."[20] The members at that time were full of expectation that the Lord would gain oneness among all believers by calling out more and more to live a similar testimony of the cross and the reality of the Lord's desire, His Body.

At this time, Mr. Sparks sought a place away from the English winter in order to more fully recover from his operation. He went to the island of Malta. While he was there, he was struck by a recurrence of his physical problem and was again taken into the hospital. George Paterson, who was now very busily engaged in the administrative affairs of the Center, traveled to Malta to aid Mr. Sparks in his distress and to further help him, by the presence of a familiar face, in his recovery. Mr. Sparks returned by Easter of that year, partially recovered and able to attend the Easter conference, although not yet strong enough to minister. After his return, the only possible avenue of communication for Mr. Sparks could be found in writing brief messages that would appear in *A Witness and a Testimony*. It was not until August of that year that Mr. Sparks fully regained his strength to the point that he could minister at the August conference, which took place over the long bank holiday. Throughout the time of Mr. Sparks' incapacitation, the needs of the wider ministry were being met by the brothers the Lord had raised up to give an experiential message of the cross, like George Paterson, Edwin Goodwin, A. S. Crowe, Victor Thomas, Gresham Speedy, brother Oliphant and of course T. Madoc Jeffreys.

In June of 1928 the calls for ministry from outside the Center became almost constant and were not able to be answered fully. The Lord was raising up more from within the fellowship to meet the need of many hungry seekers for the word of the cross. Conferences began to be held in Northern Ireland. And more consistent, regular gatherings for ministry were being established in many places in Britain that the brothers had been only intermittently visiting. The needs everywhere were growing. The fellowship also undertook a more definite gospel work at Swalwell, near Newcastle. Additionally, the weekly and monthly conferences continued under the rich ministering of these same brothers. Together the brothers upheld a rich realization that the testimony of the cross and the Body of Christ did not depend on one man alone, but could be borne by those raised up by the Lord in the local assembly to meet His needs.

The Fuller Meaning of the Cross of Christ

Nineteen twenty-eight proved to be another significant spiritual advancement for Theodore Austin-Sparks. His new realization may have taken place during his sickness and near death experiences, where he had much time to consider his life and work before the Lord. Or it may have come after August, when he was back at Honor Oak ministering on the cross of Christ. It may also have come in August of that year, when he decided to fully publish his messages on *The Centrality and Universality of the Cross of Christ*. Whenever it was during that year, Mr. Sparks referred to his new realization of the meaning of the cross as a turning point in his ministering. After this point, Mr. Sparks felt that he could no longer speak simply because he was scheduled to speak. From this point onward, he could only speak if the Lord led him

to speak and gave him the words to speak. In 1940 he
shared this testimony,

> It was after years of Bible teaching,
> evangelical ministry, and other Christian
> activities that the Lord brought me to see,
> as I have never seen, the fuller meaning of
> the cross of Christ. Gradually it became
> clearer and clearer that the cross was God's
> starting-point for everything that He
> planned to do. It is the starting-point be-
> cause the cross of Christ is not an end in
> itself, but rather the beginning of every-
> thing. As regards its objective meaning I
> had no reason for adjustment because the
> great values of the Lamb slain for our sins
> was already an established foundation. I
> knew the reality of the righteousness which
> is by faith in Jesus the righteous One who
> offered himself without spot to God for us.
> My appreciation of that has never ceased to
> grow and today is stronger than every.
>
> Atonement by Jesus' substutionary
> death is an essential foundation for faith
> but much more needs to be said. What Je-
> sus did on our behalf destroyed an outward
> bondage, our involvement in the doom of
> the world, but there still remained an in-
> ward bondage. Like Israel in the wilder-
> ness we are indeed God's people: re-
> deemed, yes, heirs of promise, yes, but
> never getting very far. We remain ineffec-
> tive, unfruitful, living an up-and-down ex-
> istence, always looking at the life-sense
> and even sometimes looking back regret-
> fully to Egypt. It is an oddly inconsistent

state for people who are sure they were redeemed by God. A bias to sin is always there.

It was the sense of despair from repeated failure that led to the discovery of the fuller meaning of the cross. Thus it happened that I turned in my need to Romans chapter six and saw, almost as if someone were saying it audibly, 'When I died, you died. When I went to the cross I not only took your sins but I took you, and I not only took you as the sinner that you might regard yourself to be, but I took all that you are by nature—your good as well as your bad, your abilities as well as your disabilities, yes every resource of yours. I took you totally, as a Christian worker, a preacher, an organizer. My cross means that not even for me can you be or do anything out from yourself. If there is to be anything at all it must come from me. That means a life of absolute dependence and faith.'

Let me now take you back twelve years to 1928, to a moment when all of the above was transformed from a mental grasp in to a devastating experience of reality in my personal life. Prior to that time I preached and taught these truths of God's great movement in history, centered in the crucifixion, death, burial and resurrection of Christ, crucial to all the Bible's other doctrines, and fundamental to our Christian lives, both for forgiveness and for deliverance from the destructive power of our sinful natures.

The day came, in that fateful year
of 1928, when all that sound head knowledge rose up like an enormous poleax and
hit me between the eyes, leaving me as
good as dead. I was brought to the point
where the door was shut on all the past and
the key was turned in the lock. Without
something new from God I could not go
on. In that anguished hour I came to see
what the cross of Christ means in reality.
All the boasted Bible knowledge, all the
main lines along with myself were smitten
and floored, and in that day there was an
end. I knew I had to tell my church elders
that I could no longer preach just because I
was paid to do so, or because it had been
planned and my name was publicized.
From now on I would speak only if God
gave me a message and the words to say
it.[21]

It is hard to say what the immediate impact of this
subjective realization of the cross had on Mr. Sparks' ministry. He continued that year giving conferences entitled
"The Meaning and the Message of the Cross" and "The
Cross, and the Release of the Holy Spirit in Service." He
published, in book form, the series of messages he had
given the previous fall called "The Centrality and Universality of the Cross." Mr. Sparks also spoke a series of
messages at this time that were to become a masterpiece
of his works entitled *The Release of the Lord.* However,
the long term impact of this experience on Sparks' ministry was surely great. After this point, he would begin to
testify that he had the sense that he was speaking under
"an opened heaven." Previously, he felt many times that
what the Lord showed him in his spirit could not be ut-

tered or conveyed freely to his audience. Afterward, he possessed a new-found liberty to speak exactly what God had shown him in his own heart. Now his speaking had no other motive, not for glory, not for career, not for advancement, not due to others' advice. His speaking found liberty because it was given over completely to God. If God gave him a message, and gave him words to speak, then Mr. Sparks would speak. If God did not, then he would not speak. With such dependence there was liberty under an "opened heaven."

Jeffreys Leaves and the Lord Provides

In October 1928, many calls from both near and far came to the Center asking for ministering of the rich message of the cross and the Body of Christ. Mr. and Mrs. Jeffreys took the unusual step of leaving the Center to engage in an extended period of ministry in Holland. The reports that came back were extremely positive, causing much praise to be given to the Lord. Jeffreys ministered in quite a few centers around Amsterdam and reported that there was an earnest hunger for the word and also that nine believers decided to take the step of being baptized. In November Mr. Jeffreys' presence was sadly missed at the monthly gathering because he was on a further ministry trip, this time in Ireland. In December, he felt led to return to Holland to continue the work that the Lord accomplished through his first visit there. This was to be his withdrawal from the fellowship and from his responsibilities at Honor Oak. In the March issue of *A Witness and a Testimony*, a notice appears concerning Mr. Jeffreys. "As many are making enquiry we feel that we should let friends know that our brother, Mr. Jeffreys, has felt it necessary to withdraw from us. This is a matter of no little regret to us and we have done everything in our power to make it otherwise, but without avail. Our brother continues to have a place in our heart and prayers."[22]

The exact reason for Jeffrey's leaving is not clear. Perhaps the pressure of carrying the ministry during Mr. Sparks' frequent illnesses was too much. Perhaps the work in Holland and the doors the Lord was opening through him were a great call to him. Perhaps it was simply that the Lord led him and his family away at this time. Surely this must have been a loss for Mr. Sparks. Jeffreys had been with Sparks from the Honor Oak Baptist days and had led the congregation side by side with Mr. Sparks to take the step of faith in leaving their Baptist denomination. Together they had established the clear vision of the testimony at Honor Oak. Together they had set forth a strong message of the cross and the oneness of the Body of Christ. Together they testified that their oneness was something of the Lord's doing. Sparks clearly was thankful to the Lord for the ministry of Mr. Jeffreys, which he felt met so many needs, especially during the frequent illnesses when Sparks himself could not minister. Mr. Jeffreys was the chief editor of *A Witness and a Testimony*. He wrote monthly articles concerning the ministry and the fellowship at Honor Oak. Over half the messages appearing in the 1928 edition of the journal were spoken by Mr. Jeffreys. Surely his leaving was a great loss for Mr. Sparks.

But the Lord provided more and more brothers and sisters to rise up to fill the loss of Mr. Jeffrey's portion. In fact, in 1929 even more were added to the fellowship at Honor Oak and even more were called out to be trained at the Center. It was a sign that their testimony did not depend on one man or a group of men but was out of the Lord's working in the assembly. The Lord would raise up those He needed to meet His current need. Through all this, Mr. Sparks was a prominent figure, mainly because of his greater gift of ministering and his great clarity of

what the testimony of Honor Oak was standing for. However, one does not get the sense that he was the center of
what was going on. One gets the sense that the center was
the Lord Himself and that as the Lord of the harvest He
could raise up and thrust out workers into the great field
of the world to meet the need of the hungry.

There were changes after Jeffreys left, especially
to *A Witness and a Testimony*. It went from a monthly
journal to a bi-monthly journal. The "ministers' letter"
was discontinued, to be replaced by infrequent "letters
from the editor" signed by Mr. Sparks. The cover, which
previously displayed a globe and a cross inside two open
doors, now was changed every issue to reflect the current
theme. A new section entitled "For Girls and Boys" was
started as a way to share the gospel to young people
through many stories and illustrations. Other messages
from great teachers, not from Honor Oak, regarding the
cross were included in almost every issue. Every issue in
1929 contained an article on the fundamentals of the experience of the cross by A. J. Gordon. The two great series, which were later to become books, and that appeared
in the 1929 edition were, "The Release of the Lord" and
"God's Reactions."

Between 1929 and 1939 the fellowship at Honor
Oak grew. A good number of young men who were gifted
by the Lord in various ways felt led to join the fellowship.
A number of these brothers passed through a period of
training at Honor Oak and a number more began to join
the band of brothers ministering and speaking out the
message concerning God's desire for a corporate Body. It
was not a mushrooming movement, but the fellowship had
a steady increase, as the Lord added. In September of
1929 messages by Brother Alexander began to appear in *A
Witness and a Testimony*. In December Mr. Frank Davies
began a weekly ministering time in Newcastle at the request of the local brothers and sisters there. During the

month of January 1931, Mr. Faunch, Mr. David Davies and Mr. Paterson were all among those planning to minister along with Mr. Sparks. Harry Foster, a brother who would stay and serve with Mr. Sparks until Mr. Sparks' death in 1971, was met in 1931 and was sent off by the fellowship to South America as a missionary. He returned to London a few years later and his first of many messages appears in *A Witness and a Testimony* in September of 1935. C. J. B. Harrison felt led to add himself to the fellowship and work at Honor Oak. He was to become a close co-worker of Mr. Sparks until his death in the 1960s. His first message appears in the January 1939 issue of *A Witness and a Testimony*.

Generally these brothers were young men when they came to the fellowship. The message being sounded out from Mr. Sparks and others was more than a simple heaven and hell gospel. It was something that caused these young men to see something to which they could give their whole lives. As they eventually grew up and got married, many continued serving in the same way with their families. Brother Oliphant married a sister from Syria and continued to serve with his family. Mr. Speedy met his wife on one of his trips to New York. They got married and moved to Ethiopia to preach the gospel. Overall, Mr. Sparks had a way of raising up many young men to serve the Lord and to be useful to the Master.

In January of 1930 there was another group of young brothers ready for a period of training at the Honor Oak Center. These trainings were not constantly being held; they were held according to need, when the Lord would so lead people to give themselves. In 1930 these trainees testified "We are a happy little band of those who have our faces set to His glory wherever He may appoint. The 'training' is intensive but full of life, and rather than have to set ourselves with effort to do the work we find ourselves in a rich and deep stream which carries us on."[23]

These trainings produced people who desired to go on with the Lord. As the principle of the training was to always have a definite spiritual application in view, part of the training of young workers involved giving them a definite field of labor in which to learn. There were opportunities for traveling to other places to minister and to preach the gospel. These times would be as much for the brothers' learning as they were to accomplish anything in those they met. One such example was a caravan of five brothers that set out in June of 1931. They visited towns to fulfill different ministry engagements, they spoke in missions, they held open air gospel meetings, they distributed tracts and they visited people from house to house. The brothers posted signs on their cars like "In Christ...No Condemnation" and "In Christ...a New Creation" and "Seek Ye the Lord While He May Be Found." A write up in *A Witness and a Testimony* comments, "Not the least valuable part of such a period of ministry is the education of the workers themselves in spiritual discipline, and our brethren have borne their testimony to the very great blessing that they themselves have received along this line—precious fruit that will yet yield more in the days to come when, if the Lord wills and tarries, these brethren will go forth into wider spheres of activity at His bidding. How much there is of practical spiritual knowledge that can only be acquired in the school of hard experience."[24]

At Honor Oak these brothers found fertile soil for their growth in the Lord and for their development in becoming servants of God. Under the brothers who were their mentors and who had gone before them and who had considerably advanced in the knowing of the Lord, these young men found a rich supply of the word, clarity of the burden of the Lord, many opportunities for prayer, and plenty of fields open for them to learn Christ "in the school of hard experience."

Many Missionaries Receive Help at Honor Oak

Not only were young men and women raised up during this time to meet the need of ministering at Honor Oak and in other parts of the United Kingdom, but many, many missionaries were in fellowship with the brothers at Honor Oak. There were no formal arrangements of support at the fellowship Center, nor was there a plan devised by a mission board to send people to certain places. It was all under the spontaneous and somewhat free leading of the Spirit. Many missionaries returned to England for rest and found real spiritual renewal while residing at the Center's guest house and enjoying the frequent ministry gatherings at Honor Oak. These would return to the mission fields invigorated and charged by a new seeing of the Lord and His purpose. Many others, who began following the Lord with the fellowship at Honor Oak, eventually felt a call to set out to many different countries in order to preach the gospel. This entire process and spread was without arrangement and mostly based on the inward leading of the Spirit. It was the spontaneous result of the rich feeding on the spiritual food served so often during the ministering times at Honor Oak. Just like when a child is well fed, he can do well at school and live an active life, the spontaneous result of the believers being well fed is seeking the Lord and action taken for the Lord.

One example of what happened to a missionary who was resting at Honor Oak suffices to give the flavor of such respites.

As a missionary on my first furlough, to whom the Lord has given two months here at the Fellowship Center for a time of waiting upon Him, there is a deep desire in my heart to bear witness to what the Lord has made this time mean. This testimony has

not been asked for but is quite a spontaneous 'overflow' in the Lord....I praise God
for a new, fuller vision of our Lord Jesus,
our Sovereign Lord, as the One with a
strong, strong love for that which is wholly
according to God—a new revelation of the
object of that love—even that ultimate object—'the city'—'the house of God'—
'God's   people'—'God's   dwelling
place.'...So, God willing, I return to Africa
after this furlough, with a new vision, a
new impetus, a new everything, for I return
with a new reality of WHO the Lord is.
The Lord, who reigned, beholds His inheritance in the nations—May He have more
full possession, yea, complete possession of
His rights, His inheritance in me, in all of
His 'sent ones' that through us he may take
out of the nations a people for His name,
and build them up together with us, for a
'habitation of God in the Spirit,' that He,
our Precious Lord, may see of the travail of
His soul and be satisfied—even according
to the Eternal Purpose which God purposed
in Christ Jesus, our Lord.[25]

Such a testimony was not uncommon among missionaries who sought respite at Honor Oak. They returned
to the mission field with a fresh charge and a new vision
of who Christ is and what He wants, i.e. a house to dwell
in. Additionally, they returned with the strong prayer support of many faithful brothers and sisters at Honor Oak.
This, perhaps more than any other thing, became a rich
supply and blessing to them and to their labor.

Spontaneous Expansion

The phrase "spontaneous expansion" seems an apt description for the spread of the fellowship at Honor Oak to much of the world. In a few short years a small fellowship that felt led by the Lord to leave their denominational distinctions to begin a small testimony in non-descript South East London suburb gained a fellowship of believers in almost every country on the face of the earth. It was all done with no advertisement, no propaganda, and no call for workers. It was all done based on the move of the Holy Spirit Himself. It was almost a prophetic fulfillment of a series of messages spoken by Sparks in 1928 entitled *The Release of the Lord*. In that series, Sparks compared the spread of the church in Acts with the spread of the churches at the present time. In Acts there was never a record of one believer telling another believer to preach the gospel. It happened spontaneously and powerfully. There were no mission boards, no organization of workers, no campaigns for the preaching of the gospel. It was a spontaneous outflow of exalting Christ as the Head and of being filled with the Holy Spirit. Mr. Sparks remarks,

There is no precedent in the New Testament for appealing for workers or missionaries. This is at best a sorry alternative or necessity. When the Holy Spirit is really in possession and the life is manifested then He takes the initiative in all work and worker, saying 'Separate Me....unto the work whereto I have called them.' Great emphasis is laid in the New Testament upon receiving the Holy Spirit. The Holy Spirit is the Spirit of the universally Sovereign Lord—'The Heir of all things.' His mission is world-wide, kosmic. To have Him Lord within must inevitably result at once in world-vision, world passion, world vocation. It cannot be otherwise....The Lord's purpose and method in this age is to bring into resurrection union with Himself two or three in every place and 'add unto them such as are being saved.' It is an accretion of life, not enticement, 'attraction,' advertisement. Here again the Holy Spirit takes the initiative when a true testimony is borne. The greatest need of the hour is a revitalizing of the Lord's people with His Risen Life by the Holy Spirit. May they soon see it and come to the place where everything— tradition, system, common acceptance, forms and molds, prejudices, personal interests, reputation, prestige, compromise, the opinions of others, policy, etc. will be sacrificed, if needs be, for LIFE, and the true and living.[26]

So, without any direction, gathering of workers, advertisement or mission boards the following spread took place between 1929 and 1935. More countries may be included but they at least included these missions. Mr. A. S. Crowe moved to India in January of 1929. Mr. Douty, after spending almost half a year at Honor Oak, moved back to the USA and established a house of ministry called Hephzibah House in New York in March of 1929. Miss Gow moved to India in March of 1929. Ruth Rogers, a missionary to Lebanon, and Mr. Gallimore, a missionary to Italy, shared with the fellowship in the summer of 1929. The brothers visited Scotland in July of 1929. Mr. Oliphant held an extended time of ministry in Syria in July of 1929. Miss Marcovitch moved back to

Serbia in July of 1929. Mr. Oliphant traveled to Lebanon in July of 1929. Mr. and Mrs. Holloway were commended to the Lord by the fellowship at Honor Oak upon the eve of the travels to Sudan for missionary work in September of 1929. These two were members of Willesden Green Baptist Church, but enjoyed fellowship in Spirit with the brothers and sisters at Honor Oak. Miss Cowie, who had spent some time at the Center, was sent back to India in October of 1929. Mr. Oliphant visited Jerusalem and Egypt in December of 1929. Miss Grace Bard was sent off to Nyassaland (currently called Malawi) in January of 1930. Brothers Speedy and Harper held a conference for young people in Ireland in January of 1930. A sister who we only know as I. R. was sent back to Africa, after a two months furlough at Honor Oak, in March of 1931. Mr. and Mrs. Harry Foster were sent off to Columbia, South America, in September of 1931. Miss Sinclair was sent off to Spain in November of 1931. Mr. and Mrs. Speedy, recently married, were sent off to labor in the gospel in Addis Ababa, Ethiopia in September of 1932. Mr. Yankowski was engaged in a gospel work in Poland and was in close fellowship with the Center in December of 1932. Brothers Graham and Birbeck moved to Quibdo, South America in December of 1932. Miss Sinclair began laboring with Sister Margaret and Mr. and Mrs. McKay in Spain in March of 1934. Miss Agnes Milne joined Mr. and Mrs. Speedy in Abyssinia in March of 1934. Misses Clarke, Featherstone and Taylor were in Shanghai China and were in fellowship with an assembly of Chinese Christians in Shanghai in March 1934.

In addition to the spread of the fellowship throughout the world by missionaries, a number of indigenous Christian groups began to have more fellowship with the brothers and sisters at Honor Oak between 1929 and 1939. These included brothers from China, France and India. Watchman Nee, a brother who was raised up by the Lord in China and who established many local assemblies of Chinese Christians (including the one that Sisters Clarke, Featherstone and Taylor fellowshipped with in Shanghai) visited Honor Oak first in 1933 for a short time. He came for about a week at that time and was not able to meet Mr. Sparks, who was out of town engaged in ministry. He later came to visit for almost one year in 1938 and was hosted by the fellowship at Honor Oak. During that year, he spent significant time with Mr. Sparks, he ministered often at the Center and he visited other places in Europe for ministry. Many of his messages appear in subsequent issues of *A Witness and a Testimony*. Brother Jacot of France also had a very intimate relationship with the brothers at Honor Oak. Since 1926, Mr. Sparks had visited France and gave a series of messages at the Dieulefit conference. This resulted in quite a hunger for the word developing among the Christians there. Brother Jacot shared with the fellowship at Honor Oak about the history of the recent work of the Spirit among the Christians in France and he looked forward to yearly extended visits by Mr. Sparks. Many brothers and sisters associated with the fellowship at Honor Oak went to India, where they came into fellowship with groups of native Christians. One group that had particularly sweet and close fellowship with these brothers was raised up by Brother Bakht Singh. This group maintained a very close fellowship and contact with the brothers at Honor Oak.

The frequent conference gatherings at Honor Oak also were means to reach the world. Many of these gatherings attracted attendees from all over Britain and from many different countries. In early 1929 it was recorded that conferences had representatives from Scotland, Wales, France, Switzerland, India, Africa, China and the USA. In the summer of that same year Syria, South America, Serbia, Canada, and Italy were added to the growing international representation. Brothers from

Honor Oak also held conferences for ministry away from the home base. These places included Dunoon, Scotland; Syria; Mazemet, France; Greystones, Ireland. In all ways it seemed that the kosmic world-wide vision was being lived out in the exercise of the fellowship at Honor Oak.

The result of the traffic between Honor Oak and the many countries in fellowship was that publications began to spread. The missionaries who received timely help during their furloughs at Honor Oak returned to the mission field with a new vision and with Witness and Testimony publications. The result was that by the end of 1939 *A Witness and a Testimony* had readers in almost every country on earth and some countries had more than a few subscribers. In 1928 a list of contributions toward the maintenance of the publication of *A Witness and a Testimony* included cities from England, Ireland, and Scotland and from one city in the USA. In comparison, a 1939 list of countries from which gifts came includes cities in Australia, Ireland, England, USA, Ceylon, China, Denmark, Scotland, Holland, Hong Kong, India, New Zealand, Switzerland and Canada. The range of distribution was wide, but the number never was large. In 1959, at the peak of distribution of the magazine, a total of about 3000 copies were mailed out each issue.

In addition to subscribers to the English version of *A Witness and a Testimony* other Witness and Testimony literature was translated or otherwise made available by Christians in different countries. In September of 1932, Brother Jacot of France began translating and publishing the French edition of *A Witness and a Testimony,* which was called *Christ Our Life.* The brothers and sisters who traveled to India found such a demand for the literature there that they established a house in India from which literature from Honor Oak could be distributed. In November of 1936 application for literature could be made to Mr. F. Young at The Soldiers' Home, Wellington, Nilgiris

Hills, South India.   In China, Watchman Nee translated
several titles of Mr. Sparks into the Chinese language.
These included the titles *The Meaning of the Gospel, The
Three Main Principles of the Cross, A Manifested Mystery, Victorious Life is a Real Fact, Resurrection Life and
the Body of Christ.*[27]

Widening Ministry Under the Lord's Dealing Hand

The flow of people and literature from Honor Oak
opened up a worldwide ministry to the brothers in the
Christian Fellowship Center.   Mr. Sparks, healthier now
than before, also began to travel more widely to give conferences and to meet with small groups of believers who
were attracted by the taste of the riches they received
through the literature.   In 1929 Mr. Sparks traveled
throughout the United Kingdom and to Continental
Europe to fulfill conference ministry, usually in coordination with other brothers.   In September of 1929 Mr.
Sparks held conferences in Dunoon, Scotland where he
took as his theme the eternal purpose in Christ and examined both the personal and corporate aspects.   From
Dunoon he traveled to Mazaret, France where a few hundred believers gathered and where Mr. Sparks took the
afternoon sessions to share about the specific thing which
is in God's mind.   In October, Mr. Sparks went to Dublin,
Ireland for another time of ministry where he shared on
"the persistent purpose and the specific method of God."
Others, including Dr. Pace of the USA and Mr. R. B.
Jones and Mr. Douglas Brealey, shared on topics supportive of this general theme.

As the Lord was using the instrument, He was also
working on it, as a potter works to shape the clay according to his desire.   It was this realization that governed Mr.
Sparks' December 1929 review of the first three years of
the fellowship at Honor Oak.   In the midst of the growth

and expansion of the work, the greatest work was done by
God "without hands" on the very instrument through
which He was operating. Of the first three years Sparks
writes

> With this issue of the Witness and Testi-
> mony we complete three years since we
> came into the 'Center.' The story of these
> three years will be better written if reserved
> until it finds its setting in the larger period
> and purpose. While the work and message
> has in that time become world-wide, so that
> there are very few lands into which the
> message has not gone and is not being ea-
> gerly sought after, and while there are
> many other phases of divine blessing and
> attestation, we are mostly conscious that
> the clay has been on the wheel during that
> period. Pressure, cutting, elimination, and
> many other methods have been employed
> by the Potter to shape and conform this
> vessel to a greater meetness for His use.
> He has worked—as He ever does—in the
> light. We have sometimes only been con-
> scious of the mystery and of our own in-
> ability to know what He was doing.
> Withal, the supreme recognition has been
> that His hand held us ON the wheel. We
> have not been without a conviction of the
> necessity for much of this divine activity;
> rather has the conviction very often been a
> strength to endure. Now, however, we
> have reason to believe that this first cycle
> of preparation is issuing in a fuller, freer
> and more definite ministry. It is a tremen-
> dous story is the story of those three years;

but, as we have said, the issues have to justify it, and the telling must therefore await
the setting in the larger story. When that
time comes, be it in time or eternity, we are
assured that it will be the occasion for mar-
veling at the wonderful work and ways of
God, and it will be to His glory abundantly.
If ever three years have been packed full
with education, these three have been for
us, and we are quite certain that the
Church—the Body of Christ—is to be
greatly enriched by it. God's method of
education is always experimental, never
theoretical. It is costly, therefore valuable.
Salvation is free, but the truth has to be
bought. 'Buy the truth and sell it not.' If
God takes pains and does not leave us in
His contempt apart we may take it that
great issues are at stake. Thus we confi-
dently believe that after three days there
will be a reviving and a new loosing.
There is 'a sound as of a going,' and we
believe 'the Lord has gone forth.'[28]

It was true that the decade of the thirties witnessed
a great spread in the message of the testimony. Much of
this spread was due to the work God had done and was
indeed still doing in the vessels he was preparing for His
use. Throughout the thirties, the ministry of the Word became far richer and the vision could be expounded far
clearer than before. Seeds were sown that were to become
testimonies to the specific work God was accomplishing
through the testimony at Honor Oak.

In May of 1930, Mr. Sparks embarked on his first
visit to America since the fellowship had moved to the
Center at Honor Oak. The way for his reception in Amer-

ica was paved by the subscribers to *A Witness and a Testimony* and by a particular brother, Mr. N. F. Douty, who spent about six months at Honor Oak and returned to America to establish a conference center for Christians named Hephzibah House at 51 West 75th St. New York City. Sparks' schedule for this first visit included ministries in Chicago, Boston, Michigan, Pittsburgh, Philadelphia, and conferences at Hephzibah Heights, Monterrey, and several days at the Canadian Keswick. We also know that during his visit to Boston he made it a point to visit Mary McDonough of Boston and to spend an afternoon with her. Mr. Sparks had received light from her book *God's Plan of Redemption.* The two began to have infrequent contacts at this point. Mary McDonough was to recommend Sparks' Journal to many young seeking Christians that she came into contact with.

Sparks' trip to America left an overall impression on him concerning the general state of Christians in the church at large. He lamented that there was overall a lack of "inwardness" among believers and that, in general, believers dealt with the many deep things concerning the Christian message in a very "superficial life." Mr. Sparks felt there was a need to have a corresponding deep life experience in order to truly handle and bring through the deeper things of God. He felt that this condition was not limited to the people in the states, but was surely exhibited by them. Furthermore, he felt that only through paying a price and through a certain amount of suffering could the situation be turned around. Only through cost can the fullness of God be attained.[29]

Mr. Sparks further outlined his views on the state of the church in the next issue of *A Witness and a Testimony.* He noted a common yearning that existed in many different Christians for a revival. But then he asked a difficult question, what kind of revival do most people want? And furthermore, how does this contrast with what kind of revival the Lord desires? Sparks notes that every time the Spirit moves it is toward the end of making things "more utterly according to Christ." Sparks comments on what this means in today's time and notes "Evangelism has become mainly a matter of getting men saved for the sake of their being saved. The 'deepening of spiritual life' has become a matter of having Christians sanctified. These and other things have become ends in themselves. In the New Testament it is not so. The Apostles and first Christians had a definite vision of a heavenly pattern for the fellowship of the Lord's people and their corporate vocation and everything was related to that. The end in view was not individualistic in any sense; it was the church conformed to Christ."[30] This was to be Spark's theme for his entire ministry.

After a period of further ministry close to home and most likely on the Continent, Mr. Sparks again sailed for America in June of 1931 with Mr. Speedy. Here he ministered and held conferences in Darby, Swarthmore, Hephzibah Heights and Grand Rapids. Before he could finish his full itinerary, Mr. Sparks became ill in the extreme heat of the summer and, because of his worsening condition, returned to London early for an extended period of rest and recovery.

After returning to England and recovering, Mr. Sparks, in fellowship with the brothers at Honor Oak, felt the need to acquire a property away from the Honor Oak Center that would be suitable for retreats and special times of fellowship. In December of 1931, the brothers acquired a conference center in Kilcreggan, Scotland. This was to become an oft used facility for summer conference gatherings, retreats with special guests for special fellowship, and longer trainings for desirous seekers of the Lord. From this time onward, a good portion of Mr. Sparks' ministry would be conducted at this northern conference center.

In the fall of 1932, Sparks spent three weeks on the continent, one week in Switzerland, one in Dieulefeit, and one in Paris. In Switzerland Sparks gave a joint conference with Pastor Imburg, which was well attended and which included a question session. In Dieulefeit Sparks attended the tenth annual convention with the "Brigade Missionare." He commented that the believers there were facing many problems due to the perplexity caused by certain religious movements that were gaining popularity in France. In Paris, Mr. Sparks was warmly welcomed by Pastor Urban and a group of Russian brethren. Here he shared on the resurrected Christ's relationship to the believers. In October, Sparks traveled with Mr. Alexander to the annual Y.M.C.A. convention in Dublin, Ireland for another session of ministry. Travels like these, in America and in Europe, were to become a regular custom for Mr. Sparks throughout the 1930s. His visiting and ministering became a source of spiritual life and encouragement to many who looked forward to his fellowship.

In 1933 Mr. Sparks wrote an editorial in *A Witness and a Testimony* describing what the Lord had done thus far and also hinting at some of the opposition that faced the testimony held by the brothers at Honor Oak. The stand that the brothers at Honor Oak took was that of becoming a ministry to the whole Body and to minister something that would bring in God's full thought concerning the church. However, because they had been standing apart from traditional Christian circles for over the past five years, suspicions and prejudice toward them had grown among God's people. Sparks writes, "It never was our thought or desire that this should be a center of a new organized movement or a new 'sect.' To this we most strongly adhere to this day, and always shall do so. We have many enemies, mostly amongst the Lord's people, and they seem to think that to say the opposite of what we have just said will injure us most."[31] It was not at all the desire of those at Honor Oak to lead a movement of leaving denominations, although many mistook this as their intent. The real intent was to have a fellowship with all of God's people and to encourage them to put Christ and the leading of the Spirit first, at any cost. If the Lord would so lead to leave denominations then so be it. But if not, the fellowship of seeking spiritual food together could still be very loving and unhindered.

This stand was becoming clearer and clearer within Mr. Sparks. Throughout the thirties, the clarity and stand of the testimony grew. At the same time, the opposition among other Christians throughout this decade also grew to unthinkable proportions. Mr. Sparks and the rest at the fellowship took the opposition as a suffering ordained by the Lord for their personal and corporate growth and perfecting. In spite of the opposition, the 1930s marked a great increase in worldwide readership of *A Witness and a Testimony* and the gathering of a good number, probably a few hundred, of God's seekers to join with the brothers there to hold forth this specific testimony.

In this same editorial, Mr. Sparks announced some changes that would be made to *A Witness and a Testimony*. Mr. Sparks decided to separate the spiritual messages conveyed in the paper from the news concerning the Honor Oak Center and the work. The goal of this separation was to present the message of the testimony purely, without any tainting from the knowledge of the success or advancement of the work. Mr. Sparks did not want people to become interested in the testimony being held forth by Honor Oak merely because so many others were receiving this ministry. Rather, Mr. Sparks desired that people would be drawn to Christ and to the message of the deeper life for the procurement of the Lord's desire of the corporate body. Because of this decision, there is a great void of information concerning the travels, inner feelings, and impressions of Mr. Sparks during the major part of the

1930s. It was not until World War II began that Mr. Sparks again began to write editorials containing his feelings and impressions of the work, of the Lord's current move and of the world situation, both inside and outside Christianity.

Because of this decision, we know little of Mr. Sparks' doings between 1933 and 1939. We know that conferences continued to be held at Honor Oak, although the monthly conferences were slowly phased out in favor of emphasizing the longer gatherings held on various holidays. Regular, large conferences were held on Easter, Whitsun and the August Bank Holiday. We also know that in November of 1934 Mr. Sparks held another conference in Switzerland. Besides this one, we surmise that Mr. Sparks continued his travels to America and the Continent until wartime conditions limited and restricted him to his base at Honor Oak.

Watchman Nee and T. Austin-Sparks

During the 1930s a relationship developed between Watchman Nee and T. Austin-Sparks. Watchman Nee was an eager reader of *A Witness and a Testimony* and had taken the step of translating at least five books of Mr. Sparks into Chinese. These included *The Meaning of the Gospel, The Three Main Principles of the Cross, A Manifested Mystery, Victorious Life is a Real Fact, Resurrection Life is a Real Fact.*[32] In 1933 Watchman Nee traveled to England as the guest of Charles Barlow, who was associated with a group that came to be known as a branch of the Exclusive Brethren. During Watchman Nee's visit to England, he took leave of his host for a week to conduct some business in London. On the Lord's Day, he visited Honor Oak in hope of meeting Mr. Sparks. At that time, Mr. Sparks was out of town attending a speaking engagement, but Watchman Nee enjoyed the ministry with the brothers and sisters at Honor Oak, broke bread with them, and had a good time of fellowship with George Paterson.[33] This visit, particularly his partaking of the Lord's Table at Honor Oak, was to become one of the issues that caused the Exclusive Brethren to eventually terminate their fellowship with Watchman Nee and the churches in China.

After his visit to Honor Oak, Watchman Nee spoke of Mr. Sparks in one of his conferences in China. In January 1934 Watchman Nee mentioned T. Austin-Sparks in a message entitled "What Are We," which he gave during his third Overcomer Conference. In that message Watchman Nee refers to T. Austin-Sparks who was previously a pastor in a Baptist chapel in London and comments that, "Later the Lord showed him different truths concerning the meaning of resurrection and the meaning of the church life."[34] Watchman Nee continued a description of what he himself, had received from the Lord up to that point in his ministry. He writes of himself, "Despite the above revelations, it was not until 1934 that we realized that the centrality of everything related to God is Christ. Christ is God's centrality and God's universality. All of God's plan is related to Christ. This is the truth that God is pleased to reveal to us in these days. It is also the message we are preaching during this conference. This is what God showed Brother Sparks also. He saw much of the truth concerning God's overcomers."[34] Later in his message Watchman Nee refers to the responsibilities that he sees the churches in China bearing and of the testimony they are bearing in relation to Christ being preeminent in all things. He mentions that "Today this testimony can be found in America, England, France, Spain, Africa, and everywhere."[34] His reference here to England most likely was in reference to Mr. Austin-Sparks and the brothers at Honor Oak.

In 1938, Watchman Nee again visited the brothers at Honor Oak, this time for a more extended period. In that year Watchman Nee accompanied a few sisters from the China Inland Mission on their return to Europe. Upon arriving in England, he proceeded immediately to Kilcreggan to meet Mr. Sparks face to face, having previously only corresponded with him by mail. They took the train southward together and attended the Keswick Convention. It was here that Watchman Nee, who was suffering with the rest of his Chinese countrymen under the Japanese invasion, prayed neither for China nor for Japan but for the interests of God's Son both in China and in Japan. After Keswick, Watchman Nee returned to Honor Oak and used the fellowship center as the base for his visit. Here he talked with Mr. Sparks and the other leading brothers at Honor Oak. Watchman Nee was then invited to Denmark, where he gave series of messages that were to become the books "The Normal Christian Life" and "Sit, Walk, Stand." Upon returning to Honor Oak, he felt that he should spend more time with his "friend and counselor," T. Austin-Sparks, discussing their views on the practical outworking of the Body of Christ.[35]

After leaving Honor Oak, Watchman Nee received a telegram from China while he was in Paris. Upon receiving this telegram, Watchman Nee delayed his return in order to make an English translation of his recent book, "Rethinking the Work." He then returned to Honor Oak for four more months of fellowship with T. Austin-Sparks and the brothers there. In May of 1939, his book, "Rethinking the Work" appeared with another title "Concerning Our Missions" and had the Witness and Testimony imprint under the title.[36] The book, later published under the title "The Normal Christian Church Life," was of immediate interest to many missionary societies of the time. In May of 1939 Watchman Nee departed from

Honor Oak and was never again to see Mr. Sparks face to face.

Crucial Truths Unveiled Under an Open Heaven

The decade of the 1930s was a time when many foundational truths were spoken by Mr. Sparks. Quite a number of his books written during this period withstood the test of time and still convey clear revelations of many crucial truths. A brief look at the titles shows how Mr. Sparks advanced in revelation and in clarity during this decade. Mr. Sparks emphasized the experience and revelation of Christ in His vast dimensions. He portrayed Him not only as the individual redeemer and head of the Body, but also as the corporate Christ—"The Christ" as revealed in 1 Corinthians 12:13. His books of this decade unveil the Body Christ (1932), a thorough look at the believers' prayer life (1934), a heavenly expounding of the gospel of John (1935), Jesus Christ as the center of everything in this universe (1936), the eternal purpose of God—the corporate expression of His Son (1937), the vehicle of expression and representation of this corporate man—the local church (1938), and the composition of man as spirit, soul, body with God's full salvation in relation to all these items (1939). While we have little to say of Mr. Sparks' doings during this time, we can surely see his advancement in ministry, as he himself testified that he was speaking under an opened heaven. We encourage the reader to take note of the summaries of his books from this time period recorded in the last chapter of this book. The regular gatherings for ministry at Honor Oak, especially during the longer conferences, provided the setting for this spiritual food to be released for the benefit of the listeners and of the entire Body even up to the present time.

Wartime Interlude
1940-1947

The fiery tumults of World War II drastically altered life for the little company of believers at Honor Oak and for Theodore Austin-Sparks. On September 3, 1939 Britain, along with France, Australia and New Zealand, declared war on Germany. This war would soon claim millions of lives, uproot even more, and would change the political landscape of the entire globe.

Another effect that directly affected the fellowship at Honor Oak was that for many people all over the world, traveling was first limited and then no longer possible. Outwardly, the worldwide fellowship that had grown from the little company at Honor Oak was greatly limited. In 1939 Mr. Sparks did not leave Great Britain. The 1939 *A Witness and a Testimony* includes announcements for ministry gatherings in Kilcreggan, Newcastle, Birmingham, Crawley, Sandown and, of course, Honor Oak. In 1940 through 1942 all the announced ministry gatherings were held at Honor Oak. The steady stream of believers from far off lands stopped; missionaries, speakers and servants of the Lord who once routinely frequented and enriched the fellowship at Honor Oak weathered the storm in their own lands. Conferences were no longer attended by seekers traveling from distant lands. Rather, the gatherings assumed a more local character and included some long term guests who, being displaced by the war, resided at the guest house. Impressive is the simple fact that the gatherings and the ministering continued for such a long time span during the war.

Man's work may stop or be disrupted, but God's work continues. Mr. Sparks writes in a 1944 editorial "We are never off the wheel as a vessel finished, but somehow the Lord combines the molding and the using."[1] Throughout the war, God never stopped using Mr. Sparks through his uninterrupted publishing of *A Witness and a Testimony* and through ministry at Honor Oak. Throughout the war, God also seemed never to have stopped molding Mr. Sparks and the company of believers at Honor Oak. During much of the war, Sparks' schedule was free from traveling and he had more time to consider, to read, and to ask questions. He writes that these years from November 1940 to November 1944 "have been the most agonizing years of my life, in which the bottom seems to have been touched many times."[2] Hemmed in, uncertain of the future, uncertain of the continuation of his ministry, uncertain of the duration of his human life, Mr. Sparks was being worked on by God to become a vessel more fit for the Master's use.

In his 1941 book, *The School of Christ*, Sparks writes how a fresh revelation of Christ is always bound up with a practical situation that the Lord has arranged for us. "You and I can never get revelation other than in connection with some necessity...We have to come into New Testament situations to get a revelation of Christ to meet the situation. So that the Holy Spirit's way with us is to bring us into living, actual conditions and situations, and needs, in which only some fresh knowledge of the Lord Jesus can be our deliverance, our salvation, our life, and then to give us, not a revelation of truth, but a revelation of the Person, new knowledge of the Person, that we come to see Christ in some way that just meets out need"[3] The war definitely brought Sparks into many situations that required a fresh revelation of the person of Christ to meet his present needs. His limitations on travel and ministry revealed a hidden Christ that would become food and light for the next decades of speaking.   Such experiences changed and deepened his ministry. A comparison of His ministry before and after the war reveals a growth and advancement of the minister. His message does not change. God's eternal purpose is still that—His eternal purpose. But the war wrought a greater ability into Mr. Sparks to clearly utter words describing the entrance to that purpose and concerning the experience of a person desirous to learn in the school of Christ. His messages become more than a clear, grand depiction of God's plan in Christ. They are as if the minister, who has passed through crises and depths with God, is speaking directly of his interaction with God in the process God led him through.   The messages contained in the book *The School of Christ* are clear examples of Mr. Sparks calling the reader into his realm and showing the way to enter. Threads of these utterances run through his subsequent messages on all sorts of topics. After the war, other books with similar themes followed.

In addition to the marked deepening and increase in experiential nature of Sparks' sharing, the war brought about another change in Sparks. He began to "take his pen and share" with his readers what he called "the exercise of my heart." Fellowship via traveling and many other forms of communication was severely limited at that time and updates on the situation at Honor Oak and with Mr. Sparks himself were needed to maintain fellowship with his many readers. This was a marked departure of his 1930s practice of not including personal notes in *A*

Witness and a Testimony. This departure was to remain for the rest of Sparks' life. After the war, many issues of his bi-monthly journal contain letters from the editor of an increasingly more personal nature. Before the war, the last note from Sparks appeared in January 1933. Here he included a letter from the editor describing some of his personal experiences in being led by the Lord out of his position as pastor to take up a testimony at Honor Oak. However, from March of 1933 to September of 1940 Sparks followed his principle of not including any personal references in his magazine. He desired simply to present the messages and revelations of Christ that he and others had seen and not let the reports of the work or the advancement of his ministry become a banner, attracting people to join a new "movement." However, the war situation became more acute. On July 10, 1940 the battle of Britain began, on August 23 German bombers dropped their first bombs on central London and on September 15 massive German air raids ravaged London, Southampton, Bristol, Cardiff, Liverpool and Manchester. At times the conference center at Honor Oak was ringed with fire to within a few feet. Sparks had no idea which issue of *A Witness and a Testimony* may be the last. He did not even know if the ones he sent out would reach his readers. In these conditions he abandoned his previous principle and wrote.

From his letters we gain insight into his views of the war, his thoughts about what God was trying to unveil through these massive worldwide convulsions and his thoughts about his own ministry in the context of such widespread disruption and destruction. Towards the end of the war, he gets even more personal in his letters and reveals some of his thoughts on his own experience in light of current events. It is enlightening to go through his letters year by year, piecing together Sparks' observations with the major world events and with the subjects he ministered at that time.

The Battle of Britain

1940 was the first full year that Britain was engaged in the war. During the first half of the year, the world watched as the Nazis, allied with Italy and in league with the Soviets, occupied Denmark, Norway, Netherlands, Holland, Luxembourg, Belgium and finally France. During the second half of the year, Britain felt the full force of German air raids, which were supposed to pave the way ultimately for the German invasion of Great Britain.

At Honor Oak, there was a great searching of heart before the Easter gathering of that year. The brothers felt hemmed in, not only by the world situation, but more so from obtaining a fuller liberty in the work of the Lord. They felt they needed a new spiritual position and thus gave themselves to prayer for one week before the Easter gathering. During the prayer, they felt the Lord pointing more and more to their own hearts as the barriers to greater fullness. The brothers gave themselves to putting right many things that grieved the Lord in their attitude and conduct and to seeking a greater fellowship with Him. Out of the prayer, the theme for the conference emerged which was "The heavenly calling, conduct and conflict of the church," based on the revelation given in Ephesians. The conference attendance was strong, the guest house was filled and the Lord's presence was rich throughout the whole weekend. Mr. Sparks ministered the whole time, supported by a number of brothers who were also exercised in the word along with him. Even though Mr. Sparks was experiencing another of his frequent illnesses, the Lord supplied him and gave him strength to speak the entire duration of the conference. A good summary of the

Lord's speaking throughout this gathering is, "If, when you were alone with the Lord, He came to you and said, 'My child, I have an immense piece of work for you, no less a piece of work than to be My agent to administer all My authority and moral glory in heaven and on earth throughout all the ages of the ages,' how would you feel? On the authority of the Word of God, I can say to you that He has said that to you."[4]

A few months later, during the Whitsun conference in May, the Lord released more messages concerning the responsibility of the Church to stand in the gap between the kingdom of God and the kingdom of Satan and to minister to God's glory. World events, looming ever more ominously, pressed the attendees to more earnestness and gave them a sense of finality. A strong feeling rose up that at this time the Lord must have a people in union with Him as their unique Head. He also needed people fighting the prayer battle, which is the church's supreme obligation while days remain. This gathering was anything but a routine, general assembly. Earnestness was worked into those who felt the privilege of being able to continue to gather with other believers to enjoy God's word and receive ministry.

The brothers and sisters held two more gatherings that year at Honor Oak, one was in July and the other in August. No more gatherings were announced or reported upon in the later 1940 issues of *A Witness and a Testimony*. By mid-August, the Nazis were bombing British factories and airfields, sending daylight air raids over London and other cities and establishing a naval blockade of all of the British Isles.

In September of 1940 Sparks writes that he does not know how many further issues of *A Witness and a Testimony* will be possible and that maybe this one will be the last. Under these conditions, he comments that now is the time of the one crucial test: "How much of all that we have is just teaching and interpretation; and how much is the Lord Himself, and of practical working value?"[5] He reminds his readers of the many times the brothers at Honor Oak have emphasized the oneness of the Body and that, because of the fact of this oneness, they would not be cut off from spiritual, prayer fellowship, even if other forms of communication are made impossible. He ends by giving a word to those not yet involved in the conflict, warning that if this conflict is related to the final Satanic battle for world domination (which may not necessarily involve any man as yet in view) then the world, specifically America, must get involved. This being the case, all the believers not yet facing the same conflict as those in London should ensure themselves now that the Lord Himself is their life and everything, and not merely "Christianity in any one or more of its mere externals." God's object is to make "spiritual people of believers; a spiritual church, a spiritual ministry, with a glorious spiritual consummation in rapture and the receiving of a spiritual body."[5] Because of this being his aim, Sparks took comfort that in the midst of this most severe test he had so little of "the material and temporal side of Christian work to lose." He concludes, "The measure of Christ is ultimately the criterion with God. The Lord give us all grace to abide *in Him* when all *things* crash around us."[5]

On September 3, Hitler planned operation Sea Lion, the invasion of Great Britain. By mid-September, in preparation for the invasion, the Nazi air raids over London and other British cities became massive. Due to the heroic acts of the Royal Air Force, in October operation Sea Lion was postponed until the spring of 1941. The preparatory air raids continued with periodic surges of intensity throughout the fall and winter.

In November Sparks again includes a letter in *A Witness and a Testimony*. He began, "I am writing this letter to you in the midst of the most acute situation."[6]

Some years later, he described how at that time Honor
Oak was ringed by fire to within two feet. He further described how much of Christian activity in its outward
forms had come to a halt and that even the gathering of
the Lord's people had become difficult. The difficulty
first was due to evacuations of hospitals, schools, etc. and
then was due to "destruction and assault." He asked what
all this means. And, more specifically, "What does the
Lord mean by it?" In this letter he tried to convey what he
believed was the divine meaning of all that was being allowed to transpire on the earth. He did not consider it a
kind of "emergency purpose" that God had in store for
just this time. Rather, he saw it as "the intensifying and
pressing home by these conditions of what has been the
first and pre-eminent thought of God since His Son
came." From the time Jesus came, God had desired true
worshippers to worship the Father in spirit and in truth.
Jesus said "The hour cometh and now is, when the true
worshippers shall worship the Father in spirit and in
truth." Sparks interpreted this as "the thought for this dispensation is that relationship with God, whether it be personal or corporate, individual or Church, shall not be a
matter of places, buildings, forms etc., but spiritual, a matter of 'he that is joined to the Lord is one spirit.'"[6] However, man's tendency and even his "persistent course" was
to "bring things down to earth, to make something of temporal power, reputation, glory, appearance. One result of
this has been to associate Christian life with outward customs, forms, places and activities as entirely to confuse
spirituality with these things."[6] At that time many of these
places were being destroyed and many of the outward
forms and customs were suspended indefinitely. The test
then was how much of the Lord they really had and how
much did they really know *Him*. "It will be just the measure of Christ in us that will decide the issue." Sparks
ended the letter, "Beloved, our spiritual fellowship re-

mains and will be of great value when earthly communications are suspended, and all things here are under eclipse."[6]

What Sparks meant by spiritual people and spiritual means and a spiritual church is not that believers become isolated, introspective and irrelevant to their surroundings. Sparks' meaning must not be taken only from his short letters but is more fully defined in his book "God's Spiritual House," which is a collection of messages spoken during this later part of 1940. His comments in this book describe that the issue confronting all was not merely the fall of London but the real possibility of the domination of the entire world by the German-Italian-Soviet-Japanese alliance. God wants a spiritual house, one that is practical in that it can be seen in the relationships among believers and testified by local representations of Christ in every place. But this spiritual house is not essentially dependent on earthly, temporal things. Its foundation rests in the spiritual interaction resulting from each individual being born of the Spirit and it grows as these individuals gather in spiritual relationships in the Body of Christ. Sparks gives an example in this book of how Watchman Nee, in the beginning of his stand for the churches in China, had a great exercise before the Lord concerning God's testimony there. After waiting and seeking the Lord, God added another and then another and continued until a testimony grew in that country.[7] The example was of a practical representation of Christ in every place growing out of a spiritual exercise before the Lord. Sparks comments that God's spiritual house thus formed cannot be torn down by earthly, temporal affairs, no matter how intensely they may rage.

1940 closed with a massive German air raid on London on December 29 and 30. Honor Oak remained untouched; the gatherings for prayer and ministry endured; and the little paper, *A Witness and a Testimony*, continued to reach many of its seeking readers.

The School of Christ

Nineteen forty-one began with continued Nazi bombing raids over London and other British cities. During the first half of the year, the Nazis expanded their empire to include control of Greece and Yugoslavia while many battles with British army units took place in the deserts of North Africa. Britain itself continued to front much of the full force of the Nazi air war machine. By midyear, after failing to gain control over the British air space, the Nazis indefinitely postponed operation Sea Lion, the land invasion of Britain. In June, the Germans began their invasion of the Soviet Union and thus began a two front war, which gave Britain, and more specifically London, some measure of relief.

Mr. Sparks' March letter from the editor expresses thanks for prayers and letters of appreciation and support from many readers of *A Witness and a Testimony*. The bond that Sparks felt with his readers went far beyond simply providing them with a magazine; he had personal acquaintance with many and he felt a sweet bond of fellowship with others. He remarks how a large number of friends in England who used to gather with the brothers and sisters at Honor Oak were scattered and could only be reached via letter. He also remarks how he longed to travel among them and visit for fellowship and building up. However, war time fuel restrictions prohibited him from doing so. In this limited state and in lieu of traveling to them, he reveals a bit of what the Lord had been exercising in his heart. Recently he had been dwelling upon the fact that God's family is the Church and local families are the churches. Churches are not companies constituted by a certain New Testament technique, or a certain doctrine or practice. Rather, families start from the inside (they can start with only two spiritually responsible ones), they grow by spiritual birth and organic oneness, their success is determined by their spiritual life and measure of Christ, and there is nothing professional, artificial or formal about any true family. Sparks asks the question if this fact may be the thing that God is getting at in allowing all the widespread disruption of the traditional framework of Christianity. God wants to get down to the fact that the Lord's true people are a family. This family is to arrive at God's goal of attaining spiritual fullness. "We are quite certain that spiritual fullness is only possible by emancipation from the artificial and man-made system of procedure which obtains today, and a return to the simple but powerful basis of organic life kept pure by the direct government of the Holy Spirit, as it was at first."[8]

The brothers at Honor Oak sought the Lord's leading as to whether or not to continue the Easter conference gathering. They felt an encouragement from the Lord to do so and were thankful to Him that He gathered such a large company of believers. Most were from England, but some were able to travel from Scotland and four other countries were represented—Bulgaria, France, Germany and Romania. With thankfulness the brothers and sisters also noted that by day and by night the skies were free from assaults and attacks during their gathering; before they came together, hostilities were severe and they recommenced after the weekend. Brother Harrison and brother Faunch began the conference with messages focusing on God's way of exulting Christ as the unique Head and on the cross being the means for us to know the Holy Spirit. Mr. Sparks then gave messages covering the revelation of the cross in the first five of Paul's epistles, Romans through Galatians.

After the conference, Mr. Sparks sought the Lord's will in how to occupy his time. Hemmed in by the war and rationing, he began to review writings by various authors expressing the feelings of Christians throughout history. His observation was that one common theme found expression in almost all of them: most thought that their time was the most ominous, foreboding time and that surely the Lord would come back soon. Now, facing the current drastic situation and contemplating the real prospect of world domination by an evil power, Sparks drew a parallel between Christians of history and Christians now. Now surely was an intensifying time as the age progressed and as Satan's time grew short. Surely, near the end, examples of antichrist's coming world domination were to become more and more severe. But then Sparks brought up this verse: "This gospel of the kingdom shall be preached in the whole world for a testimony unto all the nations and then shall the end come." The word testimony means "setting the evidence." But, Sparks asks, "Is the church as it is 'setting the evidence'?" In order for the end to come we cannot merely look at the outward situation, no matter how drastic it may be. God must have a testimony, a vessel to "set the evidence" before the end will come. In Sparks' observation the churches at the present time fall far short of setting the evidence and the Lord must therefore call out overcomers to meet His need. Sparks therefore issues a challenge to his readers to go the Lord, to have a deeper working of the cross in them, to enter into a spiritual travail for God's testimony. "Will you seek the Lord that there may be just where you are in the nations a vessel of this testimony and of this heavenly nature, which really does 'set the evidence'?"[9]

The Whitsun conference, a couple of months after Easter, came with no thought of suspending the gathering due to the war. The brothers were full of faith and very thankful to the Lord for His faithfulness and goodness. Throughout their gathering, the conditions were as if they were in peacetime and very little disturbance took place.

A good number, probably around 200, brothers and sisters attended and quite a few joined the conference for their first time. But the real joy of the time was a sweet and real sense of God's presence and recognition of hearing His voice. The emphasis of the gathering was "that the Lord's desire for all His people is the fullness of Christ, and that fullness is inescapably bound up with the true unity of the spirit in the Church—a unity not in doctrine but in love."[10] A living experience of this unity was sought in how to "be set on God's full thought and at the same time keep an open heart to all God's people."[10] The way for the fulfillment of this dream is the cross working in us, as seen in the apostle Paul's experience in Philippians. We, individually and corporately, are in a process of being brought out of bondage and into divine fullness. This journey is described in Paul's epistles where he details how our relationship should grow in Christ.

The theme of unity among Christians was constantly on Sparks' mind throughout the summer of 1941. In his July-August letter from the editor, Sparks took some time to again put forth the position and purpose of the testimony at Honor Oak. His dominating objective was "The fullness of Christ as the goal of all God's concerns for His people."[11] He sought to lay this out to allay fears and dispel mists of suspicion and prejudice that were continuing to grow concerning the ministry at Honor Oak. He reiterated that Christians were wary that the fellowship at Honor Oak was seeking to establish a new movement. However, Sparks had no desire to start a movement; he felt to never impose a system upon others or never obligate people to follow any practices in imitation of the fellowship at Honor Oak. He sought to have unity with all the believers. The uniting factor can only be the divine life and cannot be light (the seeing of a particular doctrine). If we make anything else besides life the uniting factor we will at once "divide and move apart." Sparks writes "there is all the difference between our telling people that they must do this and that in the matter of their connections and the thing coming up as a living issue resultant from a work in them of the Holy Spirit. The latter is the only way of life, and the only safe way for the future."[11] Sparks closes by wondering if the widespread disruption to the "shell of Christianity" that was taking place would tear down many of the walls of division and give believers a true hunger for being united solely around Christ and solely for the purpose of reaching the fullness of Christ.

In August the brothers and sisters gathered again at Honor Oak for fellowship and ministry. No details of the conference preparation are given, nor are we told what the local wartime conditions were during the gathering. During this August 1941 conference, Mr. Sparks released the series of messages entitled "The School of Christ." These describe a "course of education" that every born again believer must undergo. Christ is the subject which is to be learned and the Holy Spirit is the teacher. This series of messages was a substantial advancement in Mr. Sparks' utterance and description of the process that every believer must undergo to learn Christ. The messages did not emphasize so much the objective doctrine or teaching of the believers' oneness with Christ and conformity to Him. Rather, they were principles that could be derived only from personal experience in the classroom. These messages were as if Mr. Sparks was speaking directly concerning how he learned, what he felt, and what principles he discovered throughout his many years of being taught by the Holy Spirit. His sharing was as if he is able to utter exactly what is on his heart in relation to his experience of the Spirit. He talks about his past experience of having the sense that he was unable to utter his true experience, but now he testified that he felt he was touching an open heaven. It is significant that no reference to the war or to the world situation was given in these messages. This was a sharp contrast to many messages given the previous two years. It was as if God's glory was shining to reveal Christ as the focus, above every other situation, no matter how pressing it may be. The storm of the political and military world was raging, but Christ, transcendent and peaceful, was in the boat pointing towards Himself as the eternal One.

The 1941 November-December issue of *A Witness and a Testimony* expressed that the brothers were full of praise and wonder that after two years of war the magazine could still be sent out to so many parts of the world. The little company at Honor Oak had passed through "dark and strenuous times,"[12] enduring months of intense air raids and sometimes having destruction rain from the air just a few feet from their premises. But to their wonder and praise, they were all still there. And through it all, the magazine did not miss one issue, not one conference was discontinued, the regular ministry was not interrupted and the amount of literature that was sent out by request was more than any previous year. The letters accompanying gifts for the maintenance of *A Witness and a Testimony* were a great support for the brothers and sisters at Honor Oak. They felt that these were truly help from God. "Having received help from God, we continue until now."

While the military battle raged over much of the world, there was also quite a spiritual battle taking place. Sparks writes, "Although our own all-dominating desire is that the absolute Lordship of Christ, which means the ground of His fullness in the saints, should be a realized thing by all of His own, we are bitterly hated and opposed by many children of God. They are praying hard against us."[12] Sparks emphasized that the only solution to this problem set forth in the word of God was Christ and a life "according to Christ." Though it may sound simple,

Sparks felt it was the only way to heal the wounds and stem the tide of opposition. "The evil germs of suspicion, prejudice, fear, jealousy, and many other such like things will be killed by the radium-like power of this new Life. The dislocations between people will be quickly and effectively adjusted." Sparks concludes "Oh, for the ability to show how the Lordship of Christ in a life, or in a church, and in all the churches, is the solution to every problem and difficulty! Will you ask the Lord to impress you, firstly with this fact, and then to lead you into its reality? To this ministry, by His grace, and as helped by your prayers, we give ourselves until we—with all saints—'attain unto the measure of the stature of the fullness of Christ.'"[13]

Spiritual Sight

Nineteen forty-two was the first full year America was involved in the war. American troops began arriving on British soil on January 26. By August 17, the American war machine was able to launch from its bases in Britain the first all-American air raids in Europe. In the first part of 1942, the air war against civilians worsened in intensity. On April 23, Hitler ordered the bombing of Cathedral cities in Britain. York, Essex, Canterbury were bombed with the sole intention of inflicting massive civilian casualties to break the morale and the will of the English people. The royal air force responded in force on May 30 by flying a 1,000 bomber sortie to lay waste the German city of Cologne. In June the Nazis began to implement their "final solution of the Jewish question," the mass murder of the Jews. This fact was publicly reported to the British House of Commons in December.

The entrance of America into the conflict caused Sparks to include several observations in his editor's letter in the 1942 January-February issue of *A Witness and a*

Testimony. He refers back to his 1940 letter where he said that if what is taking place on earth relates to the spiritual life of the Lord's people, then the conflict could not be confined to a limited area of the world. America had now become involved. Sparks noticed a number of items which, for him, pointed to the fact that this conflict was a spiritual one as well as material.

(1) The very wide-spread acknowledgement by leaders, political and religious, that this is pre-eminently a spiritual issue in its essential nature. (Note the use of such terms as "Satanic," "Antichrist," in public utterances.)

(2) The destruction of properties, without discrimination for places of long and world renowned evangelical traditions. An immense amount of the fabric of organized Christianity has been demolished and wiped out, and very much of that which is the material means of Christian propaganda has just gone up in smoke.

(3) A great deal of the established order of Christian activity and procedure has been suspended and rendered impossible.

(4) On quite a number of occasions loud, boastful and proud declarations as to our strength, our ability, our material and moral resources as a guarantee of victory, etc. have been swiftly followed by some setback, disaster, or more serious outlook.

(5) On several occasions united prayer has been followed by a marvelous deliverance, yet in such a way as to leave little room for man to take the glory, but to which it is

only possible to attribute the intervention
of God (e.g. Dunkirk)

(6) Another, and to many of us, a very impressive, feature of this time is the way in
which the Lord is causing so many of those
who are affected by the Government orders
to hold themselves for Him for disposal,
without prejudicing their course by adopt-
ing a set position as to what they are willing or unwilling to do. We have seen this
attitude of faith resulting in tremendous
spiritual values to those concerned and,
through them, to many others.[14]

Sparks' feeling was that the wider issues of God's
thought, those dealing with the questions of national sins,
godlessness, and unrighteousness etc. were undoubtedly
involved in the divine mind for this time. But, as he had
sought to convey many times in past letters, he felt that
the divine meaning of all these events for the Lord's people was a call to seek after the increase in the inward
measure of Christ and not merely the varied outward associations so often confused with spirituality. "Things, activities, institutions, programs, etc. may have been the
conscious or unconscious standard by which spiritual
measure has been judged: the 'things seen' being the sole
or predominant factors. The fact remains that with the
Lord spiritual measure, the measure of Christ as positively
expressed in the life and experience of His own, is the
only and ultimate concern."[15] Sparks ends by stating a
yearning that he frequently put to words in his editor's
letters for a prophetic voice from God emerging in this
generation, who would make God's thought and heart
known to all His people.

In a September editor's letter, Sparks introduces a
new series of messages entitled "Spiritual Sight" spoken

in early 1942 at Honor Oak. Sparks' emphasis in these messages is to convey the need for the eyes of the Lord's people to be open. The biggest tragedy would be to pass through the entire world war, experience all the suffering, yet not learn what the Holy Spirit meant by all the disruption and tumult. Sparks saw the war as a time where there could be a great spiritual advance among all of God's people. Old lines of division could be torn down, old prejudices buried and Christians could emerge from the war with one dominating desire: to reach the fullness of Christ, a spiritual goal that does not depend on temporal and earthly institutions, buildings, societies, and customs. So if the war would tear these things down, who should shed a tear for the passing of the divisive things? Why not learn from God and from the situation and build on a firmer foundation after the war? However, what Sparks observed among the Christian leaders as a result of all the destruction was "the only positive thought among the responsible leaders seems to be to rebuild what has been destroyed and resume on the old line and in the old way. We have eagerly watched for, but have so far failed to discern any real enquiry—let alone explanation—as to what God might mean by it all. If He is really Lord and is interested, then surely He has not allowed, and is not allowing this for nothing. But there is worse. In so many of these greater fields of Christian occupation...the Lord's people, in spite of all, still find it possible to allow Christian *things* to take precedence over Himself."[16] Sparks' cry and over-riding burden at this time for God's people was for spiritual sight. He remarks, "Is there not a possibility that the Lord may be seeking to bring His people to the place where they realize that nothing short of an altogether new and fuller knowledge of Himself will save them from being put out of the fight?"[16]

The 1942 exercise among the brothers and sisters at Honor Oak was marked by a faithful continuation of regular conference gatherings, regular ministry and a regular sending out of *A Witness and a Testimony* to readers all over the world. There were no conferences held away from Honor Oak that year. However, near the beginning of each month of 1942 there were gatherings for the ministering of the word. The continuation of these gatherings was becoming a reason for increased gratitude and praise to God for His goodness and faithfulness.

A Witness and a Testimony underwent some wartime changes in 1942. A rather acute paper shortage began early in the year. The January issue was about 30 pages in length, the same as its prewar size. By the end of the year the magazine had shrunk to half that size, the November issue being 16 pages. All available space was used in these issues; the front and back inside covers were used for space for additional message content and the back cover was used to publish the Witness and Testimony book list.

We should remind the readers that Mr. Sparks was not the only speaker of the messages published in the magazine. The speakers represented an entire group of leaders at Honor Oak and others. In 1942, in addition to articles by Mr. Sparks, articles were included by Harry Foster, Watchman Nee, C. J. B. Harrison, George Patterson, K. P. O., C. O. Excerpts from F. B. Meyer and other writers were also included. In the 1942 issues 34 messages were published in this magazine, 15 were spoken by T. Austin Sparks and 19 were spoken by other brothers who had either visited Honor Oak or who were laboring along side of Mr. Sparks. This shows that Mr. Sparks was by no means alone. Conferences were supported by a large group of brothers, the ministering at Honor Oak was shared, prayer was entered into together, and the testimony to keep God's thought for the fullness of Christ in fresh view of God's children was upheld by more than Mr. Sparks alone. This was a real strength as well as a real testimony during these war-time years, with destruction raining from the sky and with a surge of opposition from fellow believers who were sowing suspicion concerning the brothers and sisters at Honor Oak.

In July of 1942 Mr. Sparks included another reminder of the ministry that the brothers at Honor Oak felt they had been committed with by God. He acknowledges that "many have prejudiced our ministry by misapprehension, misrepresentation and precipitate action."[17] He also writes that such opposition was not unexpected and that the brothers have no desire to vindicate themselves. Rather, he first reminds his readers what their ministry is not. It is not a new movement, it claims no new revelation and it does not desire to cause people to leave their current attachments to any "church, mission or society." The brothers at Honor Oak recognized that theirs was not the only ministry of God and that they recognized the value of other work which "has the knowledge of Christ as its object." Secondly, Sparks reemphasizes to his readers what the ministry of the brothers at Honor Oak is: a ministry to bring in the divine fullness of Christ. Sparks relates his and others' experience concerning this ministry. "divine fullness is only going to be reached by a progressive and ever increasing revelation of Christ and His significance. Such a revelation—unless we misunderstand the record of God's ways from of old—comes firstly to an apprehended instrument which is taken into the deeps with God: then it is given forth as His truth for His people: and then it becomes the inwrought experience and knowledge of such as really mean business with God—not as to their blessing, but as to His purpose and inheritance in them."[17] In the war-time year of 1942, such was the stand of the brothers. Their expectation was that with proper sight, much spiritual progress toward this end could be made by all Christians who were exercised by the conditions the war produced and by the corresponding work of the Holy Spirit in their hearts.

On November 10, 1942, two days after the Americans launched their invasion of North Africa, Churchill uttered his famous words: "This is not the end. It is not even the beginning of the end. But it is, perhaps, the end of the beginning." And, true to his words, 1943 became a turning point in the war with Germany. The Nazis suffered their first large defeat on the Soviet front; Nazi armies retreated from North Africa under the intense pressure of British and American forces. Meanwhile, the German homeland felt the weight of the more frequent assaults of a rapidly expanding and increasingly accurate allied bomber force. Bombing raids on German cities were crippling infrastructure and severely hampering resupply efforts. By the end of the year the allies had firmly established themselves in the southern part of the Italian Peninsula. At the end of the 1943 the vice was set to close in on the Nazi war machine.

Cast Down but Not Destroyed

For the little company standing for a testimony unto the fullness of Christ at Honor Oak, 1943 was a year of conflict and struggle. It was a year of more than usual spiritual struggles and the fourth long year of bearing the disruption and anxiety of the grinding world conflict. Air raids over London continued, but not to the same extent as before. In March, more-or-less-monthly conferences began to be held in the North in Glasgow, as well as at Honor Oak. This was the first time such travel was possible since the summer of 1939 and it showed a general easing of the war limitations and restrictions on travel. The Easter and Whitsun conferences continued as well as the regular gatherings for ministry and fellowship. The encouragement throughout this year was a steady growth in requests for Witness and Testimony literature and many encouraging letters from around the world. It seemed that many Christians seeking a greater fullness of Christ expressed genuine appreciation for help received from the rich ministry.

The paper shortage further affected the appearance of *A Witness and a Testimony*. The blue paper of the prewar cover was no longer available and was replaced by simple white. The January 1943 issue was 17 pages long and by June the size fell to only 10 pages, a length that would be maintained through the end of 1945. Two series of messages previously spoken by Sparks were continued in the 1943 issue of *A Witness and a Testimony*: "Spiritual Sight" and "The School of Christ." Two new series of messages by Sparks, spoken during 1943, began to be published also: "The Cross, the Church, and the Conflict" and "The Representation of the Invisible God." The first series centered on the issue that "the Cross of our Lord Jesus Christ is meant by God to lead immediately and directly to the Church, and that, when the Cross and the Church are really brought spiritually into view, then an intense state of conflict is set up." The second series dealt with God's eternal principle of having a representation who is one with Him; the fact is first seen in the Lord Jesus and then in the church, His Body. Although both series of messages are very rich, Mr. Sparks never chose to make them into books, like other series (e.g. "The School of Christ") that he spoke during the war years.

During this year, 1943, Sparks also chose to rewrite and reprint the first book ever published by Witness and Testimony publishers, *The Centrality and Universality of the Cross of Christ*. This book was to become a clear foundation of teaching representing a universal view of his ministry.

But when Mr. Sparks looked back over 1943, a year of harsh conflict, he was simply thankful that they were still there. Throughout all of 1943, Sparks only wrote one editor's letter, so it is difficult to ascertain the details of what transpired, but one surmises that opposition and problems from all angles assailed the little company at Honor Oak. At the end of the year, the advancement of the work was not their criterion for success or failure; they were simply thankful they were not destroyed. A longer quote from one of his letters written at the end of 1943 appropriately captures the feeling of this little company.

> As we pass over another landmark of years, we would record our gratitude to the Lord for all that He has been to us and enabled us unto, both directly, and through His people, until now. We can truly say that "if it had not been for the Lord," we would have been swallowed up. There is no doubt that the enemy hates with a bitter hatred that for which we are standing. It would be difficult to think of any fresh ways in which he could seek our quenching, although doubtless he has them. But "having received help from God we continue until now." If we want witness borne that the Lord is with us and for us, it is mainly found in this, that, although we have nothing on the natural side to support and substantiate us, we have not been destroyed, though all hell seems to have been moved against us, both in spiritual ways and by many outward means. We can simply echo the word, "The witness is this, that God hath given us eternal life..."
>
> Not only have we been kept alive as an instrument and a ministry (I refer to that

which is corporate, not merely personal),
but there has been continual growth. Despite the restrictions and limitations of a
fourth year of war—in a country so much
affected—there has been a steady increase
in the calls upon all that is available, so that
the past year has seen more literature going
out, and more demands for the "Witness
and Testimony" than in any previous
year.[18]

From Mr. Sparks' many attempts to answer criticism of his ministry we can glean that these criticisms
centered mainly on two stands that were taken by the
brothers at Honor Oak as a result of what they had seen in
God's word. There may have been, and probably were,
other points (false or true) used by people in opposition
concerning the character or actions of brothers at Honor
Oak or Mr. Sparks himself. However, the brothers never
sought to vindicate themselves or their reputations. But
when some person would attack a point related to the
spiritual testimony that was being born at Honor Oak, then
the brothers felt the need to make defense for the sake of
the Lord's testimony and not for the sake of their own
reputation in the sight of men. Two points that seemed to
frequently be defended are 1) their stand as a fellowship
open to all Christians but with no thought of becoming
something separate from the rest of the Body and 2) the
fact that there is a subjective experience of the cross in
addition to the objective fact of the work of the cross. The
first charge accused the brothers of asking people to leave
denominations, societies, missions, etc. and to form a new
group.

It was true that the brothers were very clear that
God's desire is not a denomination, society, institution, or
mission, but a heavenly, universal church expressed in

many local churches. The fulfillment of this desire has nothing to do with denominations, missions etc. But it was never the brothers' encouragement to ask people to leave their previous connections. However, they did encourage seekers to be faithful to the moving and leading of the Spirit within. And, if the Lord would lead people to leave their denomination, that is up to the headship of the Spirit within. The second criticism was based on the brothers' strong emphases on the subjective experience of the cross. All Christians were initially justified through the act of Jesus on the cross, but all Christians also need to continually live in a way such that their old man, their self, is crucified that they may walk in spirit. For this we need the Spirit to make the cross real in our experience. This stand was not accepted by many Christians, who considered this view to be casting doubt on the effectiveness and efficacy of the cross. In fact the cross was effective in our objective justification but needs to be experienced by us in our subjective walk with God.

It is fitting to end this short description of 1943 with the entire editor's Letter included in the September *A Witness and a Testimony* issue. We include this to see concisely what the little company at Honor Oak was standing for and what the enemy was raging so bitterly against. Succinctly, Sparks writes.

Beloved of God,

Space permits only a few lines. The question which is occupying the minds of many of the Lord's people in these times is, "What is *the* object which God has in view particularly?" and therefore "What is *the* message for the hour?" While we will not claim to possess any special knowledge in this matter, with some conviction we would present the following for serious consideration.

(1) God's object in this dispensation has never changed, and it is the same as ever.

(2) From time to time His emphasis has rested more particularly on different phases of that object, and He has thus sought to recover its fullness.

(3) At the end of the dispensation there will be a divine concentration upon the *whole* object, and less upon mere aspects of it.

(4) The inclusive object is His Son and "the One New Man" ; Christ as Head and the "called out company" as "Body" = one corporate man ; organic, living, related, interrelated, interdependent, and spiritually authoritative under one anointing—Head and members.

(5) To this all "*things*" must give place, whether they be teachings, traditions, institutions, missions, organizations, etc. The Lord will not be interested in anything only in so far as it *directly* and *immediately* ministers to His sole and utter purpose.

God is after a Man, a Race-Man, a Corporate Man; "conformed to the image of His Son"; to "have dominion"; and this demands that—as not since the beginning—Christ should come into His place as Lord and Head. The great 'movement' at the end should be a "Christ movement"! *Everything* in the world points to this necessity.

The Lord Give us a new apprehen-
sion of the greatness of Christ!
Yours in His fellowship
T. Austin-Sparks[19]

The Destruction of the Honor Oak Conference Center

Almost all the war news of 1944 announced allied
victories and a gradual shrinking and weakening of the
ferocious German war machine. Russian troops advanced
into Poland, the siege of Leningrad ended after 900 days,
and the allies flew the first daylight bombing raids over
Berlin. On June 5 the allies entered Rome on their push
through Italy and on June 6 the allies landed on the D-day
beaches of northern France and began to fight and march
their way to Berlin. By fall, French troops had reached
the Rhine River; the Allies had liberated Athens in the
south and Brussels in the north, among many other cities.
Hitler's top general, Erwin Rommel committed suicide.
In December, the famous Battle of the Bulge in Ardennes
began, which was to be the last massive ground conflict of
the war in Europe.

For London, the beginning of 1944 was marked by
relative calm. The Nazis were facing a shortage of both
planes and trained pilots to fly raids over the city. However, Hitler was looking for some way of relieving German cities from the full attention of allied air power. In
June a secret weapons program finally gave Hitler what he
wanted—a pilot-less, flying bomb called the V-1. The
bomb was launched from northern France, was propelled
by a simple engine and had a crude guidance system that
roughly led it somewhere into the city of London where it
dived and indiscriminately delivered its 1900 pound bomb
payload. For Hitler this was a big success. At times almost 40 percent of the allied air power was aimed at de-

stroying V-1 launching sites in France. On June 13 the
first of these flying bombs was launched, in July 120 a
day were terrorizing London, and by late August the allies
had begun capturing the launching bases in northern
France and thus eliminating the major threats from these
weapons. London was terrorized once again during the
summer months of 1944, but afterwards was relatively
peaceful. The V-1 attacks continued into 1945, but with
far less ferocity and much reduced magnitude. The Germans were on the defensive and, as most in England believed, allied victory was only a matter of time.

For the company of believers at Honor Oak, 1944
began with a conference for Christian workers. Gatherings for regular ministry continued throughout the beginning of the year including the two big conferences at
Easter and Whitsun. A thought from the Easter conference was, "'What is the service of God in this dispensation?' The deliverance of an elect people from this world,
for the Lord, and the bringing of them into the fullness of
Christ."[20]

What was most occupying Mr. Sparks during the
first half of 1944 was the distressing situation among
Christians. He wrote in a July-August editor's letter,
"While the world is torn with disruption and warring fac-
tions, both in international war and in national internal
strife - political, industrial, social, and other ways - the
people of God are no less disrupted and weakened by
schism, divisions, suspicions, prejudices, personal and
party interests, jealousies, rivalries, and misunderstandings."[21] Mr. Sparks recognized a general cry among some
for revival and power among the Lord's people, that they
would be a proper testimony to the world. He felt that the
revival would only come if the Lord's people would re-
pent, realize how far they have strayed from the revelation
in the New Testament and return to that revelation.
"There is no promise of revival apart from adjustments to

the Lord's revealed mind."[21] To this end he felt that the Lord's people had fallen from God's revelation in two main aspects. First, they had fallen from the experience of the cross of Christ, which meant "the setting aside of man by nature and the exclusion from the realm of God's things of all that is of the Adam creation." Secondly, the Lord's people had fallen from "The oneness of the believers as an organic body, interrelated, interdependent, by the power of a common life and the government of a common Head in the anointing of the Holy Spirit."[21] Sparks strongly felt that the only hope of a recovery of the testimony of the Lord's people to the people in the world was in returning to these two main aspects of the New Testament revelation. Sparks' feeling and desire was to see more of God's people to rise up and respond to this call to become those who "follow the Lamb withersoever He goeth."

In July of 1944 the situation for the little company of believers at Honor Oak drastically changed. Up to that time, they had been proceeding with regular gatherings and ministry even in the midst of the direst destruction around them. Suddenly, the Honor Oak conference center was hit by one of Hitler's flying bombs. The conference center, the residences and all the other adjoining premises were no more. Mr. and Mrs. George Paterson and Mr. and Mrs. Foster were both in residence at the time the bomb hit and the bedrooms in which they were sleeping were destroyed. However, they emerged unscathed, save only some minor scratches. Not a single life was lost in the attack. The brothers and sisters at Honor Oak felt this was the wonderful, protecting hand of the Lord. When Mr. Sparks arrived to see the destruction, he found so many of the brothers and sisters far from despairing and even somewhat triumphant and buoyant in the spirit. In the days immediately following the attack they banded together to sift through the rubble and retrieve what was not destroyed. Through it all, the Lord gave abundant grace and did not allow their spirits to fall to despair. The attack destroyed the meeting facility but left all the printing equipment, literature, and much of the office equipment safe. These were soon transferred elsewhere to continue the production of *A Witness and a Testimony*. Conferences at the center were suspended indefinitely, but the local assembly still regularly gathered on the grounds in the basement of the old Center.

Mr. Sparks moved to Kilcreggan, Scotland, to the retreat center that had been purchased by the brothers and sisters in 1931. He was to remain there for the remainder of the war, and as far as we know, no conferences were held during the later half of 1944 and for the entire year of 1945. As to what was the Lord's meaning to all this, Sparks admitted he was not yet clear. Up to this point, the Lord had marvelously preserved them in the midst of destruction raining from the sky and reaching to within a few feet of their premises. They were able to maintain their gatherings, conferences and the publication of *A Witness and a Testimony*. Now, it seemed, the Lord saw fit to allow the destruction of the conference center and the cessation of much of the ministry of the word at Honor Oak. Sparks wrote that the Lord had recently been emphasizing to him "the essentially spiritual nature of His work in this dispensation."[22] Although he realized that at times temporal items are used in this world for spiritual ends, in Sparks mind, the spiritual essence must always prevail over the material. In this sense Sparks testified that he was "glad that with us there is such an extensive and strong spiritual ministry and testimony that we do not feel that the real values need be affected by such happenings as these."[22]

What Sparks was to do outside of London was not at all clear. At this point he was a person seeking the Lord to find what His mind was. Sparks was evaluating before the Lord his ways of ministering, his form, the location of the place he was ministering, the size of his meeting hall, whether to rebuild at all. He was wondering if his time should be occupied with traveling to many of the countries where brothers and sisters were receiving his ministry, or should he stay in Kilcreggan. It is significant that he did not immediately make plans to rebuild and resume his pre-war service to the Lord. Rather, he sought to find out what the Lord's mind was. This was a time of great searching before the Lord to see how these circumstances could bring Sparks' person and ministry more fully into the thought that God revealed to him in the Bible. Sparks realized that there was a great heart movement in many people that caused them to seek after reality and fullness. This heart movement did not find expression in an outward movement that could be seen. Rather, it was an inward attitude or yearning that caused people to realize the food they were getting in traditional circles of "Christianity" was not able to bring them through to God's full thought. Sparks' consideration before the Lord was how his ministry could be more fitted to reflect the need of God's people and the thought of God in the fulfilling of His purpose.

Mr. Sparks did not travel widely during the later months of 1944. His post-war comments indicate that this isolation was due more to lack of possibility for travel than his desire to settle in Kilcreggan till the war ended. He remained thus in Scotland under a feeling of being greatly limited by the Lord. In his November editor's letter, Mr. Sparks recounted the Apostle Paul's limitation during his imprisonments. Although Sparks would not even dare to compare himself with Paul, he did emphasize this principle about Paul's imprisonment. "When the earth side of things, with all its time features and human factors seemed to be breaking down and becoming so disappointing and heart-breaking, the flood gates of the heav-

enly, eternal and spiritual realities were opened."[23] Sparks
noted how this same situation was true with so many
Christians and that even for himself this was a time of
pressing, limitation and hedging up resulting in serious
soul-searching. Sparks writes of the people in this situation, "When all the incidental matters are dealt with by the
fires of his soul-searching situation, the ultimate intention
of the Lord will be reached—a clearer, fuller, and more
fruitful revelation."[23] While Sparks admitted that this may
not be the case for many in America, in Europe and the
Far East many servants of God found themselves in this
very situation. Sparks writes, "For ourselves this is intensely true, and speaking personally, I can only say that
the past four years have been the most agonizing years of
my life, in which bottom seems to have been touched very
many times."[23] But what did Sparks see in his situation?
What was the counterpart to what Paul saw in his prison?
As Mr. Sparks often looked out from his window and saw
the first rays of light rise over the mountains and water, he
contemplated what, to his mind, was dawning in God's
work for the present hour through the hearts of believers
scattered over the whole earth. Sparks writes, "I believe
there is a new movement of God on the near horizon. It is
not a movement which can be put into sectional, departmental, or phasial terms, such as 'revival,' evangelistic,
doctrine, missionary, or reform. But rather it is a movement to Christ."[24] Further he writes, "Much is breaking
down, much is being suspended. The war has created
conditions both negative and positive which would foster
and point to a new place for Christ Himself; and the manifest development of antichrist...Christ alone will be sufficient, and the measure of Christ in believers will determine the measure of their endurance and overcoming."[24]
The Lord seemed to use these times of limitation, pressure
and soul-searching to create a longing in Sparks for a
movement throughout the world that was centered on

Christ and Him alone. It seemed also to be a time when Sparks himself was being more prepared to supply food to God's people who were living out such a movement. Only in a fresh and grand vision of Christ rests any hope for breaking down all the barriers that kept Christians divided from one another and prevented many from growing. A great yearning was in Sparks for this worldwide movement and a great preparation by the Lord was taking place in him.

In spite of the destruction of the premises at Honor Oak, every issue of *A Witness and a Testimony* was printed and sent out during 1944. The only difference was that no new series of articles appeared in this year's journal. Some series that had begun in 1943 were completed, but with no conferences in the later part of the year, new series stopped and no new books were written. For the most part, the 1944 publication included stand-alone messages from a variety of brothers in the fellowship. George Paterson, S. Alexander, C.J.B. Harrison, K.P.O., and Harry Foster contributed 9 of the 23 articles appearing that year. Mr. Sparks began a project to rework one of his earliest books entitled *The Release of the Lord*. These messages were reprinted beginning in January of 1945.

For a man like T. Austin-Sparks, who worked so hard and prolifically, this lack of opportunity both to speak in conferences and to write surely must have been a drastic limitation. For most of Mr. Sparks' life since 1913, scarcely one month would go by that he was not actively ministering in some form to God's people, health permitting. Now many months of limitation were passing by. Meanwhile, Sparks was writing how he had hit bottom many times in the past four years. Surely it was the Lord's time to work in hidden ways, in soul-searching ways and in ways that only such a situation would allow.

Rebuilding with a Deepening Life

Nineteen forty-five witnessed the end of the war and a rearrangement of the world political situation on a scale that few other years in the history of mankind could rival. The beginning of that year saw the Russians closing in on Germany from the east and the Americans, British and French closing from the west. In January Warsaw fell to the Russians, by March the Allies had taken Cologne and established a bridge across the Rhine. On April 16, the Soviet troops began their final offensive on Berlin. On April 28 Mussolini was captured and killed by Italian partisans, two days later Hitler committed suicide. May 7 witnessed the unconditional surrender of the German forces to the allies. The war in Europe ended.

A few months later, on August 6, the United States dropped an atomic bomb on Hiroshima, Japan. On August 14, the Japanese agreed to an unconditional surrender to the allies. The greatest war ever, one that had engulfed almost the entire world, was over. And a weapon which had the real possibility of destroying all mankind was now in the hands of nations.

This year witnessed many changes to the world political landscape. Roosevelt died before the German surrender and was replaced by Truman. Churchill was not re-elected and was succeeded by Atlee as British prime minister. An east-west polarization of the post-war world was emerging. Western Europe began the tremendous task of rebuilding, while Eastern Europe slowly realized that their liberators were to become their occupiers. A large part of the world was being brought under the sway of communism. China, now free from a brutal wartime occupation, was quickly being entangled in civil war between nationalists and communists. And behind it all was the startling realization of the destructive power of the atomic bomb, which for the first time in history gave mankind the real power to utterly destroy himself.

Mr. Sparks' January 1945 editor's letter reveals his continued quest before the Lord as to the meaning of the intense conflict occupying the whole world. Previously, Sparks wrote of how the war could be used by the Lord to strip away Christians' reliance on anything other than Christ and thus bring many Christians together under a fresh and powerful revelation of Christ as the one Head. Now he framed his reasons in light of the Lord's return. The present world conflict could be a preparation of those overcomers the Lord needs for His coming. Or, it could be the process bringing about the very coming of the Lord Jesus Himself. Sparks writes, "Either the Lord is preparing for some fresh, and perhaps final, movement to the consummation of His purpose on the earth; which movement requires a state that will guarantee depth, strength, and lastingness, so that real fullness shall mark the ingathering to glory at His appearing; or else this *is* the end of a phase and the Lord is coming for the ripe fruits."[25] If either of these were the case, then the present, earthly conflict would have a spiritual cause, a spiritual process and a spiritual result. The result would be "Now is come the salvation, and the power, and the kingdom of our God, and the authority of His Christ: for the accuser of our brethren is cast down...." There was a renewed yearning in Sparks for the necessity of fighting this conflict in united spiritual strength, so that the accuser would be cast down in both specific situations and eventually from his position in the heavenlies. In this way the war became an environment in which real spiritual growth and fullness could be experienced by God's people. Eventually the Lord could come for the ripe fruits of His harvest. Characteristically, Sparks veered away from making specific predictions using the current events to fit into Biblical prophecy. Instead he chose to emphasize the spiritual re-

ality and experience of the process of the Lord return. As
he was considering the real possibility of the Lord's imminent return, this view caused him to seek the Lord more in
prayer and to encourage others to do the same. In this
way God's spiritual aims would be met by people who
were attaining a lasting spiritual fullness, and neither
Sparks nor the ones he ministered to, were to be caught up
in excitement over the outward course of events leading to
the Lord's coming.

Pressed by the course of events to long for the final spiritual fullness among God's people before the
Lord's return and prevented from traveling by circumstances, Mr. Sparks continued his publication of *A Witness
and a Testimony* from Kilcreggan. He began to publish
the series of reworked messages, *The Release of the Lord.*
Only Harry Foster and Mr. Sparks published messages in
A Witness and a Testimony until the October issue of that
year when one message was included by S. Alexander.
This was a clear result of the suspended conferences and
regular ministry gatherings. No new series of messages
were introduced in early 1945; rather all the new messages
were stand-alone. Despite the destruction of the Honor
Oak conference center, literature was still sent out on demand at a level higher than any time before. Many of
God's seekers in countries around the world were even
hungrier for a ministry that could give them food.

May 7 witnessed the unconditional surrender of all
German forces. The war in Europe was over. Mr. Sparks
returned to London and wrote his September editor's letter
in the midst of peace celebrations. He was truly thankful
for the end of the war and he breathed a sigh of relief for
the end of the conflict that had caused so much strain and
suffering over the last five years. As he looked back, he
was also full of thanks that the Lord enabled the publication of every issue of *A Witness and a Testimony* throughout the entire war. Sparks comments "The Lord is able to

maintain what He wants, no matter what the conditions."[26]
He also looked forward to the coming days of greater freedom to continue the Lord's work "in outward ways"
through travel and the further expansion of the literature
work. There was still a paper shortage in Britain which
limited the size of the Journal to about 10 pages per issue,
far below the pre-war length of 30 pages per issue. Sparks
looked to the Lord and ask for the prayers of his readers to
open the way to expand the magazine to its pre-war size.

A very moving experience accompanying the end
of the war was the appearance of letters from the "hushed"
countries telling a story of suffering and God's faithfulness through the trying years. There were many hungry
seekers in these countries who received *A Witness and a
Testimony* and carried on correspondence with those at
Honor Oak before the war. The war had totally cut off
any form of communication. Mr. Sparks was now receiving letters from France, Holland, Belgium, Norway, Swe-
den, Denmark, Japan, etc. telling stories of God's preservation and faithfulness in the midst of intense upheaval
and suffering.

Mr. Sparks' ministry was never a matter of simply
presenting truths that he had learned or had recently studied. It was a matter of his personal experience. Concerning his ministry he writes "Ministry and living experience
have been kept very strictly, severely, and deeply in oneness."[26] The price of all the sufferings he withstood for his
ministry was far too great to merely be peddling some
truths that he had picked up from books or research. The
truths he ministered were his very own experiments in divine grace and revelation. The war brought him into an
experience that he had never been in before and this
pressed him to the Lord to see the Lord's desire in a fresh
way. One of the fruits of his later war experience was a
series of messages on overcomers that began to be published in the September 1945 issue of *A Witness and a*

Testimony. Here Mr. Sparks further described what God really wanted at that time and indeed since Jesus Christ came, that is "a people living in the good of the greater fullnesses of Christ!"[26] These people live for God for the sake of all the rest of God's people.

At the same time, Mr. Sparks expressed grave concerns for the current state of Christianity and felt that the current system greatly limited the Lord from bringing many believers through to His full purpose. Mr. Sparks' intention was simply to give food to God's people and to sound out a call that God seeks those who overcome. He hoped all the practical outworkings of where and how Christians should meet would be decided by a personal living revelation of Christ within all those he ministered to.

In November of 1945 Mr. Sparks looked back on the year with wonder and astonishment at all the changes that took place in world affairs. 1945 was a year that would set the disposition of nations for many years to come. Thankfully, Mr. Sparks did not find himself in need of changing any prophetic predictions that he had made during the war. He did not make any predictions of the political ramifications of the war, nor did he point to specific prophetic portions to ascertain the arrangements of nations after the war. But he did realize that with such a rearrangement of nations a corresponding rearrangement of thinking was required. The advent of the atomic bomb was a great impetus forcing an entirely new thinking of what the world was and how the political landscape would operate hence forth. Now mankind had the real capacity to destroy itself from the face of the earth. Sparks likened this kind of rearrangement in thinking in the political sphere to what was required in the spiritual realm. In the spiritual realm God's truth could never be boxed in and set. It could never be such that the established official evangelical institutions could have the final say in all decisions of what was of God and what was not. With such limitations it was very difficult for the Lord's greater and fuller purpose to be realized at that time. Mr. Sparks was not advocating a new set of truths but neither was he saying that once a truth is in the books of evangelical doctrine, no further seeing of that truth was possible. In fact he was saying that truth should always be freshly unveiled with a "wealth and fullness of meaning and value that is commensurate with its infinite Source and Fountainhead."[27] It is this kind of seeing that is revolutionary and it is this kind of seeing that a set and atrophied system would never allow.

Mr. Sparks observed that after the war there were a great many young people hungry for "the real and true life of God."[27] Traditional Christianity was losing its hold on such people and on many other true seekers of reality. It was only a new seeing of truths (not new truths but a new vision of the limits and outworkings of these truths) that could bring in God's freshness to this seeking young generation. Such a fresh unveiling results in a willingness to adjust one's life to that unveiling and brings with it the real possibility that God's goal of a people after the greater fullness of Christ could be attained. In this way God may gain from that generation a people that truly live and desire one thing, "That I may know Him." But this could only be gained by a greater, fuller and richer application and appreciation of the eternal truths in the word. Mr. Sparks' continuing concern was that in these post-war years the Lord would truly gain a people for the fullness of Christ.

Sparks' observations of a young, God-seeking generation turned out to be true. Many young people were spiritually hungry after the war. Billy Graham remarked of his 1946 visit to Britain, "The people, still reeling from the war, were starved for hope and hungry for God."[28] Billy Graham's Youth for Christ gospel campaigns drew large crowds everywhere he went. And the next few years were to see a great increase in the number of people in the fellowship at Honor Oak. There was a general hunger for God among many of the people of Britain at that time.

1945 ended with hope and assurance for Mr. Sparks and for the local assembly with him. All the brothers and sisters in the fellowship had been preserved throughout the entire war. Every issue of *A Witness and a Testimony* had been sent out in spite of the air assaults, paper shortages and the destruction of the conference facilities and guest houses. Demand for literature was more than ever before. Many people who were shocked by the war were hungry for a real and living God and a high purpose to their Christian life. Communication was becoming easier and travel was soon to be possible to visit many of the seekers throughout the world. And now many sweet ties of fellowship both from the European continent and the Far East that had previously been suspended due to the war were opening again. There was a great thankfulness to the Lord for His faithfulness and his protection through six years of the largest conflict that ever engulfed the earth.

Post-War Advance

Conditions in London in 1946 were those of a nation emerging from rubble. Billy Graham writes of his visit "The whole city of London looked to us as if it had been destroyed...We were there less than a year after the end of World War II, and we encountered shortages, hardships, and rationing everywhere. Food especially preoccupied us, as it did most people there...Wes observed that the only eggs in London were in the museums..."[28] Paper was still in short supply forcing Mr. Sparks to keep the journal at its wartime size and to use every available square inch of the magazine, even the inside front and back covers, for content. The entire city was making due the best it could as the immense job of rebuilding proceeded. The brothers felt from the Lord to try and rebuild the conference center at Honor Oak. However this did not take place in 1946. So they, like so many others in London made the best of it and began to operate as much as they could with their limited facilities.

Letters continued to pour in from many seekers in countries cut off by the war. Other brothers and sisters returned to Honor Oak after years of captivity to more fully tell their stories of God's wondrous faithfulness through intense suffering, uncertainty, and pressure.

But among the brothers and sisters at Honor Oak there was a great hope and expectation for a greater expansion of travel and work and a true thankfulness for the cessation of the conflict. The banner published for 1946 by Mr. Sparks spoke, "I will do better...than at your beginnings....A latter end and a hope." And it was a time of hope, not only in the improving political situation but in the God of hope. Sparks writes "Our God is so often called 'The God of Hope;' as such, He never despairs, never gives up; He never accepts a verdict of hopelessness. He always has a way of reaching His end; and so long as any heart will trust Him, no situation is impossible."[29] Laying hold of the God of hope, Sparks' prayer was that this year would be one of "enlargement upward, and victory all along."[29]

In the January issue of *A Witness and a Testimony* Mr. Sparks included an announcement that he was again considering holding a training for Christian workers. He describes it further; "The provision will be for instruction in the Word of God in a spiritual way with a definitely, practical aspect, and it will be exclusively for those who have the service of God definitely in view." In addition to an opportunity for those who could apply themselves exclusively for the training for a number of months, Mr.

Sparks also announced shorter vacation Bible conferences aimed at training those who had a similar desire but more limited time. These were aimed to fall on the vacation times of young men and young women who desired to participate. These kinds of trainings held by the brothers at Honor Oak were never regular features nor did they have large numbers of participants, nor were they structured as a theological school would be. They were held within the context of the local assembly as the need arose. They had a definite view of an immediate practical issue of all the Bible knowledge that the trainees were exposed to. In 1946 vacation Bible conferences were held in Kilcreggan each month during the summer from June until September.

Meanwhile, many seekers of the deeper things of God were appearing all over the world. Mr. Sparks saw this move of the Lord to prepare so many for a message of the fullness of Christ. So he felt the need to attempt once again to break down any barriers that may have arisen that would prevent many of those seekers from receiving his ministry. In three of his 1946 editor's letters Mr. Sparks yielded to an appeal by some trusted friends and tried to address a few of the misunderstandings and wrong reports that were being circulated about his position concerning various matters. Previously he had refrained from a strong defense of his position, but simply continued to publish messages in order to allow the truth to speak for itself. Now he felt that a defense would be helpful, not to vindicate himself, but to open the way for more to receive help from what the Lord had given to him. In this way, he could have confidence that his defense was of and for the Lord's interests. He was mainly addressing the rebuttals to three classes of people. First, there were those real and genuine servants of God, who actively opposed Mr. Sparks' ministry, yet had never been to any conferences or never had never personally talked with any brother from the fellowship at Honor Oak. Second, there were a greater number of people who had heard things that cast suspicion on Mr. Sparks' ministry and who became perplexed and confused concerning the whole situation. Finally, there were those who were friendly toward the ministry of Mr. Sparks and were receiving it with joy, yet were imposing it on others in an improper way that resulted in more opposition.

In an attempt to educate all three of these classes of people Mr. Sparks addressed three issues in three different editor's letters. First, there was an accusation that they did not have any active care for the unsaved. Second, they were accused of trying to call people out of their Christian connections to form new churches. Third, they were accused of being exclusive in their teaching, attitude, and in their practice of laying on of hands.

To the first accusation of having no care for the unsaved Mr. Sparks replied that, while they did not feel that their ministry was a direct evangelism ministry, they had much care for the unsaved. Missionaries who had gone out from among them brought the gospel to many unsaved people, both in Britain as well as in other parts of the world. And the local assembly at Honor Oak was also quite exercised in the gospel. Few of these activities were published, but many prayer gatherings focused on true concern for salvation of the unregenerate.

To the second accusation, that of trying to cause people to break their connections with other Christians and form new churches, Mr. Sparks reiterated the following. His ministry was not to form new churches, new assemblies or special fellowships. He stated that if he wanted to do this it would be an easy thing to do. However, some have begun to meet on the ground of Christ and Christ alone as a result of fellowship they received from the ministry of *A Witness and a Testimony*. To this Mr. Sparks says that it was never out of an encouragement from his ministry. Rather they could have done it out of lack of understanding or out of reaction to the lack of food in their Christian circles, or they could have done it out of a revelation of the Living Christ within them. In any case, they were not being brought into a "fellowship" with a membership role. The most that was being done with them was that Mr. Sparks or someone else may visit them on an occasional basis. On the positive side, what this ministry represented was the fullness of Christ and God's eternal purpose in Him, the objective and subjective aspects of the cross of Christ, and the church which the Body of Christ in its spiritual and heavenly essence and universal nature. This ministry was to all Christians, regardless of connection or involvement in any Christian organization. Such a ministry to all of God's people is what the stand on Christ and Christ alone allowed and opened up.

The third accusation of exclusivism was a little more complicated to address. Firstly there were no special beliefs, practices, forms or teachings that needed to be ascribed to beyond that which was related to a new birth and a union with Christ by faith. Next there were no membership roles either of the local assembly at Honor Oak or of any wider fellowship. Thirdly there was no fellowship based on light received from the Lord, rather fellowship was simply based on life. If you have the same life you are in fellowship no matter how much light you have received from the Lord that caused your understanding of the truth to develop. This charge of exclusiveness was partially from the fact that the ministry at the Honor Oak conferences was not something that was typically heard from many of the devoted servants of God of evangelical faith. To this Sparks simply replied that his ministry was one which was the product of his particular history and experience with the Lord. His ministry was to bring people into the fullness of Christ and for this purpose he had passed through many sufferings to bring such a distinctive ministry to all of God's people. While Mr. Sparks did respect and see the value in other ministries, he also could not forsake the responsibility for the particular ministry that the Lord had entrusted to him. Thus, it was not Mr. Sparks' intention of becoming exclusive or developing an exclusive fellowship, but of being faithful to the portion that God had given him. The final item related to the charge of exclusiveness is the practice put in place at Honor Oak of laying hands on a person immediately after they were baptized and praying for them as a sign that the Body is one. It was this practice that caused those opposing to accuse Honor Oak of creating a special, exclusive fellowship, distinct from the rest the rest of the Body. To this Mr. Sparks replied that while he himself practiced this, he in no way forced others to practice this and furthermore he in no way regarded this practice as a basis for fellowship. If the Lord would lead others to practice it or not to practice it then Mr. Sparks would still fellowship with them.

Finally, Mr. Sparks gave a more personal word to address these issues. People were confused and wondered why were so many devoted and greatly used servants so much opposed the ministry of Mr. Sparks and others at Honor Oak. With all this opposition how could Mr. Sparks not be wrong? To this Mr. Sparks could only give his personal testimony.

> Years ago I was unquestionably stretched out to the full for God's best (as I trust I am now), and there was no doubt whatever as to my devotion to the Lord. I was right in the full tide of every kind of evangelical activity, and especially in conventions everywhere for the deepening of spiritual life. I was a member of many Missionary

Boards and Committees, and was greatly in demand because it was believed that I was a man with a message. This is putting into very few words an immense amount of truly devoted activity and concern for the Lord's interests. Being a man of prayer, I was open to the Lord for all His will, I believed. But there was a certain realm of things against which I was deeply prejudiced. It was really the very essence of the original ''Keswick'' teaching, but I would not have it at any price. I fought it and those who taught it. To make a long story short, the Lord took me seriously in hand along another line, and brought me into great spiritual distress. The very thing that proved my emancipation was that which I would not formerly have touched for anything. That proved the key to a fuller life and a worldwide ministry. I came to see that my judgment had been wholly wrong, and that I was blinded by prejudice. I believed that I was honest and right, and seemed to have evidence of it; but, no, I was in my ignorance shutting out something which was of great value to the Lord and to myself. Thank God for the grace to be perfectly honest when the fact of prejudice was brought home to my heart.... No man is infallible, and no one has yet "apprehended" nor is "yet perfect". Many godly men have had to adjust in the presence of fuller light given when a sense of need made such necessary.[30]

Many letters of thanks returned in response to the publishing of these three editor's letters. In the long run, it is hard to say what effect they had and how many people were less opposed. We do know that as the testimony at Honor Oak grew, especially over the course of the next ten years, the opposition to the ministry also grew and Mr. Sparks found himself addressing the same issues again and again.

Nineteen forty-six closed with two items that were indicative of the return to a normal post-war situation. Firstly, at the close of 1946 Mr. Sparks asked for prayers concerning his personal ministry in the coming months. Many request for visits for ministry had come to him from all over the world and he was very much before the Lord as to which ones to accept. This was a clear sign that the war-time conditions were over and now the Lord was opening again the possibilities of more travel and a reuniting of the fellowship with many seekers of God from around the world. The possibility of such travel was a great relief to Mr. Sparks, who had remarked so many times during the war how pressed he was to have face to face fellowship with so many that had been receiving his written ministry all over the world.

The second item indicating that the situation for the local assembly was returning to normal was the first conference held at Honor Oak since the conference center was destroyed. In October of that year, the brothers and sisters gathered in the salvaged basement of the Center for a joyous time of ministry of the word and fellowship. It may have been here that Mr. Sparks spoke a series of messages called "Four Greatnesses of Divine Revelation," a series that was made into a book in 1970 when Mr. Sparks was in his last days of life. This conference was the beginning of a truly heavenly time of ministering in many gatherings that were to follow after the war.

Nineteen forty-seven marked a year of restoration of many of the outward means through which the work would advance. Conferences were resumed in Kilcreggan for the purpose of training and equipping workers who were seriously set on serving the Lord; *A Witness and a Testimony* now returned to about 70 percent of its prewar size; and Mr. Sparks began traveling again to visit the growing number of seekers in different parts of the world. The post war period was to become a period of rapid growth in the number of people who were receiving and affected by Mr. Sparks' ministry.

In 1947, regular ministry was resumed by Mr. Sparks and by many other brothers. The conference center at Honor Oak was still not rebuilt, as the brothers were waiting on financial help from the war damage reparations fund. Meanwhile, many seekers expressed a great desire to come and partake of the ministering at Honor Oak. The brothers felt that the rebuilding of the conference center was a great priority to meet this growing need. In spite of not being able to accommodate many who were desirous, the local assembly at Honor Oak still gathered in the basement of the former Center. Here Mr. Sparks and many other brothers began to minister as they had before the war. Mr. Sparks also began holding longer conferences in Kilcreggan during the summer months. These were intended to be training sessions for those with serious intentions to enter the Lord's work. With the growing numbers of people hungry for something living and real of the Lord, Mr. Sparks sought to meet the need by training more workers who could minister, understand spiritual things, and be a part of a practical church life.

Mr. Sparks emphasized in his January editor's letter that their burden was the fullness of Christ and not the extension of any movement. He reminded his readers that his ways were different from the majority of Christian works because he sincerely felt that the system in which many Christian workers operate severely limited the Lord. He felt that many replace God Himself and His work with "things." Sparks stated that he had no desire to see his own work furthered if it did not please the Lord. "We have no tradition to keep going, and nothing here on this earth that we want to preserve."[31] Rather he sought to allow the Holy Spirit to operate in "direct spiritual ways" and thus not allow "things" to replace the genuine operation of His Spirit. Mr. Sparks was a man seeking to stand for Christ and His fullness alone and not even for his own work or the building up of his own following. Now that the world situation was much freer for the work to operate outwardly, he felt that he needed to emphasize that the essence of the work was the Holy Spirit's move and that these outward things should always take a lesser place to the greater work of the Spirit Himself. Thus he embarked with the little company of believers into a new year.

In 1947 *A Witness and a Testimony* returned to almost 70 percent of its prewar size and also experienced a great increase in demand. Paper shortages continued throughout this year making it a subject of prayer that the Lord would provide the paper to meet the growing demand. Because of the conferences and the greater freedom to hold regular ministry, longer series of articles were again being published in the journal. 1947 saw the publication of two series of articles: "God Has Spoken" and "Four Greatnesses of the Divine Revelation." In "Four Greatnesses," Mr. Sparks spoke on the theme of and need for enlargement. In these series, Sparks commented that many had been pressed and straightened outwardly and inwardly by the war but how many saw the fulfillment of the verse "In pressure hast Thou enlarged me"? Enlargement was the key to solve many problems among Christians in their relationships and in their Christian walk to fulfill God's purpose. These messages were fruit of experience that Mr. Sparks went through during the six year war-time period of outward straightening and "so intense and bitter spiritual pressure and conflict." 1947 also saw the resumption of articles by other brothers in fellowship with Mr. Sparks at Honor Oak. Out of the 36 articles published in 1947, 13 of them were spoken or written by C. J. B. Harrison, Harry Foster, S. Alexander, George Paterson and others. This was the result of the resumption of regular ministry at Honor Oak and showed that through the war Mr. Sparks was not alone in his service to the Lord.

The column entitled "For Boys and Girls" also resumed in 1947. This continued to present simple spiritual principles to children using many illustrations. In the first series of articles, aspects of a Christian's life with God were presented through the stories of Captain Scott's 1911 voyage to Antarctica. This column was to become a regular feature of the journal. It shows that there was concern and effort expended to reach young people in Mr. Sparks' ministry. The brothers and sisters were concerned that the spiritual truths and principles that the Lord gave them would be presented in a way that even children could understand and enjoy.

Nineteen forty-seven also marked a year in which Mr. Sparks could finally visit many children of God from around the world who had been receiving benefit from his ministry. Throughout the war, he had a yearning for this kind of fellowship and wrote of it in his editor's letters. Now the contact which was previously confined to letters was able to be made face to face. He received an invitation to Nilgiri Hills, India to speak at a series of annual conventions. Mr. Sparks felt it was of the Lord to go. So from May 5 to 23 he ministered to missionaries from America, Australia, Great Britain, Canada, New Zealand as well as local Indian believers at that series of conferences. After Mr. Sparks' visit, an announcement appeared in *A Witness and a Testimony* that now Witness and Testimony literature was available retail from Evangelical Literature Service 1/24, Vepery High Road, Madras India. The contact people in Madras were given to be Donald J. David and C. R. Golsworthy. India was to continue to be a place where there were many who received help from Mr. Sparks. Around a dozen missionaries who went to India had resided or fellowshipped at Honor Oak for some period of time. Now books were being sold retail in India. In the mid 1950s the brothers at Honor Oak were to further extend their work by buying a center for training and teaching to meet the growing need for the deeper truths in that country.

Upon arriving back in England, Mr. Sparks set off to spend the summer months in Kilcreggan where he gave many conferences for the training of workers. In September of that year Mr. Sparks along with his wife set sail for America and Canada. Before he left, he did not arrange a particular program for his visit. Rather, he left it to the Lord to open doors for his speaking engagements and to bring him into contact with those whom the Lord desired at that time. He was to travel over 16,000 miles on this journey and to give messages to seventy gatherings and have many personal and private meetings with seekers.

In America Mr. Sparks was hosted by Dr. Thornton Stearns of New Jersey. Dr. Stearns had been a missionary to China where he became acquainted with Watchman Nee. He was made an elder of the church in Shanghai by Watchman Nee and served the Lord faithfully in that capacity. During the war, Dr. Stearns was imprisoned by the Japanese and had become very involved in taking care of his fellow prisoners. He did this to the point of seriously jeopardizing his own health. In 1943 the Red Cross arranged an exchange of civilian prisoners. Dr. Stearns was released in this exchange and returned to New Jersey to recuperate from his exertions. Before leaving, Watchman Nee told Dr. Stearns to find T. Austin-Sparks when he got out of China and came to

America.[32] Taking Watchman Nee's advice, Dr. Stearns made contact with T. Austin-Sparks from his new home in East Orange, New Jersey. Their fellowship was very good to the point that Dr. Stearns hosted Mr. Sparks on his first visit to America after the war. Mr. Sparks announced his visit to the United States and Canada in an issue of *A Witness and a Testimony* and indicated that Dr. Stearns was the person to whom correspondence should be addressed if any brothers or sisters wished to fellowship with Mr. Sparks on his travels.

During this first trip, Mr. and Mrs. Sparks began in New Jersey, then traveled to Toronto, Vancouver, Los Angeles, and returned the same way with a stop in Minnesota. His trip was a testimony of the Lord's work. There were no advertisements, nor any other attraction, except for a truly significant presentation of Jesus Christ. Many who had been receiving help from Mr. Sparks through his journals and publications desired to further their fellowship. Generally the size of the gatherings increased as he went on. He attributed this to the Lord and to the rightness of his message which met a real need of God's people. Before his trip, he wondered how the ministry would be received. But the response was a strong encouragement to him. People received the ministry with an open heart and it was "acknowledged to be the very need of His people."[33]

The travels to India and America and Canada also gave Mr. Sparks an opportunity to form an impression of the current state of the Lord's people in these parts of the world. He felt that, on the whole, the church was very busy doing things but was unable to influence the world as it should. It did little to seriously shake the hold that spiritual forces had on so many people of this world. What was needed was a turning away from things, institutions etc. and a strong movement "to bring His people to know the fullness of Christ!"[33] He pointed out that there were many great evangelical and missionary movements in the past and the essence of what they did was to bring people into a greater measure of Christ. However, now these movements have drifted far from their original source and have become institutions, methods and formalities. What is needed now is a movement back to Christ and back to His fullness. Such is the only way that the church can hear a strong testimony and make an impact on the world. It is the only way the church can really affect Satan's work and the many operative sources of evil. How much we must be delivered from things to be brought back to the fullness of Christ.

In many ways Mr. Sparks was a different man than when he visited these places before the war. Through many experiences, God had worked as the potter, to make Mr. Sparks' vessel more fitting the ministry committed to him. He was shaped by the intensities of war; the evil reports circulated about him due to his presentation of the truth the Lord had given him; and the pressures of near constant uncertainty. It was over 20 years since he had set out with the little band at Honor Oak Baptist church and began to meet at the Honor Oak Christian Fellowship Center. What a twenty years they were! In another visit to America in the late 1940s, Mr. Sparks again visited Mary McDonough in Boston. He had last seen her about 20 years earlier on his first visit to America after he left Honor Oak Baptist. Upon seeing him two decades later, Mary McDonough's comment was, "You've Changed."[34]

And, yes Mr. Sparks had changed. Now he was entering his 59th year and was quite mature in the Christian life. Since he had last seen Mary McDonough, he had suffered separation from his close co-worker T. Madoc Jeffreys, was joined in the ministry by many other very solid brothers, and had witnessed a great expansion and spread of his ministry to reach seekers in almost every country in the world. He had published books and messages touching God's eternal purpose. One set of books, "The Stewardship of the Mystery," was to be his clearest unveiling, an encapsulation of the divine vision of God's eternal purpose. He had learned of the suffering accompanying the release of this kind of revelation. During the war years, he suffered greatly from the many evil reports circulated about him due to these books. Meanwhile, he had lived in uncertainty and sometimes in real fear of death in a city which bore the brunt of brutal air assaults for five years. He had witnessed shortages and severe limitation in his outward work and even the destruction of his conference center. Throughout his prolific service and energetic ministry, he suffered from a chronic and recurring physical ailment that forced him to trust God for even the most basic matters. Through all this, he had learned much of Christ and was made clearer about his own commitment to the Lord. By the end of the war, he was able to say that he desired nothing on this earth to remain that was not pleasing and useful to the Lord; this included any part of his own ministry. The price he was paying for his ministry was too great for there to be no reality in what he was doing. In his view he was for no "thing" but only for God's interest, which was that believers would be brought into a real and genuine experience of Christ resulting in the fullness of Christ. Such was the only hope for the church to make a genuine impact on the world and bear a strong testimony in this age.

As he visited places, he seemed different to many. He had a presence with him of being a person who knew the Lord to some degree and who also knew how to follow Him in the way of life. It was this growth through the law of the grain of wheat falling to the ground and dying that was to bear fruit over the next ten years of his ministry. He was to see a further worldwide expansion, to see many capable young men gained at home, and was to see groups around the world greatly appreciate the ministry of life and truth that he would unveil to them. The twenty years of preparation, including learning Christ in the midst of world wide reception of his ministry and in the midst of limitation and shrinking during the war, produced a man who could somewhat understand God's mind and could be used by God for His fuller work.

Expansion and Enrichment
1948 – 1958

The decade from 1948 to 1958 was the one where the building ministry of T. Austin-Sparks and his co-workers grew in both scope and depth and reached more hungry seekers than at any time in the past. These years were in many ways a contrast to the war-time experience. The situation created by World War II saw Mr. Sparks' travels limited, *A Witness and a Testimony* reduced in size and distribution, many believers from "hushed" countries cut off from practical fellowship, and the conferences at Honor Oak suspended after the conference center was destroyed. God had many lessons for Mr. Sparks and his co-workers during the war years. They learned not to trust in movements, open doors, capabilities and buildings. Just as Paul counted all things as loss and then suffered the loss of all things, the war brought Mr. Sparks through a similar experience with his ministry. Many times before, he mentioned that he was not for outward matters pertaining to his ministry. During the war years, he was greatly limited and continually faced the very real and physical possibility that his ministry would be terminated. Upon passing through this test, Mr. Sparks and his co-workers could genuinely say that they desired only Christ Himself. They could declare based on experience that as soon as their service was no longer of any use to Him, they would gladly allow it to be put aside to emphasize again that all things will be headed up in Christ and that Christ will be all in all.

After such an experience where they learned not to trust in outward success, the Lord gave the brothers at Honor Oak a ten year period where those benefiting from their ministry grew in number both at home and abroad. The conference center at Honor Oak was rebuilt to over twice its pre-war size and conferences there averaged over four hundred guests. Some even larger conferences were held during this time in local conference centers, because the facility at Honor Oak could not handle the growing number of seekers from Britain itself, not to mention those from many places abroad. Honor Oak once again became a gathering place for ministers of Jesus from all over the world, who would visit to fellowship and further enrich the ministry of the gatherings. Hundreds of salvation experiences were witnessed as a result of the ministry at Honor Oak. The attendance at conferences and regular ministry gatherings increased to three or four hundred, a large fraction of which was young people. Demand for literature grew each year and the distribution of *A Witness and a Testimony* grew to reach almost every country with a total number of subscribers exceeding three thousand. Mr. Sparks began sending out tapes of his speaking to many hungry seekers who requested them from all over the world. He also renewed contact with native Christian groups in China, Africa, India and South America. He traveled widely and regularly visited the Far East, India and North America. Distribution centers for Witness and Testimony literature were established in Minneapolis, Minnesota and Los Angeles, California. The Witness and Testimony trust obtained a property in Mysore State India that served as a distribution center for literature and a center for ministering the greater riches which were able to build up churches in that country. Mr. Sparks was warmly welcomed by large groups of believers in Taiwan (at that time called Formosa), the Philippines and Hong Kong. Mr. Sparks traveled to the Far East twice to visit the churches where he was warmly welcomed and spoke on occasions to congregations of over three thousand seekers.

At the same time that the world-wide expansion of his ministry was taking place, the Lord was also allowing even more suffering and persecution for Mr. Sparks and the company at Honor Oak. These situations were to do their work in molding Mr. Sparks to make him more of a living example of the ministry he preached. In 1951 George Patterson was unexpectedly taken to be with the Lord. The loss of such a close co-worker was a blow to Mr. Sparks that is hard to describe in full. Also the 1950s saw opposition to Honor Oak reach unparalleled proportions even to the point of the evangelical community publishing a book of warning against the Honor Oak teaching.

This period saw Mr. Sparks as a minister who had reached a very mature stage. He was in his sixtieth year and had learned many lessons in the school of Christ over the last forty years, since he first began announcing Christ with that group of young gospel preachers on the street in Glasgow. Many who attended the post-war conferences at Honor Oak testified that the ministry was so rich that they felt as if they were under an opened heaven. If we look at Mr. Sparks' ministry, we could divide it into a number of stages, from the time Mr. Sparks ministered at Honor Oak Baptist to the present decade of the 1950s. In the first stage of ministry, up to and immediately after leaving Honor Oak Baptist, Mr. Sparks' messages were full of Bible verses and included many terms, like 'superhistorical' or 'the kosmic cross' describing the wondrous implications of the cross of Christ. In the second stage, encompassing most of the 1930s, his messages more profoundly and powerfully expounded God's eternal purpose—to head up all things in Christ—and the way God would gain His purpose—through the exaltation of Christ who is the center and content of the Church. The interlude of the war gave Mr. Sparks time to consider what he saw from the Word and what he saw of the world situation, both politically and spiritually. His books during this war-time period began to open the way to see that God's way of fulfilling His purpose was by the operation of His divine life in the believers who were all in the school of Christ being taught the riches of Christ by their tutor, the Holy Spirit. The fourth stage of His ministry falls roughly between the years 1948 and 1958. In this stage we find Mr. Sparks' clearest expounding of the way believers can enter into God's eternal purpose and fulfill God's eternal purpose. In this stage, Mr. Sparks ministered to hungry audiences both at Honor Oak and around the world. These Christ seekers drew out many riches that Mr. Sparks had learned from the Lord. In this period Mr. Sparks revealed what it is to be a real prophet in this age, what the pathway is of a pioneer of the heavenly way, what true service to the Lord is, how we can stand with the Lord as He recovers His testimony, and what it is to build the church with the everlasting gold of the sanctuary. In the 1950s Mr. Sparks also reprinted a book from the late twenties, *God's Reactions to Man's Defections*, and added seven messages to it that described the life necessary for a person to stand with the reactions of God in this age. On the whole this period was the richest period of Mr. Sparks' ministry that unveiled the practical steps of a believer interacting with God and entering into God's eternal purpose.

This period combines many ingredients necessary for a rich, experiential ministry to be spoken. First there was a mature minister, Mr. Sparks, who had learned many lessons from the Lord and who was full of riches from the Word and from his experience. Second, this period gave Mr. Sparks a setting conducive to the speaking of his riches. The brothers and sisters at Honor Oak greatly appreciated his riches and were fully supportive of his ministry. At the same time, the world was becoming opened to him with many groups inviting him to speak in North America, India and the Far East. Third, this period provided Mr. Sparks with audiences of believers who had grown in their spiritual life through much of his ministry over the past years. This provided a way for him to speak about matters beyond the basic spiritual experiences of salvation. While he shared with a congregation, Mr. Sparks would not speak beyond the spiritual level of his listeners. As he was ministering to an audience, he could tell by their reaction how much they were receiving and would repeat or illustrate various points until he felt they had come to a spiritual understanding of them. With this kind of exercise it was necessary to have a group of listeners who were maturing and growing in their Christian life in order to speak of any higher or more experiential aspects of the Christian life. All three of these factors were present during Mr. Sparks' ministry between 1948 and 1958. Thus, his books during this time are rich, profound, clear, practical, experiential, simple, pure, and focused on Christ and His eternal purpose. These messages were keenly intended to bring to full growth many believers who would constitute the church as the instrument with which God could fulfill His eternal purpose.

Laboring at the Base in Honor Oak

In 1948 London was a city still recovering from massive wartime destruction. Upon returning to Britain from his visit to North America, Mr. Sparks felt from the Lord that he should remain in London to take care of the

Lord's great need there. Many seekers expressed strong desires to visit the Center at Honor Oak for fellowship and ministry. However, the authorities still did not allow any repairs to be done, pending further review of the situation of the conference center. Furthermore, a new paper shortage was threatening to limit the size and distribution of *A Witness and a Testimony* as well as the distribution of other Witness and Testimony literature. This shortage hit amidst a rapidly growing demand for the journal and other literature worldwide. All these matters were subjects of much of Mr. Sparks' prayer and energy during the late 1940s. Except for a brief visit to India in the spring of 1949, the years of 1948 through 1950 saw Mr. Sparks put all his energy into the ministry and the work at Honor Oak.

Eventually, in late 1948, the conference center at Honor Oak was rebuilt with the help of funds from the government War Damage Reparations program. The conference room was enlarged to almost twice its prewar size, with overflow rooms in the former dormitories. The facility could now comfortably accommodate gatherings of over four hundred people. The guest house and kitchen facilities were also enlarged to accommodate twice the number of people compared with their prewar size. The hospitality provided at the guesthouse was augmented by a number of private properties nearby, which together housed attendants who came from afar to the five yearly conferences held at the center. For the next twelve years the conference center was used for five yearly ministry gatherings. It began with a January conference, part of which was dedicated to the needs of Christian workers, then came the Easter gathering followed by the Whitsun gathering fifty days later. In the summer was the August bank holiday gathering. Finally there was a conference in the fall in October. Notice for each gathering would be posted in *A Witness and a Testimony*. These yearly conferences were to become places where many seekers of the word of God from all over the world would come for fellowship and ministry. During these three years, 1948-1950, Mr. Sparks sought to labor in a way where he could remain in London and minister to people who came to enjoy the rich ministry at Honor Oak. He saw this as the Lord's present way to fulfill his ministry and therefore chose to turn down many invitations from abroad requesting his presence. In May of 1950, Mr. Sparks debates in a letter to the editor, whether he should continue this kind of "home base" exercise or whether he should once again travel to visit believers in a yearly circuit. For the rest of the 1950's Mr. Sparks chose to travel a significant amount and to meet believers where they were instead of asking them to come to Honor Oak to enjoy his ministry and the ministry of his many co-workers.

While Mr. Sparks was taking care of the needs at home in London, his written ministry was being distributed by more and more brothers and sisters in many far off lands. In 1947, after Mr. Sparks visit to India, Witness and Testimony literature began to be distributed in that country from two brothers in Madras. In 1948, after Mr. Sparks visit to America, his literature began to be distributed from two different places in the States. The first was by a brother in Minneapolis, a Mr. H.E. Almquist of the Christian Literature Store, 3025 Irving Avenue South, Minneapolis Minnesota.[1] The second was with a brother in Los Angeles, a Dr. James Graham of Olivet House, 1505 South Westmoreland Avenue, Los Angeles CA.[2] Both of these addresses were announced in issues of *A Witness and a Testimony*. The Los Angeles group was to continue to support and receive Mr. Sparks' ministry for more than 20 years, until his death in 1971.

The regular church life at the center also flourished during this time. Many new people, who had been prepared by the war to take serious steps with Christ, were brought into a loving, close family of believers. Together this family grew to hold a view that they were there for a testimony of a preeminent Christ to the entire world. A brother who came to know the Lord during this time at the center at Honor Oak testified that a big difference between the fellowship at Honor Oak and other Christian gatherings was that these people knew one another so well. It truly felt like a close family, with Mr. Austin-Sparks as a father figure.[3] There was fellowship in the weekly gatherings and also at other times throughout the week, which created a close bond between all those gathered there. Prayer meetings were held twice a week at Honor Oak and they were of special note. Prayers in their gatherings were not supplications from poor beggars. Rather, many would gather to pray prayers of authority as ones joined with Christ sharing the throne with Christ. Name after name and situation after situation from around the world would be brought to the assembly where one by one the prayer of authority would be exercised before God until a feeling emerged that the prayer had been heard. Many times, a few weeks after praying a prayer, news of an answer would come to the joy and encouragement of those at Honor Oak.[4] The assembly surely had a loving church life and shared a common, worldwide view that this Christ was for the whole earth and that God was moving for His interests across the entire globe.

In 1948, while Mr. Sparks was focusing his energies on his base at Honor Oak, he also was very concerned for the way the world political and spiritual situation was evolving. He wrote in a May editor's letter to express his feeling of the current circumstances of God's people. At that time only the United States had nuclear weapons, but the very real possibility of a nation having the power to eliminate tens of thousands of people in a split second was a significant change in the world political situation. Also Mr. Sparks saw that many countries were rapidly becoming closed to the gospel and even actively prohibiting Christian worship. There may have been a deep feeling in Mr. Sparks for Watchman Nee and all the churches in China, who now were in the midst of a bloody civil war with a powerful, religion-eradicating, communist party. There was a feeling in him echoing the words of the Lord Jesus, "Except those days be shortened, there shall no flesh be saved."[5] These events caused him to consider that the Lord may be near and that the church must intensify its work in the believers to meet the present need of the world situation. He felt that at this time there was a pause in the unfolding of events, as if it were time to wait for something from the heavens to be carried out on the earth. The church however, in its present condition, was largely conscious of only "bafflement, smothering, and inadequacy."[5] As a response to these circumstances, Mr. Sparks encouraged corporate and individual prayer that 1) "the work needing to be done both within the church and through her unto His appearing shall be intensified and perfected" and 2) "the restraining work of God shall be exercised in and over the nations until the above is accomplished."[5] This, he felt, was the responsibility of Christians facing the pressing world situation of the time.

On February 24, 1949, Mr. Sparks made a brief visit to India, possibly to share at an annual conference for missionaries and native believers. Notice was given in *A Witness and a Testimony* requesting prayer for Mr. Sparks in view of the spiritual burden he was bearing and in view of a very real physical need. It was at this time that Mr. Sparks' sickness resurfaced once again. He struggled to continue to minister and serve throughout that spring and summer, in spite of the recurrence of his physical ailment. He arrived at Honor Oak in time to minister at the Easter gathering and then continued his speaking at the Whitsun gathering. Throughout the summer, he proceeded to hold special week-long conferences at Heathfield, in Kilcreggan.

In the fall of 1949, Mr. Sparks' illness became even worse and resulted in him being admitted to the hospital in November. On November 8, he underwent an operation, and on November 28, he was in need of another, more serious operation. He spent the following months recovering from these. For more than twenty years previous to this, his illness made him frequently prostrate with pain and unable to carry on his work. Some of his travels to minister were cut short due to a recurrence of his illness. Sometimes he would literally rise up from his sick bed to carry out some aspect of his service to the Lord. In Mr. Sparks' life, this illness was a big part of the cross that the Lord had graciously laid out for him to bear. Those around him testified to the increase in his spiritual measure from the suffering of this physical ailment. During the frequent surges of the intensity of his pain, the many brothers and sisters at Honor Oak prayed more fervently for him. After these struggles, they surely saw a deepening of his spiritual life and a deeper reliance on the Lord Himself to enliven his mortal body. It was not until these operations, in late 1949, that Mr. Sparks was finally completely released from his physical pain. These operations proved to be God's means of grace to relieve Mr. Sparks of his physical limitation. For the next 20 years Sparks was able to vigorously serve the Lord through tens of thousands of miles of travel and while keeping a busy schedule of ministering and writing. He was truly an example of how the divine life can energize the mortal body.

In May of 1950 Mr. Sparks wrote a letter of thanks to his readers for their support of him by prayer and other means throughout his long recovery. He also expressed his optimism that the limiting suffering of the many past years finally would be eliminated and that upon his full recovery he should be much stronger than he ever was before. He also expressed how much was owed to the many brothers who "carry so much of the burden of the many-sided ministry."[6] While he was indisposed, much of the work went on smoothly showing that the ministry he was engaged in was not dependent on one single man. He was standing in oneness with many other brothers who were devoted to the same vision of the ministry that was committed to him. At this time Mr. Sparks also sought prayer from his readers that he would be clearly led by the Lord into the next phase of his labors. He wondered if he should stay at Honor Oak and minister to those who traveled to him or whether he should respond to some of the many invitations he was receiving from all over the world. He writes, "The question is whether to keep to a base and seek to meet the wider need through personal contacts here and the printed ministry, or to do what Samuel did—have a house from which to go 'in a circuit from year to year, and return.'"[6] As we will see, in the very next year Mr. Sparks began to travel increasingly, responding to the many invitations from around the world.

Later in May, Mr. Sparks found himself strong enough to minister the full three days at the Whitsun conference in London. It appeared that his hopes had materialized and that he would indeed more than recover; he would be stronger and more able than he had been in the past.

Throughout the period between 1948 and 1950 seven series of articles appeared in *A Witness and a Testimony*. These series, which were mainly written transcriptions of the conference ministry from that time, vividly portrayed the rich ministry that Mr. Sparks was presenting. From these we begin to see how his messages pointed the way for seekers to grow in the divine life and to have their Christian life conform to God's timeless purpose in Christ. In these messages Mr. Sparks speaks very much from his personal experience and relates the pathway that the Lord led him on during his rich and experiential walk with Christ. These series included Prophetic Ministry; The Cross, the Church, and the Kingdom; A Way of Growth; Behold My Servant; A Candlestick All of Gold; The Gospel of the Glory; and Spiritual Hearing.

World Travel and the Loss of a Close Co-Worker

Nineteen fifty-one began as a year of optimism. While there was a dramatic increase in opposition and suspicion from the evangelical community towards the brothers at Honor Oak, there was also a real sense that the Lord was with them. In a January 1951 editorial, Sparks echoes the Apostle Paul's word that he was very aware of God's presence with him and especially of the "exceeding greatness of His power to us-ward."[7] When Mr. Sparks considered the great might of the enemy arrayed in so many ways against his ministry, he could only say, "Having received help from God we continue unto this day."[7] There was a genuine feeling that as the magazine was entering its 29th year, only God could have preserved the ministry through so much opposition. Mr. Sparks also felt grateful to his readers for the many letters testifying of the help they received through the ministry and of its real value for them in attaining unto a fuller enrichment in the things of God. Such letters came from many ministers, missionaries, experienced servants of the Lord, and others. Mr. Sparks also was full of thanks to the Lord for the widespread distribution of his written ministry, which had spread to places way beyond where he could personally reach. He hoped his written ministry would work to accomplish God's desired goal "till we all attain unto the (full) knowledge of the Son of God, unto a full-grown man, unto the measure of the stature of the fullness of Christ." Then Sparks summarizes the intended effect of his ministry, "It is so little realized that the Lord's ordained and normal way is through a Church in life and oneness, and that the 'fullness of Christ' is *the* goal of all."[7] Then he exposes the enemy's scheme against this end. "The great enemy is very busy against that, and more than ever - the end being so near—should the Lord's people be on their guard against the suspicions and misapprehensions which serve the enemy's purpose to divide, and thus defeat the divine end."[7] Sparks began 1951 aggressively and optimistically pursuing the burden the Lord committed to him. In the January conference, Mr. Sparks spoke a rich series of messages, which were to become the book entitled "The Work of God at the End Time." The remainder of the year was to be one of expansion, traveling, greater opposition from without and a great, unexpected loss from within.

In the first half of 1951, Sparks made his first trip to America since his previous visit in 1947. In a September editor's letter Sparks thanks the many friends who prayed for him during his travels and the many more who greeted him with love and fellowship. He had a very full schedule and was disappointed by his inability to stay longer and minister to more of the great need facing him in the States. He describes his general feeling from his travels as being impressed with a "deep" and "appealing" and "heart-breaking" need.[8] Sparks had an unusual vision of the fuller purpose of God for His people. In light of this vision, he saw the situation of Christians in America and felt that in America, as in almost all parts of the world, Christians were far short of an aim that would produce God's fuller thought—the fullness of Christ. Sparks asked his readers to "Pray with us that, yet, He may have His 'eternal purpose' brought into fuller expression in a concrete way in many places."[8] For this Mr. Sparks felt a deep need for his travail "the fellowship of His sufferings." This travail was not for simple salvation of souls but was a suffering that would lead to fullness, "a suffer-

ing of Christ for His body's sake, which is the church."
One impression that Mr. Sparks received from his travels
was the necessity for the ministry entrusted to him. From
his extensive familiarity of the current spiritual condition
he felt that the ministry given to him was able to touch the
condition of believers and to answer a deep need voiced
by many who were not satisfied with the way things were.
Mr. Sparks was truly concerned for the many readers of
his magazine, not for the success of his ministry but for
the "fuller satisfaction of the Lord," which his ministry
would bring people into.

In the same issue of *A Witness and a Testimony*
came an announcement of unspeakable grief and utter surprise to Mr. Sparks and others at Honor Oak. George
Paterson, late assistant editor of *A Witness and a Testimony* and faithful co-worker from before the time the
brothers left Honor Oak Baptist, died on Saturday, July
21, 1951. Four pages were dedicated to describing his
life, his contribution, and the gathering they had to remember him. George was a man of unusual physical vitality and energy. The brothers were aware of his continual outpouring of himself for the affairs of the work and
of the particular exhaustion of all his reserves in the more
recent months. They were surprised when in a period of
48 hours the effects of a pneumonic virus were first seen
and ultimately culminated in his being taken away from
his earthly service to the presence of the Lord. The brothers had a gathering for his remembrance at the Center and
a simple graveside service "in which the beauty of the
Lord was felt."[9] The following night, a large crowd gathered for a remembrance of this brother's life and contribution to the Lord's work.

Mr. Sparks testified how he had known George
Paterson for more than thirty years and witnessed him
growing from a very young stage in the Christian life to
become a believer who was quite mature in Christ.

George was very instrumental in the spread of this ministry from its small and local beginnings to the worldwide reach that it held today. George Paterson lived a life full of sacrifice for Christ. Even though he possessed a good civil service job and had won recognition by national honors in his office, he heeded the Lord's call and stepped out to serve Him in a full time capacity. His time truly was full and was marked by outpouring and paying a cost for the Lord's interest. Of more note than his participation in "the work" was his real ministry of Christ, which only came from what he was in the Lord. Many thousands who had met him and had interacted with him felt as if they had met the Lord. It seemed that he had picked up the essence of Mr. Sparks' ministry—that God values who you are in Him much more than what you do for Him. It was this prominent characteristic, which caused Mr. Sparks to appreciate the labor and support of George Paterson. He lived a life exhibiting what Mr. Sparks taught.

Mr. A. G. Taylor also spoke about his appreciation for Brother Paterson through his many years of serving side by side with him, often in prayers. Brother Paterson was a man "wise in heart" and many sought his counsel, grew much in the Lord because of it and leaned hard upon it. Now that the Lord took Brother Paterson away, Mr. Taylor felt that we all must learn to lean even more upon Christ Himself. In the last months of his life, Mr. Paterson was especially concerned for the next generation to be raised up with an utter commitment to Christ and to the particular testimony that the brothers in the fellowship had been called to bear. Mr. Taylor pointed out how quickly the first generation could pass away and therefore how important raising up a new generation was for the continuance of this testimony.

Mr. Harry Foster described Brother Paterson with three words: meekness, reliability and loyalty. In meekness brother Paterson was one who would speak honest words with people without a condescending attitude toward even younger brothers and sisters. Brother Paterson's reliability was the source of confidence for many brothers, near and far, who were aware of the great number of problems facing the ministry both from without and from within. Brother Paterson's loyalty was manifested because he knew so many weaknesses of the brothers around him, but still remained loyal to them and to the Lord's interest that was being carried out through them.

Finally, C. J. B. Harrison added that he appreciated exceedingly the continual fervent and fresh spirit that Brother Paterson had. His inner fellowship with Christ was the source of his persistent gladness and cheer and his continual fire.

Some would say that the passing of Brother Paterson was the beginning of increased misunderstandings between the brothers at Honor Oak. The description of him at this gathering highlights some crucial characteristics he had, which greatly helped in keeping a fellowship together. When working so close to one another especially under the weight of almost constant Satanic attack, a brother who is fresh with the Lord, meek, and loyal to the other brothers in spite of the others' faults becomes a balm to heal many wounds. Without such an attitude, baseless suspicion, something the enemy uses frequently, can grow to become a real barrier to fellowship. The seeds of mistrust, suspicion and accusation constantly sown by the enemy within the fellowship at Honor Oak were to find fertile soil near the end of the 1950's. Had Brother Paterson not been taken, these seeds may have never taken root. However, the Lord's timing is His and we must trust that it is always right. Possibly the loss of brother Paterson at this time caused a further increase in spiritual measure and riches in Mr. Sparks' ministry and the ministry of others at the center. Only in eternity may we fully know the impact of the loss of this brother at this time to the little band of faithful followers at Honor Oak.

When George Patterson died, the insert circulated in *A Witness and a Testimony* was four pages long. No other brother was given this much space when he passed away. We surmise that no other brother was so close to Mr. Sparks. Brother Paterson was called his closest colleague. His passing must have been a great blow to Mr. Sparks and must have pushed him even more to lean upon Jesus and Jesus alone. Mr. Sparks' life was unusually full of sufferings of all kinds and from all angles. Here at this juncture of time, the Lord saw fit to include this particular angle in the suffering life of Mr. Sparks. As Mr. Sparks himself testified, in the school of Christ one learns much more by suffering than by studying.

During the second half of 1951, Mr. Sparks continued to minister in both the local conferences and abroad. In late August he traveled to Switzerland to give a week-long series of messages in addition to the normal week-long conferences held in Kilcreggan during the summer months.

In 1951 one new series of messages was published in *A Witness and a Testimony* in addition to "The Work of God at the End Time," which was published directly as a book in the same year. Mr. Sparks began to publish a series of articles called "His Great Love." In this series he explores God's relationship with man based on His great love in contrast with the self-interest so many times prevalent in God's people in the Bible and today. Mr. Sparks also spoke two other messages that were to become booklets in 1952. These were called "The Service of God" and "Some Principles of the House of God." In "The Service of God," Mr. Sparks outlines his view of true service of God and describes the training he regards as crucial in producing a spiritual person who is capable of serving God. True service of God leads to the increase of the measure of Christ both in the servant and in those being served. For people who desire to be trained to serve God, Mr. Sparks outlines that their training must be both Biblical and practical. Biblically, God's word must not simply be presented in a series of lectures, but must be spiritually taught and apprehended. Practically this training must take place alongside other believers, where crucial lessons of cooperation and forbearance can be learned. The training should also not be detached from everyday tasks and work fitted for different ages and sexes. There could be many lessons found in washing dishes and digging gardens. Finally, the training is most profitable if done in the setting of a local church, where practical lessons can be learned and immediately applied to the corporate life of a group of believers living together on the organic basis of the Body of Christ.

God's Purpose Verses the Sad State of Christianity

We will divide the remainder of Mr. Sparks' ministry in the 1950s into roughly two time periods: from 1952 to 1954 and from 1955 to 1958. These time periods see Mr. Sparks in much improved health after his operations. During the first time period, he traveled much more extensively than ever before and thereby became more intimately acquainted with the state of Christians all over the world. He sadly reported the lack in expressing the standard of God's testimony and he was impressed even more for the need for God to raise up an instrument through which He could obtain His purpose in His believers and thus bring in the fullness of Christ. To this end Mr. Sparks ministered messages that touched God's testimony, the fullness of Christ and the pathway for pioneers to walk on in order to obtain that testimony. These titles include: *The Recovering of the Lord's Testimony in Fullness, Union with Christ, The Significance of Christ, The*

Service of God, and *Pioneers of the Heavenly Way.* The emphasis in his many editorials during this period was on the condition of the church in general and on the need for such a ministry to feed God's people and to bring in God's purpose.

The next period of his ministry, from 1955 to 1958, was one seriously concerned about the heavenly nature and practical expression of the church. This period was marked by two visits to the island of Formosa, where Mr. Sparks witnessed a great scene of God's working. He saw here that the emphasis of this work was on the church as God's instrument for His testimony. This view encouraged Mr. Sparks and even confirmed his commitment to the church as God's unique instrument. He had seen this matter of the church early in his ministry and had even spoken about it at Honor Oak Baptist, during the last meeting he held there before the little company went up the hill to Honor Oak Fellowship Center. Now he had seen an example of it and was deeply affected. This time period begins with editorials describing the emphasis of his ministry being the fuller meaning of the cross, life in the Spirit, and the heavenly nature, vocation and destiny of the church. Furthermore he states that the New Testament makes it clear that "God has bound Himself to the church in a very full and utter way. He has made it clear that His means and method of fulfilling His eternal counsels concerning His Son is 'Churchwise.'"[10] This period ends with a long series of editorials on the essential nature and function of the church. All these events and writings show that Mr. Sparks was very much concerned and taken up with the matter of the church during this second time period.

We begin now to look at the first period of ministry after Mr. Sparks' operation. Nineteen fifty-two was to be a very full year for Mr. Sparks. In this one year, he was to travel 26,000 miles by air alone and even more by other means. He did more traveling this year than any previous year of his life, which possibly may have been one of the first issues of his drastically improved health. His extensive visitation and ministry to large and small groups gave him an intimate picture of the condition of Christians throughout a large part of the world and enabled him to assess the spiritual situation of many peoples and areas. The more he traveled the more he became keenly aware of the need for the ministry God committed to him. This was not a selfish realization, where he merely desired to have more followers. In fact, Mr. Sparks stated that the ministry he had was crucial to the Lord's people, but which instrument the Lord used (whether Mr. Sparks or another) was a secondary matter. Mr. Sparks was genuinely concerned that God's purpose would be fulfilled among His people. This purpose in short was to bring in the fullness of Christ through the church as the unique instrument. In the many places Mr. Sparks visited in 1952, he did not see a strong testimony up to the standard of the New Testament testimony shown to him by the Lord.

Nineteen fifty-two began with Mr. Sparks writing an editor's letter in which he mentioned his rejoicing because of the many letters reporting help received from the ministry. These letters were a source of encouragement for Mr. Sparks. Because of their continual arrival, Mr. Sparks felt "constantly checked from despairing of fruitfulness."[11] This year very few countries did not have some believers receiving *A Witness and a Testimony*. Mr. Sparks hoped that this year the Lord through this ministry would continue to work in a "spontaneous way", as He had for the past 25 years, to stem the natural trend downward, which is so evident in the realm of spiritual fullness. Sparks writes, "This ministry is reactionary in the right sense, reactionary against this whole tendency. It is thrown into battle for 'the fullness of Christ' against earthboundness, against nominalism, against spiritual complacency, false contentedness: against all that is less or other than all that Christ represents of God's eternal purpose."[11] To accomplish this it is essential that people have a ministry that keeps them in a clear vision, thus to combat the forces of evil that would try to place "position, measure, and occupation" in place of desiring the "fullness of Christ."

In May of that same year, Mr. Sparks wrote more about the current situation of God's people. He pointed out that his ministry was not one of merely teaching or of conveying a certain "technique of truth." Rather he sought to maintain in life and reality and in an "up-to-the-day vital contact with spiritual conditions and need."[12] To this end God was faithful to keep the ministers in almost continual spiritual pressure and conflict in order that they would be continually in vital contact with Him and with His people. Mr. Sparks felt that specifically for this time the church was moving into very critical times. While the Christians in the free, Western countries undertook a great effort at evangelism, already many Christians under oppressive regimes had recently come under governments that persecuted and shook them. China was a prime example and other countries, like those of Eastern Europe and central Asia, showed the same pattern. Might this not be the beginning of the "great shaking" spoken about in the Word? Already some in these countries had fallen away from the faith. This was a clear example of why a mere decision for Christ, advocated so strongly by mass evangelism, was not adequate. Rather, a deeper ministry was necessary so that some may follow the steps of those who had been "faithful unto death" in the countries where Christians were now persecuted. Mr. Sparks was truly appreciative for the evangelism that brought many to Christ but was also keenly aware of the need for building up to full growth to meet the growing pressure faced by so many Christians. How much God needs ministries concerned with the "mass of the New Testament teaching which has to do with people already saved."[13] These ministries may turn out to be the very means for the survival of faith in anything raised up by the Lord to lead to "going on."

In the last issue of 1952 Mr. Sparks looks back on his year with deep concern and consideration for the spiritual situation of God's people. Through the extensive traveling and ministry of Mr. Sparks and his colleagues he felt that they were "in immediate and direct touch with the spiritual and actual situation represented by a large area."[14] In this letter he expands even more on how the current situation among most Christians limits people from realizing God's purpose. He had no hesitation in saying that the spiritual situation is "very, very sad and deplorable." If things were going to change, Mr. Sparks felt that the only way is if there were some "great and drastic judgment from heaven of Christendom." He was convinced that such judgment had begun. This must be a reference to the state of many Christians under the recently emerged oppressive regimes covering over half the globe and encompassing well over half the population. As the letter to Hebrews was intended to detach believers from earthly things and to attach them to a heavenly Christ, so such a shaking might have the same result. Like the Judaistic system in Hebrews, the present system of Christianity had become "largely an earthly, traditional, formal, and unspiritual thing." At the same time "in a very small part of our lifetime the phrase 'world evangelization' (from one part to another) has become unusable... Countries which were until quite recently the greatest spheres of 'missionary' activity are now closed to such."[15] Mr. Sparks felt strongly that this worldwide shaking was "quite necessary" to deliver so many who call themselves Christians from an utterly false position. The object of such a shaking is not to deliver believers from one system into a better system with a better church practice. Rather it is to bring them to the heavenly Christ Himself and thus to bring them into life. "Churches, like the Church, are organisms which spring out of life, which life itself springs out of the Cross of Christ wrought into the very being of believers."[15] Then what is necessary to meet the oncoming test? One necessary ingredient is "a ministry which has its substance and object the 'rooting and grounding', the establishing, the building up, of believers; the real increase of 'the measure of Christ.'"[15] He encouraged people to pray that a new mighty move of the Spirit of God would be in the direction of "spiritual purity, strength and reality."[15] This genuinely would be a move toward Christ Himself. Thus the great shaking could accomplish its purpose and bring in the fullness of Christ among God's people.

In 1952 the annual conferences at Honor Oak continued, as well as a summer of monthly conference gatherings in Heathfield, Kilcreggan. Two conferences were also held in two towns in central Switzerland: one in Kiental for young people and another in Krattigen in early September. In September, Mr. Sparks continued his ministry on the continent during a ten-day conference in Villengen, Germany. The 1952 issues of *A Witness and a Testimony* carried two new series of messages entitled "Followers of the Lamb" and "Union with Christ." "Union with Christ" was to be published as a book and emphasized the believer's full experiential union with the personal Christ and the corporate Christ.

In 1953 Mr. Sparks continued to speak further about the significance of Christ and the crucial need of God to recover His testimony in fullness. Mr. Taylor, a close colleague of Mr. Sparks, spent the first half of this year in India in fellowship with the extensive group of believers that the Lord had raised up in that country through the instrumentality of brother Bakht Singh. The regular conference gatherings continued throughout 1953, with Mr. Sparks traveling as he had the year before. As in the previous year, the summer was occupied with monthly gatherings for Christian workers in Heathfield, Kilcreggan. The August conference at Honor Oak was on the Altar and the Name as depicted in the life of Abraham.

In the September issue of *A Witness and a Testimony* Mr. Sparks sought to remind his readers of the clear and definite purpose of his ministry. His ministry was not mere academic teaching, but a vital response to the practical situations and immediate issues facing believers at that time. But how can such a ministry be formed? It was an issue of lessons learned in the "school of deep and, often, painful experience."[16] Mr. Sparks explained that in the Old Testament God first explained a pattern and then commanded things to come into being accordingly. In contrast, in the New Testament God begins with mighty works, like the death and resurrection of Christ, and afterwards explained them, revealing more and more of their implications and realities. Mr. Sparks' ministry grew according to the New Testament pattern; God brought him through dealings related to his present environment and then taught him what those dealings mean. The content of such teaching is what composed his ministry. If he were to sum up what he learned of "the work and teaching of the Lord," it would be the following statement. The present state of Christianity has been separated vitally, spiritually, organically and immediately from the Person of Christ and has instead degraded into a crystallization, "a set, established, and accepted system, with all its institutionalism, traditionalism, etc."[16] Mr. Sparks' thought was that there was a great need for the drastic work of the cross so that what was presented by the church was Christ Himself, in His life, light, power, love, liberty and glory. The church should not present a system of Christian truth but should present Christ Himself in the power of the Holy Spirit. Expressing Christ is the function of His corporate organism—His Body.

As Mr. Sparks continued his extensive travels and became even more aware of the situation of Christianity throughout large parts of the world, he became even clearer about the shortages among Christians. Likewise, he felt that the Lord had revealed something of a remedy through the ministry of life and Spirit that had been committed to him. First, Mr. Sparks described how so much of Christianity is apart from the Person of Christ. Instead of Christianity responding to the moves and desires of a living Person of Christ, it has instead been institutionalized into a system, a set of ways, practices and ideas. As such, "Christ rarely now creates Christianity; it is Christianity that creates Christ."[17] Mr. Sparks thought was that Christ Himself would not be conformed to any national, denominational or systematic form here on earth. In fact, while He was on earth, Christ Himself only declared what he saw of the Father. However, so much practice of Christianity was about imitation or duplication of a certain system of Christian truth or practice. But there is a significant difference between imitation and duplication on the one hand and generation and reproduction on the other. It is a sectarian practice to try to duplicate churches everywhere of a particular pattern or technique. Rather churches must be born out from heaven. Each church must undergo the same process of being born, even if the original church is genuinely born out from God. "Everything with God takes its rise and form from life— and that divine life! In so far as we crystallize truth into a set compass, measure and limited interpretation, we make it minister death rather than life; bondage rather than liberty; letter rather than Spirit. God's way is once, and only once, to create—the prototype—and then to generate from that; not copy it by imitation, either mass production or otherwise. The Holy Spirit is in charge of this dispensation and everything has to be born of the Spirit if it is of God." Only in this way can the church begin to express Christ Himself in a living and vital way to bear real weight of testimony in the world today. Mr. Sparks learned such lessons in his own experience and now sought to minister what he learned. The object of his ministry was, as always, no particular work or fellowship but simply "the fullness of Christ." For this end, however, fellow men are completely insufficient to bring others to see. God must truly grant his believers a spirit of wisdom and revelation in the true knowledge of Him. Only in this way can believers receive spiritual sight to see the current situation among Christians and to see God's desire for a testimony resulting in the fullness of Christ.

In the very next issue Mr. Sparks continued this thought of seeing and expanded upon his own testimony of how he came to "see" through the dealings of God. Here he was giving a clear example that his ministry was not simply academic teaching, but rather was wrought by God's work in him in his situation. He began by saying that his ministry is just a matter of seeing the real and essential significance of Christ Himself. But this spiritual sight is a matter of the work of God and is only possible by a new birth from God. Although all believers possess the faculty of spiritual sight by virtue of their new birth, few have developed this faculty. In Mr. Sparks' experience, he was once one who did not have his faculty developed. In describing where he was, Mr. Sparks states, "All the fundamentals of the evangelical faith were most surely believed and preached. The system of denominations as 'regiments of the one army' (as it is commonly understood) was accepted, or more or less taken for granted."[18] Mr. Sparks was in one such "regiment," the Baptist denomination, and had zeal for the gospel and other work. But there was a deep and growing spiritual dissatisfaction.

He described the ensuing revolution which brought him out from the Baptists through a great work of the cross and a great seeing of the true nature of the church. At the time he wrote this, he could look back over the past 25 years and say that despite opposition, the Lord granted them increase, expansion and deepening. Thus far it has been a lonely way, but a way given by the Lord and supported by His word. Sparks' realization was that it is possible for people to have possession of all the scriptures, yet to be absolutely opposed to them, like Saul of Tarsus. Mr. Sparks was praying that many believers would be given a spirit of wisdom and revelation, which was Paul's prayer for Christians not for non-Christians. With such a seeing among believers, God's goal of bringing in his testimony of the fullness of Christ could be advanced. Mr. Sparks ends by praying that the Lord would give him courage to continue to fight this fight.

It was in this same year that Mr. Sparks spoke the messages entitled *Recovering the Lord's Testimony in Fullness*. Such a yearning echoed in his heart throughout these years, as he visited and ministered to many believers around the world. He also spoke messages in conferences and published them directly as the book, *Pioneers of the Heavenly Way*. These messages were a very rich application and description of a life required on behalf of every believer to live on the heavenly way. Both these books describe God's desire and the way each believer must find God to walk according to His desire. In his editorials, Mr. Sparks explained his testimony of his "heavenly way" and showed the result—a ministry to build up God's testimony. Nineteen fifty-three was a very rich year of ministry under an open heaven.

It was also in this year that the first German translation of one of his books was published. Die Schule Christi (The School of Christ) was now available in German from Witness and Testimony press and from a distributor in Wurrt. As opposition from the evangelical community in Britain grew even more, his ministry was finding more willing recipients from different parts of the world.

The motto for 1954 was "The Lord is Greater than All." This means, among other things: He is greater than man in his environment and condition; He is greater than Satan, although Satan is ruler of the world; and He is greater than our hearts, although we are full of self introspection. Nineteen fifty-four was a year that proved the motto true. In spite of extreme opposition and spiritual pressure, the Lord was able to enlarge, deepen and expand the work and the ministry of the brothers at Honor Oak. Concerning the opposition faced in 1954 Mr. Sparks wrote, "Never in our history have we known so much opposition of every kind. Spiritually, the pressure has sometimes reached the limit of endurance. Opposition, in the form of misunderstanding leading to suspicion, misrepresentation and positive antagonism, has seemed to reach such dimensions and violence as to be intended to bring this ministry to an end."[19] But, despite the raging of the enemy, 1954, was a year outstanding in the history of the brothers at Honor Oak. More unsaved people came to know the Lord through the various ministries associated with Honor Oak than during any other year. Both the weekly gatherings and the special conferences were larger than ever before. A large proportion of these attendants were young people, which was especially encouraging and heartening to the brothers. The demand and output of literature was increasing still more. Many different ministries emanating from Honor Oak were reaching colleges, hospitals, schools and many other countries. Conference attendants hailed from various countries around the world.

A look at a typical "Acknowledgements" column for this time was a confirmation of help received from this ministry by Christians all over the world. For instance, in

December 1953 and January 1954 gifts were received from a wide range of places and peoples. Listing their names is almost a lesson in world geography. Gifts received from the United Kingdom and America hailed from large cities like London; Dublin; Edinburgh; Bristol; Birmingham; New York; Detroit; Los Angeles as well as from small towns, like Bexleyheath; Old Bracknell; Oldham; Bexhill-on-Sea; Fremont, Ohio; Spring City, Tennessee; York, Pennsylvania. From the Continent gifts came from Switzerland and Denmark (during other months gifts came from France, Germany, Holland and other places). From farther reaches gifts came from Canada, New Zealand, Australia, India, Sarawak, Tasmania, Southern Rhodesia, Ethiopia, Nilgiris and Kenya. These gifts demonstrated a witness in many seekers from around the globe to the help received from this ministry.

Truly, the brothers' feeling during these times was that the Lord was with them and that by experience He is greater than all. Mr. Sparks was quick to point out that this ministry expanded and spread to so many reaches without the "help" of advertisement, gimmicks, attractions, propaganda or entertainment so common to many Christian movements. The only thing he boasted of was "a seeking to exalt the Lord Jesus and make His fullness known."[19] It is interesting to note the progression of this "way" of spreading in Mr. Sparks' experience. A seed of it may have begun very soon after Mr. Sparks received the gospel and participated in the 1905 R. A. Torrey gospel meetings in London's Royal Albert Hall. In describing those campaigns Torrey himself testified that he did not use gimmicks or propaganda, but relied solely on the attraction of the Lord Jesus Himself, who alone could fill that hall every night week after week. Later in his ministry, Mr. Sparks learned the same thing by the inner sense of life. In his book "The Law of the Spirit of Life in Christ Jesus" Mr. Sparks testified how he had developed his speaking style to include allusions from literature and popular culture. At one point, when he had just finished quoting a bit of Browning in one of his sermons, the Lord indicated within through His law of life not to rely or use these embellishments. Rather, Sparks learned to speak only about Christ. From his youth and through the teaching of the Lord, Sparks was brought to the place of not relying on advertisements or gimmicks but of seeking to exalt only the Lord Jesus through his speaking. Now, as he saw his ministry deepen and spread, even in the midst of terrible opposition, he realized that the heavenly One he exalted was able to overcome and give growth to what He desired in spite of what transpired on the earth against it.

In 1954 Mr. Sparks published the series of messages in *A Witness and a Testimony* entitled, "The Man God has Ordained," where he began to unveil clearly the high position of man in God's eternal plan. The model of the only true man is Jesus Christ and today He is walking amidst the lampstands, as seen in Revelation. This year Mr. Sparks also published the book *Prophetic Ministry*, which was based on messages he gave and published in *A Witness and a Testimony* in 1948. This book was a further explanation of the life needed before God to be a testimony of God in this age.

A Witness and a Testimony was the main source of spiritual food to the many seekers who received help from the ministry of the brothers at Honor Oak. By far the ministry in that magazine that held the most weight and provided the most content was by Mr. Sparks. In 1954 out of the 34 messages included in the journal, 20 were by Mr. Sparks, 7 were by Harry Foster, 6 by T. L. M., and 1 was by Angus Kinnear. In 1953 out of the 29 messages, 19 were from Mr. Sparks, 6 by Harry Foster, 3 by C.J.B. Harrison, and 1 by A.G. Taylor. Mr. Sparks still felt as if he was standing with many brothers for the Lord's work that they were specifically called to do. The testimony Mr.

Sparks gave was that so much healthy ministering went on, even when he was incapacitated due to his operation. However, there was also a marked difference in the ministering of Mr. Sparks. He had grown. And as he grew in his life and ministry, fewer servants of the Lord could minister with the same revelation and life supply as Mr. Sparks. This trend was to become more and more pronounced over the next decade of growth and ministry.

Throughout these years, Mr. Sparks would make yearly visits to small groups of believers and to gatherings for ministry in the continent of Europe and in North America. We already saw how he began to make yearly visits to Switzerland and Germany. He would also come to New York once a year and hold a conference there. At that time, many believers who had received help from him would travel to New York for the weekend conference of ministry and for fellowship. One example is a small group of about 12 believers who met in Maine and who sought the Lord's best.[20] They received the food from *A Witness and a Testimony* and every year were more richly supplied by this gathering in New York, where they received help from the ministering and were able to fellowship with more Christians who also sought something of the Lord's testimony. Mr. Sparks would also travel to other places in North America where different groups of believers had extended invitations to him. His written word through books and especially through his magazine opened many doors for face to face fellowship. Another place that he would routinely visit was Westmoreland Chapel in Los Angeles. Here a small group of believers had gathered to meet and was in sweet fellowship with Mr. Sparks and others at Honor Oak.

Since 1936, a small number of Christian workers associated with the brothers at Honor Oak were laboring for the Lord in India. Between 1936 and 1960 the total number in this category was about a dozen.[21] These brothers and sisters closely associated themselves with indigenous Christian leaders to encourage them in their gospel and church planting work.   In such association, they served in various capacities including medical and social work as well as Bible teaching. In 1954 the brothers felt to take a further step to support the move of the Lord there by purchasing a freehold property in Mysore State. (The address of this property was 6 Brunton Road, Bangalore.) This facility was used for Bible teaching and conferences as well as a center for the publication of literature by indigenous Christian authors and evangelists. The indigenous group associated with Brother Bakht Singh now had hundreds of congregations throughout India. We see how the work associated with Honor Oak was growing and broadening throughout this time in the early 1950's.

The Church and the Churches

As we have mentioned before, the 1950s ministry of Mr. Sparks roughly can be divided into two sections. The first, from 1952 to 1954, can be described as a time where Mr. Sparks saw clearly the situation among Christians and the position of his ministry. This was a time when Mr. Sparks was not encumbered by war or ill-health and therefore had liberty to travel and become intimately acquainted with the situations of God's people in a large part of the world. It was also a time where Mr. Sparks and all Christians witnessed many doors to the gospel closing in large sections of the world. Mr. Sparks saw the need of believers in the "closed" countries to have a deep walk with God and he also saw the need in the "open" countries to bear a strong testimony of the Lord. Sadly, most of what he saw was inadequate and failing testimonies among the Christians. More than ever, he saw a need for a ministry like that which the Lord had committed to him. Yes, mass evangelism had done its work in getting out the message of Jesus as Savior. But, there was also a need of a ministry to Christians, a building ministry where Christians could see the riches and fullness of Christ and bear a testimony to the world of such an exalted Christ. During this first section of ministry, Mr. Sparks saw his ministry grow and meet the need of hungry Christians around the world in spite of opposition and slander spread by many from the evangelical community. This became a testimony that there indeed was a need in God's people for the fullness of Christ and also that the ministry wrought into Mr. Sparks by the Lord could meet that need.

The second phase of ministry in the 1950's, which we mark from 1955 to 1958, is one where Mr. Sparks was intensely focused on the matter of the church and the churches. The Bible speaks of both the church and the churches. The church in its universal aspect is heavenly, spiritual and perfect. The churches on earth are representations of that heavenly church in a world of fallen man with his sinful self and corrupted flesh. Putting these two, the church and the churches, together is a matter that most Christians throughout history have met with confusion and difficulty. It is just this subject that occupied Mr. Sparks in his editorials throughout this time. It is much safer and simpler for Christians to limit their focus to the person and work of Christ pertaining to redemption and salvation. However, the Bible doesn't stop there; it unveils a revelation of the church and God's plan concerning the church. It was into this difficult territory that Mr. Sparks fully placed himself during this time. In fact, nine out of the sixteen *A Witness and a Testimony* editorials written between January of 1955 and May of 1959 addressed the matter of the church or the churches. Mr. Sparks felt that it was more than necessary to address these issues because the church is the instrument which God has chosen to fulfill His eternal purpose. In 1956 he wrote, "The New Testament can be said to be—in a large proportion of its contents—a document containing God's conception, election, calling, and constitution of the Church for its eternal vocation, and it can truly be said that God has bound Himself to the Church in a very full and utter way. He has made it clear that His means and method of fulfilling His eternal counsels concerning His Son is 'Churchwise': that the normal channel of His approach to and meeting of men is His Church."[22]

Not only did Mr. Sparks focus on this matter in his editorials and thoughts, but many situations that he saw during these years clearly dealt with the matter of the church. In 1955 and again in 1957 Mr. Sparks spent a number of months visiting the Far East, especially Taiwan, and viewing a "mighty work of God" among the believers in that country and others. Mr. Sparks remarked that this work was being carried out "not on a 'mission' or institutional basis at all, but on the true and pure basis of the Church."[23] Also during this time, Mr. Sparks saw many Christian publications take up the matter of the church. He even witnessed a world council of churches meet in Amsterdam and proclaim that "these man-made divisions must go."[24] This was a vast departure and advancement from the common thought that many divisions were useful in protecting certain aspects of the divine truth, or that they were all different regiments of the same army. Not only was Mr. Sparks confronted with these matters in his travels and in the popular Christian literature, but even those at Honor Oak became more focused on the matter of the church and the churches. Within many brothers and sisters arose a desire for fuller church life. This led to changes at Honor Oak as well as many difficulties for the decade ahead of them. We will touch this matter and its evolution for the little company at Honor Oak in much greater detail in the following chapter.

We begin describing Mr. Sparks' focus on the church and the churches by including his own description of travels to India, Hong Kong and Taiwan. We'd like to reiterate that after many of the trips he made to America, he returned with an impression of the weakness, inadequacy and confusion prevalent among God's people. After these trips, he often concluded how much a ministry like his was needed for God's people to go on and for God's purpose to be fulfilled, which ever is the fullness of Christ. After these trips to the East, however, Mr. Sparks returned encouraged, refreshed and thankful to God that he could visit such a "wealthy place." In October of 1955 Mr. Sparks started off for India, Hong Kong, Taiwan and the Philippines and was to return to London by January. This is how he described his travels in a January 1956 editor's letter:

Beloved friends,

I am writing this Editor's Letter in the Far East, and although its contents will be in the past when this reaches you, I think it good that you should know a little of this ministry—where I have been and what I have found.

The first phase was the All India Convocation at Hyderabad in October. Some seventeen hundred had gathered from many parts of India and were housed and fed on the compound. Some hundreds more came in from the locality. The larger proportion of these were the Lord's, and what a joyful multitude they were! From early morning, perhaps at 4 o'clock, when a procession of singers went forth, until late at night—often after midnight—there was an unceasing occupation with the

things of the Lord in one way or another.
The meetings would sometimes go on for
six or even seven hours, and they seemed
never to tire. The Lord enabled me to take
practically all the ministry of the Word
over four days, and, although two interpret-
ers had to be employed for two other languages (which meant every message in
three languages), there was rarely a hitch—
the oneness of spirit was so real that the
word just flowed along.

This convocation was a very great
testimony to the wonderful thing that the
Lord is doing all over India, mainly
through the instrumentality of our brother
Bakht Singh, and a body of fellow workers.
Companies of believers have been 'born' in
many places. Thousands are being 'added
to the Lord.' During my brief stay in Hyderabad there were over 90 baptisms, and
every one was prayed with personally afterward. It would be impossible to describe all the details of such a convocation:
every dwelling (and there are very many)
with its own name from the Bible; likewise
every prayer place; every path to dwellings
or meeting places; the main way from
which all others branch; the walls with
Scriptural banners all along; the perfect
organization of food, water, sanitation, and
general supervision; and the continuous
prayer relays, day and night, all through.
The send-off was a wonderful experience;
singing crowds lining the way, and hands
outstretched for a grasp. That there should
be two or three such Convocations in dif-

ferent parts of India each year, besides all the work in localities, does speak of God doing something.

From Hyderabad (Dr. Kinnear having joined me there, and Mrs. Sparks having gone to Bangalore), we moved east, via Bombay, where we had another evening with the friends, and Calcutta, with other contacts and two meetings at the 'Bible College,' to Hong Kong. As we looked from our plane we saw a crowd of eager faces strained toward it and on appearing at the door hands went up and there was a general stir. About 200 believers had come to the airport to greet us, and what a greeting it was! These radiant faces of the Chinese believers are a testimony to the grace of God. After formalities with the airport authorities, who gave us no trouble at all, we joined the procession of cars into the city, and the elders joined us at an evening meal.

Here again is a wonderful work of God. The central meeting-place is a beautiful hall, quite modern in every way, seating 1,100 people, and is usually full for the main meetings. There are a number of other halls and meetings of this work in different parts of Hong Kong. We had three meetings a day (with one exception) during our ten days there. Two in the morning for workers, of whom there were about 300, from Hong Kong, Manila, Singapore, Saigon, etc. These were times of systematic teaching. The evenings were open to all, and were very large. To look on these happy faces, with the traces of suffering in so many, is an experience, and to hear these believers sing is something not to be forgotten.

On the first Saturday evening of our time there they had a Love Feast at which nearly a thousand sat down to a real Chinese meal. There was indeed a feast of love. At the close of this we were both asked to give a message. No one could possibly have had more love and kindness shown than we had in Hong Kong, and we thank our God on every remembrance of the believers and their leaders there. The send off was like the reception—a large crowd at the airport waving and smiling until we were out of sight.

Then Formosa, and here it was the same but more so. What a crowd of eager faces and bursting into singing as we emerged. The formalities were much less happy here owing to Nationalist China's reserve over Britain's relation with Pekin. It was not pleasant! But the reception outside was a tremendous thing, and it took quite a long time to get through the greetings, photos, etc. At length the leaders and ourselves were crowded into the Gospel Bus, and we were taken to the house of Dr. and Mrs. West (now doing locum for Dr. Dale), where we had an evening of fellowship. Next morning we were taken round to see most of the other seven meeting places in the city. This was an experience! On the Lord's Day morning about 2,800 gathered in the central meeting place, and that meeting is difficult to describe. The life, joy, singing, and earnestness of that great company is very impressive. At 5 o'clock in the afternoon we had reports from other places on the Island—a story of 'the wonderful works of God.' This lasted for two hours. Then a Love Feast, followed by the Lord's Table. It was late when we closed that long-to-be-remembered day.

From then onward, during the first week, there were four meetings a day: two in the mornings for workers (about 800); one in the afternoon taken by Dr. Kinnear; and then the great evening meetings with sometimes about 3,000 present. During the second week the afternoon meetings were dropped. For the third week we are visiting all the other centers on the island, eight of them. As I write, this has not been completed. From here we go to Manila, in the Philippine Islands, for another week of conferences, and then back to India for a further Convocation—all 'if the Lord wills.'

This is an unusual kind of Editor's Letter, but I thought it would encourage you, and lead to praise. It will be appreciated that all this ministry, traveling, etc. makes no small demands, but I have to testify to most gracious help from the Lord, and am deeply grateful to Him for allowing me to see something of His goings in the earth, to say nothing of being permitted to participate. "A great and effectual door is opened, and there are many adversaries."

It is no small thing that, at the time when the opposition to this ministry has reached a point of intensity and openness unparalleled in our history, the Lord should lead us out into such a large and wealthy place and tell us so overwhelmingly that He is not done with this ministry yet. We have not sought this nor tried to bring it about. 'It is the Lord's doing.' We have positively nothing in view but the glory of His Son, our Lord Jesus, and we are sure that He will stand by that. The answer to all is with Him and we can safely trust Him to give it.

May the Lord make this New Year one of great blessing to you all, and great enlargement of His Son in all of us. Warm greetings to you, dear friends, and thanks for you so valued and needed prayer help. Yours in His grace, T. Austin-Sparks[25]

Mr. Sparks had seen church after church in India, the Philippines, and in Taiwan. He felt that the churches were truly part of "a large and wealthy place." For the year after his visit to Taiwan, Mr. Sparks included references to the church in every one of his four editor's letters. In the first one he described the emphases of his ministry, one of which was the church. In the second one, he looks at how the world council of churches published a proclamation about the need for oneness in the church. His third letter speaks of signs of the times and concludes that one sign of current Christian generation was a hunger and renewed interest in the church. Finally he concludes with a letter expressing concern and desire for healing the divided state of the church.

The first editor's letter after Mr. Sparks' trip outlined the spiritual history and nature of the ministry committed to Mr. Sparks. Here he listed three major emphases regarding which the Lord had brought him into fuller
light. It should be noted that these are not three major
teachings, but rather three matters that were the results of
a living experience of Christ. The first is the fuller meaning of the cross. He saw that the cross was the beginning
point for all the believer's realization of God's full
thought. Its objective meaning—deliverance from judgment, condemnation, and the tyranny of an evil conscience—was never in any need of adjustment or fuller
light. However, Mr. Sparks was brought into a new realization of the subjective aspect of the cross. Mr. Sparks
came upon that as he turned to Romans chapter six.
While reading this passage, it was as if the Lord said,
'When I died, you died. When I went to the cross, I not
only took your sins, but I took you. When I took you, I
not only took you as the sinner that you might regard
yourself to be, but I took as being all that you are by nature; your good as your bad; your abilities as well as your
disabilities; yes, every resource of yours. I took you as a
'worker,' a 'preacher,' an organizer! My Cross means
that not even for Me can you be or do anything out from
yourself, but if there is to be anything at all it must be out
from Me, and that means a life of absolute dependence
and faith."[26] Mr. Sparks' second emphasis and the second
matter that the Lord brought him to was that of life in the
spirit. In this matter he realized that there is a difference
between soul and spirit. Our soul is "ourselves in intelligence, will, feeling and energy."[27] The Holy Spirit dwells
in our spirit, which "renewed and indwelt spirit is the organ of divine knowledge, purpose, and power."[27]

The third matter of emphasis is the heavenly nature, vocation and destiny of the Church as the Body of
Christ. Related to this Mr. Sparks writes, "It is the Church

which is of primary concern to the Lord in this dispensation. Everything is related to that in His mind and activity. This means, among other things, that all unrelatedness and independence, all that is merely personal, sectional, exclusive or separate must certainly fail to reach God's full end or to have His seal upon it beyond a certain point."[28] The Church, in Mr. Spark's view, is something wholly organic and of the divine life. The situation in Christianity, with its many man-made divisions and other institutions, falls far short of the divine conception. In Mr. Sparks' experience he felt he had to set aside the system of Christianity. He writes, "Thus, having set aside all the former system of organized Christianity, we committed ourselves to the principle of the organic. No 'order' was 'set up,' no officers or ministers were appointed. We left it with the Lord to make manifest by 'gift' and anointing who were chosen of Him for oversight and ministry."[29] While Mr. Sparks felt clearly that divisions and denominations are "a departure from the Holy Spirit's original way and intention," at the same time he realized that so many times God has truly blessed them and used them. For this reason he did not condemn them nor ask people to leave them. Rather it was a matter of everything proceeding from the leading of the Lord and the conception of the Spirit. What should be clear to all, however, is that "It is the church, which is the primary and inclusive concern of the Lord in this dispensation." These three emphases must go together. On the basis of the experience of the cross, we can live a life truly in the Spirit. In this way the church is constituted with living believers as an organic entity representing a living Christ to the entire universe.

In the following editor's letter, Mr. Sparks again takes up the matter of the church. Here he expanded on a pronouncement made by the recently gathered "World Council of Churches," which proclaimed that divisions are man made and not according to God's original design.

During a meeting of this council, the attendants developed a certain phrase into a slogan: "these man-made divisions must go." Other prominent missionaries of the time were also talking more about the church itself being a mission, not an organization or institution. In this way the world can be evangelized, not just foreign fields. In context of all these realizations by Christian leaders regarding the church, Mr. Sparks gave testimony to what he saw in the East. His testimony was of the church as the basis of a mighty work of God and also of the great opposition faced by such a work from many evangelical leaders. He wrote,

> The present writer has recently spent some time in the East and the Far East and has seen the glory and tragedy of the above. On the one hand a mighty work of God—not on a 'mission' or institutional basis at all, but on the true and pure basis of the church—is expressing itself and reproducing itself as shown in the book of the 'Acts,' reaching far and wide until churches have been born in many hundreds of places (literally true), with large numbers of full time workers, and an order beautiful to behold, a joy that bows one to worship. One thanks God for ever having been allowed the honor of seeing just a part of this work, from the inside, and of being able to look deeply into its constitution. This is something actually in existence and still going on today. But on the other hand, this is the work that has had more opposition in misunderstanding, misrepresentation, criticism, and avoidance on the part of organized Christianity, than any other Christian activity. 'Christians' have even gone so far as

to boycott in business those who have been
associated with this work. It is happening
today, but the most evident seal of God is
on this testimony.[30]

Mr. Sparks then proceeded to write about how
much damage suspicion among Christians had done to the
unity of the church. It was this "internecine strife" and
"civil war" amongst Christians that made the testimony of
the church to the world so weak and ineffective.

In his September letter, Mr. Sparks takes a look at
the signs of the times in order to try to discern what God
is doing and emphasizing to the believers at this particular
time. Mr. Sparks made such an analysis many times in
the past, especially in the midst of World War II where he
himself was so intimately involved in the city bearing the
brunt of the Nazi air-war machine. During those conflict
years, his conclusions were that God was trying to wake
up Christians so that they would not rely on things, places,
institutions, doctrines, persons, and buildings but would
rather return to Christ alone and gather as Christians on no
other basis than the basis of their birth from above. Here,
in 1956, he adds new things that he sees among Christians
and in the world situation. One significant sign he points
out is a growing concern about the church. It is here again
that this emphasis emerges. Because of the church's continual mention, we say his focus during this period of ministry was on the church and the churches.

The four signs of the times that Mr. Sparks saw
were the following. Firstly there was a great effort on
mass evangelism. Evangelism had become more widespread than at any time in history through radio and other
means so that, for the first time in history, millions every
day had the real possibility of hearing the gospel of Jesus
Christ. Secondly, there was an intensifying and expanding
dissatisfaction with tradition. This was creating a genuine

hunger for something more in many seeking Christians. Quite a few of God's people were recognizing the weakness of Christianity because of the many divisions and were working toward finding a solution. Thirdly, in many circles, including evangelical, conservative, fundamental, and liberal Christians, there was a "new look" being taken at the condition of the church. Many of these believers were concluding that the church (not doctrine, position or organization) was God's means, method, object, and answer. Fourthly, many believers in a growing portion of the world, from China to the Middle East, were passing through a fiery ordeal. This may have been a means God was using to purify the parts of the church in these areas by making any artificial means utterly useless in enduring the fierce tribulation. These four things may have been signs that the end was near. However, through all these means, God would have reality and must have reality among His people. For God, His Son is the only such reality. "He, as such, is the End, the Amen, and God works all His works toward Him, that in all things He may have the pre-eminence."[31]

In the last Editor's Letter of 1956, Mr. Sparks again returns to the question of how to heal the divided state of Christians. His mind was very much focused on the church and how a church in oneness could be a testimony to the world. He appeals to believers that they must first take heavenly ground, as is illustrated in Ephesians where believers are seated in the heavenlies with Christ and, thereby, enjoy the reality of the "one Body." He also appeals to believers to take the ground of the cross, which is how Paul dealt with the believers in Corinth. The cross not only deals with sins and condemnation, but also deals with our earthliness, our natural ground, which is the cause for so much division and strife. "If we would take heavenly ground and the ground of the cross, the Holy Spirit would be able to cause the things which really do not matter to fade from their importance, and to give the Lord's people a loving concern for all who are His, just because they are His, and not 'ours' in any earthly way."[32]

After one year of laboring in England and one visit to America, Mr. Sparks again responded to a warm invitation from the brothers and traveled to the Far East in the beginning months of 1957. It was another time of refreshing. After facing so much opposition in Britain and seeing a hard situation among Christians in America, Mr. Sparks remarks about his visit "it is a joy in these times to be in that which has ever been our vision and prayer." We reproduce his editor's letter in full describing his journey and his impressions.

Beloved friends,

So many of you have been praying much for us over these past months of far-flung ministries, and I feel it is due to you to let you know how wonderfully the Lord has answered your prayers. It has indeed been a time of tremendous demands and opportunities, but, once again, we have a glowing testimony to the Lord's faithfulness and mercy. It is quite impossible to give a full account of these first three months in the Far East, and we feel reticent in speaking about it at all lest, on the one hand, our motives should be misunderstood and, on the other hand, Satan should react to injury. It is not boasting, but just giving you occasion to glorify God.

'Spontaneous expansion' is a term which has gained currency in the realm of Christian enterprise. It is a fascinating idea and captivates the imagination. It is the one thing more than any other which is desired and sought. The defining of it may result in conflicting conceptions and interpretations. To be absolutely true to the very words, surely it means that kind of expansion and growth which cannot be attributed—in the first place—to human effort, organization, machinery, institutions, publicity, propaganda, business acumen, financial support, etc., but is just the organic expression of life, and that, in this connection, the mighty life of the Holy Spirit. In spite of rocks, storms, blasts, and many inimical and opposing forces, human and satanic, it just goes on expanding, multiplying, increasing, and growing. Without noise, display, or demonstration, the greatest and most persistent opposition is made as though it did not exist—in the long run and ultimate issue. There is "the hiding of His power" so that, while very great difficulties and oppositions are overcome, it is never as by an earthquake, cataclysm, or display. The power of the Spirit is so great that He never has to call attention to it, and even those most closely related are left wondering as to what He has done and how He did it.

It is a wonderful thing to be in the way of these 'goings of God.' In our own case and this ministry the history of these past thirty years has been very much like that. There could not have been less of the natural factors and features which men would regard as essential to the growth which has so silently taken place; from something so small and local to something which has reached literally to the ends of the earth and into all nations; something to which people of God, servants of God, in so many different places and connections, bear testimony as to its spiritual helpfulness. On the other hand, we have wondered whether anything could have more opposition in every form, human and satanic.

But this is not about ourselves. We have just returned from a further three months in the Far East, and there, once more, we have beheld 'the wonderful works of God.' Day after day in continuous sessions we have been privileged to minister to some five hundred and more hand-picked and specially selected Christian (Chinese) workers; and night after night to about 2,000 to 2,500 believers and workers. We have, in addition, spent a whole week in visiting assemblies in many places, sometimes three or four in a day, where the believers, radiant in Christ, awaited our arrival and eagerly devoured the ministry. All this work and these assemblies—ranging in numbers from one to sixteen hundred—have 'spontaneously' arisen and are spontaneously growing. A principle and maxim of the servant of God who was His instrument in the beginning of this work—even when it was growing very greatly—was 'Try to keep things small. Never try to make the work big. If it is of God it will grow in spite of everything. We must fill the trenches with water. If it is not of God we do not want it.' That principle is held to and enunciated today. I refrain from giving many details or even a general presentation of this work, for publicity is dangerous. Our range of ministry was the Philippines, Formosa, and Hong Kong, but the work reaches wider ranges.

No work or believers could have had greater opposition, or have been made to suffer more than those related to this work. Politically, spiritually, and— grievous to say—from Christian bodies, it has suffered almost unbelievably, but on it goes by the momentum of inherent spiritual life, by the power of the Spirit of Life.

If the secrets are sought, we would say unhesitatingly and with deep knowledge that they are four.

1. The deep inward work of the cross in the life of the believers, individually and collectively.

2. The sovereignty and government of the Holy Spirit in all direction and government.

3. A true and clear conception and expression of the Church as the Body of Christ, a spiritual organism on heavenly ground.

4. 'The fellowship of His sufferings,' a counting of all things as loss for the excellency of the knowledge of Christ Jesus, a life of sacrifice and abandon to His interests and glory.

If the question is asked 'Is there no organization in such a great work?' we say at once, yes, there is, and it is as near perfect as anything we have known.   But, there is a difference. The 'organization' (if you must use that word) never produced or preceded the work or the life. It is just the order into which life must be directed to prevent confusion. A garden full and overflowing with living organisms requires direction and control to make it beautiful, but you do not begin with your controls and then try—by means of them—to get life. When someone referred to the order in their   work   and   used   the   word 'organization,'   a   leading   responsible brother just quietly said 'But we are not conscious of the 'organization,' we are only conscious of that which makes it necessary.'

Well, it is a joy in these times to be in that which has ever been our vision and prayer, albeit fraught with such cost, a work for which the Spirit of God takes responsibility. May it be preserved unsullied and unspoiled.

We do most deeply thank all of you for the faithful prayer-support and encompassing during these weeks of such heavy demands, physically and spiritually, and we are happy to say—'You have not prayed in vain.'"[33]

After reading Mr. Sparks' own description of his trip and his impressions it is difficult to over emphasize how much he was impressed with the work of the Lord that he witnessed in the Far East. Not many of his editorials or messages mention joy, but here he proclaims the joy he felt in being in "that which has ever been our vision and prayer." In the many years that Mr. Sparks saw a vision of the testimony of the Lord and prayed for such a testimony to be raised up, he rarely witnessed a situation where his vision was realized in assemblies of believers. However, here in the Far East, it may not be too much to say that he saw what he formerly only dreamed of. This was surely an impression that he never forgot. It may also have been a confirmation of his views on the full meaning of the cross, living a life in the spirit, and realizing that God desires to do all things in this age on and through the unique basis of the church as His testimony.

The three editorials following Mr. Sparks' journey to the Far East, came as a response to the comment that a servant of the Lord made to Mr. Sparks during his trip to the Far East.[34] This servant commented about the influence and value of the first book ever published by Witness and Testimony entitled "The Release of the Lord." In these editorials Mr. Sparks gave the substance of that book, which describes the effects of the Release of Jesus Christ as seen in Acts and throughout the rest of church history.

In the beginning of 1958 Mr. Sparks chose to write a word of comfort, perhaps for others and perhaps for himself, in his editor's letter about Psalm 77:19, which says "Thy way was in the sea, and Thy paths in the great waters."[35] Many times throughout history, God's people, God's servants, or God's work have come up against seemingly impossible situations where there was no way out. At that time, they realized that heaven gave them a way out and that God Himself was able to give them His way, when the earth offered none. These words, Mr. Sparks felt to be very appropriate to the present time. This may have been a word to those who were being tossed by the "sea of tribulation" of the nations or to those who were in the midst of the "waters of testing" for the church. It may also have been a word that Mr. Sparks felt appropriate for his own situation as so many problems both at home at Honor Oak and abroad confronted his ministry.

In March of 1958 Mr. Sparks continues his editorials with an appeal for reality as shown in the appearing of the Lord Jesus in the flesh in the midst of all the Old Testament practices and rituals. The Lord's question then becomes, "Is your religion a matter of attachment or adherence to a system, a historical tradition, a family inheritance and so on? Or is it born—is it a birth in you; is it something that has happened to you; is it your very life, your very being?"[36] He then describes how the coming of Christ pierced through temperament and disposition. Mr. Sparks asks the following questions: Is our following of the Lord and the way we follow the Lord influenced by what our temperament leans toward? Do we have an abstract or mystical temperament that causes us to make God, Christianity, Christ, the Bible a certain way after our own image? Or do we have more of a practical temperament that causes us to form Christ and things of God in more practical terms? Either way is not according to Christ and our relationship with Him. Our following of the Lord should be based on our new birth, that is, the new disposition of Christ who is born into the believer. Only when we respond to this living Christ (who is altogether different from who we are) will we have reality in our Christian life. There is no reality if we merely respond to our natural affinity. "With God, Christ is the only reality, and that is not temperamental, mystical, not a matter of plain or ornate, ritualistic and ceremonial, or bare and simple. Christ revealed by the Holy Spirit in the heart, as by a divine fiat, corresponding to the 'let there be light' of creation, is the only reality."[36] As the end of the age approaches, God's people will experience more and more sifting and testing. In these cases only what is real, Christ revealed, will stand the test.

In the last issue of 1958 Mr. Sparks includes a letter of thanks to all of the readers of *A Witness and a Testimony*. Apparently a group of brothers had assembled a letter of support and thanks with over 750 signatures on it and had presented it to Mr. Sparks. This was very touching for Mr. Sparks and came at a time when opposition was casting him down. The opposition and problems Mr. Sparks were facing were enormous at this time. The decade of the 1950s was the time in which opposition to the ministry of Honor Oak reached unheard of proportions. In the 1970's, after Mr. Sparks' death, the brothers remaining at Honor Oak decided to try to abate the opposition from the 1950s that was still lingering among evangelical Christians.[37] After twenty years, the prejudice, suspicion, and calumny sowed in this decade still survived. When this was added to the problems soon to surface within Honor Oak, we can see how Mr. Sparks would find himself quite cast down. It is little wonder that when this letter of support arrived, his heart must have been comforted. He writes these short paragraphs to all his readers.

I am breaking a rule which has been observed for many years, when I enter a quite personal note in this paper. But necessity is laid upon me. On a date in September of this year an event occurred, the coming of which had become known to many of my friends. The result was that, on that occasion, cables, letters, etc., reached me from many countries, from— and between—the Far East and the Far West. A memorial of over seven hundred and fifty signatures was compiled. It is impossible to write a personal letter to all these friends, so this is my one alternative.

Let me say at once that I was overwhelmed with your love, and the Lord's goodness in this. Most of those who sent a message know something of the great cost, spiritually and physically, associated with the forty years of this ministry. I confess that the conflict, especially in recent times, has often had the effect of "casting down." The Lord seems to have been secretly storing up this surprise for a certain day, and, as I have said, the testimonies to spiritual value in the ministry were simply overwhelming, and led to deep worship. No words can express my gratitude, so I give up any attempt.

I thank you, my beloved friends, for your love and kindness. May I yet receive more grace to justify your confidence.
T. Austin-Sparks[38]

In this same issue of *A Witness and a Testimony*, Mr. Sparks began a series of four lengthy editorials describing in detail his view of "the essential nature of a 'New Testament church:' how such a church is formed, what are the principles which govern it, and similar questions."[39] This series was in response to the many inquiries he had received and to the general interest concerning the church that was growing among Christians in general. He writes, "During the many years of this spoken and printed ministry, very much has been said regarding the Church. This has led to not a few enquiries for advice from many who are in difficulty over this matter. Many of the enquirers are in responsible positions in the Lord's work. It is a sign of the times that there is such a very considerable re-

vival of concern in relation to the church. Many conferences on the subject are being held, many 'church' movements are afoot, and a very considerable literature is being
published."[39] Because so much of Mr. Sparks considerations regarding the church were present in his ministry in
this period (from 1955 to 1958), and because his dealings
with the work in Taiwan and the Far East dealt so specifically with the church basis of the work, we will try to
summarize his position on the matter he so clearly laid out
in these editorials. It is of interest to note that in his future
editorials he never again addresses this matter so directly.

　　　Mr. Sparks begins his statement by asking the
question: "What is the church and what are the churches?"
By this question he refers to both the universal aspect of
the church and the local aspect of the churches as seen in
the Bible. He first points out that there is no "clearly defined and completely set out plan of the Church, its order,
constitution, methods and work"[39] in the New Testament.
There is no 'blue print' for the church life that is meant to
be reproduced and that all other churches are meant to duplicate. Yes, it is possible to piece together some doctrines, practices, work, methods, and orderings found in
the New Testament and arrive at some church practice.
However, this can truly by done in a wide variety of ways
each of which will find adherents who claim that this way
is the "Biblical way." Sadly, this "objective approach"
many times results in severe limitation to God's operation
and leaves in its wake human hands responsible for up-
holding God's work through a combination of committees, boards, machinery, appeals, names, propaganda,
press etc. When such a system is doctrinally held, it results in the Scriptures losing the ability to be interpreted
further in the presence of more light. In an attempt to protect the Scriptures, men box them in and limit the Lord
from moving them from their static spiritual position.

Sadly, so much of today's "Christianity" "has almost entirely come to be such a thing now."

The book of Acts does not set up a blue print with the intention that generations of Christians reproduce that system. Instead we see something that is "so fluid, so open, so subject to proving." This is because the answer to "What?" "Who?" and "How?" in all matters of the church is not a system outlined in the New Testament, but a living Person, Jesus Christ Himself. When He came in the flesh, He was the "embodiment of a great, a vast heavenly and spiritual order and system."[40] In Acts the Apostles did not formulate by committee or arrange an organization to determine what the church would look like or how the Lord would move. Rather this Person, Christ Himself, was taking form within them, both personally and corporately by new birth and growth. "The might, energy and urge of the Holy Spirit within produced a Way and an order, un-thought-of, unintended by them and always to their own surprise."[40] This is how the believers and their companies were becoming an expression of the Person of Christ.

In the thought of God, Christians, the Church, and the local churches exist solely for the purpose of being an expression of Christ. Christ is the personal embodiment of a vast, heavenly, spiritual system that touches every detail of our personal and collective life. The Holy Spirit knows how to bring this reality into expression through the Church. When we give the Holy Spirit preeminence, He will bring us into this reality. "As an individual believer is the result of a begetting, a conception, a formation, a birth and a likeness, so, in the New Testament, is a true local church. It is a reproduction of Christ by the Holy Spirit. Man cannot make, form, produce or 'establish' this. Neither can anyone 'join' or 'enroll' or make himself or herself a member of this organism. First it is an embryo, and then a 'formation' after Christ."[41] As a response to accusations that such talk is overly mystical or idealistic, Mr. Sparks strongly states that this is very practical and that such churches exist both "in New Testament times and in the world today." Only when we are still wedded to the traditional system of Christianity does this view seem overly idealistic. A church formed by these means fulfills its true function and vocation—"to bring Christ into any location on this earth." A true local church should ever bring in Christ and minister to the increase of Christ. With all these points in view, Mr. Sparks could succinctly summarize, "In purpose and in nature the Church is Christ, and so are the churches locally—no more, no less."[41]

Clearly the Church defined this way is not co-extensive with 'Christianity' as we know it, which is "an enormous conglomeration and mass of contradictions." Christianity embraces everything related to the name of Christ, from liberals who question the fact of the resurrection and the authority of the Bible to cruel, bigoted legalism, which would lead men to take up the sword in defense of the word of God. The church, which is Christ, clearly embraces less than this. "The Church is holy, sacred, undivided, heavenly, and all of God. Not merely ceremonially sacred, but intrinsically so."[41]

It is God's desire to bring all of His believers through revelation to an understanding of what the Church means. This is surely what the apostles labored to bring believers into. They wanted all believers to come to full-knowledge of what they had come into by virtue of their new birth. This full knowledge must "relate to Christ and His church." Concerning the knowing of the Church, Sparks writes, "All the eternal counsels concerning Christ and God's eternal purpose as to Him are bound up with the Church. There are very many and very great values in a true church life, that is, a true Body relatedness, and there can only be very great loss in not knowing or apprehending this."[42] It is this revelation, the revelation of the church, that the enemy fights so strongly against. This was also seen in the opposition that the Apostles faced in the New Testament times. Satan hates the church because "The very existence of a local church was a testimony to, and an embodiment of, Christ's victory and authority over the evil powers."[42]

The experience of a local church must therefore begin with God. He Himself would instill in us a "divine discontent," where we feel that God must make a move in order to further His purpose in the midst of this degraded situation. From our side, when we respond to God's move in us and we begin to come into contact with a local church, we should have the sense that we have found our spiritual home. From God's side, churches "should be, in their inception, constitution, and continuation, the answer to God's dissatisfaction; that which provides Him with the answer to His age-long quest in the hearts of all concerned. If there is one thing that God has made abundantly clear, it is that He is committed to the fullness of His Son, Jesus Christ. That fullness is to find its first realization in the Church, 'which is the fullness of Him.'"[42]

But in this work, God must have a free way and have no self involved from man's side. Thus, the cross is the starting place of the Church. After we arrive at the church in this spiritual and practical way, the cross still governs to ensure that in any true expression of Christ (individually or collectively) "there is no place for man by nature."[43] Too often, the natural man serves his own interest in the churches. "As the church universal rests solely upon the foundation of Christ crucified, buried, and raised, so the churches must take their character from the foundation."[44] Thus, the experience of believers in the churches must be a continual, progressive movement toward a richer expression of Christ and fuller experience of the cross. "We cannot 'form' or 'found' churches like this, but the Lord can bring into being a nucleus of well-crucified leaders, building therewith and thereon."[44] Mr. Sparks sums up this thought by saying, "That way is the organic way, i.e. through death and resurrection, in which every grain shares, and to which all the grains, severally and corporately, are a testimony."[44]

The essence of this testimony is a living Christ within us—Christ in you, the hope of glory. It is not about knowing facts of Christ's person or work. It is about the presence and expression of Christ Himself. "There is no hope for us individually; there is no hope for our companies, our churches, our assemblies; there is no hope for Christianity—unless and until the living Christ, with all the tremendous significance of His coming into this world, of His life here, of His Cross, of His resurrection, has come, by the Holy Spirit, on to the inside of things, of peoples, and churches; until it is "Christ in you."[45] Stephen was a witness of just this testimony. In his inspired pronouncement he recounted the Scriptures showing how God desired to bring forth this spiritual and heavenly system and order, culminating in Jesus. Furthermore he showed how man had made the earthly things ends in themselves and had persecuted those who sought to uplift the heavenly and spiritual. At the end of his discourse, Stephen saw the Son of Man standing, indicating that all government, authority and headquarters rested in this man, not in any place. Paul was affected by this scene, indicating that "the church universal, and its representation worldwide, took its rise from that very hour and event."[46] All this has much to say about the true nature of the church and the churches.

We see from this long description that Mr. Sparks did not see any way that the church could be a system of doctrine or practice. It only came out of a living Christ in the believers. His view was that any particular practice or teaching could be carried out or learned without Christ.

But only Christ is the church. Therefore only the leading of Christ creates a practice that is the church and only the revelation of Christ creates truth in us that is the church. This is truly the safe way and a way that ensures that no system will be formed to replace the living person of Christ.

The Local Churches

A particular matter concerning the church surfaced during Mr. Sparks' second visit to the island of Taiwan. As he was viewing the mighty works of God in that country, he was very impressed with the work that the Lord was doing through some of the Taiwanese assemblies he visited. However, an issue emerged regarding what the believers in these assemblies called the "stand" of the church or "the ground of the church." They realized that Christ is the unique foundation, but asked the question: upon what basis or ground shall we build the church with Christ as the unique foundation? Instead of building the church upon the basis or ground of a denomination, particular teaching, sect, leader, spiritual practice, or particular form of church government, they realized the church with its unique foundation was to be built upon the basis or ground of the locality or city in which the believers were. They called this "the ground of locality." Any church built on this ground or basis must be inclusive of all the believers in that locality. Thus, this stand was also called "the ground of oneness," which allows for no divisions among local churches other than the simple fact of being in a different locality.

This stand was based on their interpretation of the New Testament description of the one heavenly universal church and the many local churches on earth. The New Testament reveals that the universal Church, the Body of Christ, is one and cannot be divided. It follows then that

all the local churches, who can derive their true characteristics only from the universal Church, should express the
same oneness. Accordingly, all the local churches should
then base themselves on the ground of oneness, the oneness of the Spirit, which is shown in the one Body, the one
universal Church. Furthermore, the New Testament
abounds with descriptions of local churches as being simply the aggregate of the believers in a particular locality or
city, with each locality having only one local church. For
example, Acts 8:1 says "the church which was in Jerusalem," 1 Corinthians 1:1 says "the church of God which is
at Corinth," and 1 Thessalonians 1:1 says, "the church of
the Thessalonians." This description of a local church follows through in other passages with remarkable consis-
tency. When referring to a region containing many cities,
the Bible uses the plural "churches," as in "the churches of
Galatia" (Gal. 1:2) or "the churches of Judea" (Gal. 1:22).
In addition, Paul appointed elders in every church (Acts
14:23) and charged Titus to appoint elders in every city
(Titus 1:5). The angel told John to send a book to seven
churches and then listed seven cities to which it should be
sent (Rev. 1:11). All these descriptions indicate that the
only reason churches were distinguished from one another
in the New Testament was because of geography, the
boundary being the locality or city in which the believers
were. Churches were not distinguished by a particular
teaching, emphasis, spiritual practice, level of spirituality,
nationality, founder, or apostle. All the believers in a locality were one church, the church in that city. This stand
on the ground of oneness, the ground of locality, allowed
those in the churches in Taiwan to practice a church life in
oneness with all believers. Watchman Nee taught this in
his early ministry in the book, *Concerning Our Missions*,
first published by Witness and Testimony press (since re-
named *The Normal Christian Church Life*) and in his later
ministry in the book *Further Talks on the Church Life*.

These churches in Taiwan felt that the ground of oneness, the ground of locality, was the unique stand of the church and would allow them to practice the church life in oneness. However, Mr. Sparks felt that to include a locality or city boundary as part of the stand of the local church was to make the heavenly church earthy. He may have viewed this matter as a practice and attached to it all the usual warnings that come with the emphasis of any practice. Any practice, even one clearly set forth in God's Word, carries with it the danger of being picked up by believers merely in an outward way, without any inward revelation of Christ. The result is an empty form that eventually produces an exclusive group of believers. Only the revelation and experience of Christ in the believers can be considered the church and can be inclusive of all believers. Thus, Mr. Sparks could not embrace this stand of the church in his definition of a local church. Instead of emphasizing the need for a local church to stand on the ground of oneness, Mr. Sparks emphasized the need for a local church to seek the highest measure of Christ.

Sadly, some in the churches in Taiwan used Mr. Sparks' position on this matter as reason to separate themselves from others who stood for the ground of oneness, the ground of locality. In consequence, a work, which had been so prevailing during Mr. Sparks' visit, lost much of its impact for the next number of years due to internal turmoil. Mr. Sparks was not asked to visit again and minister to these churches in Taiwan. However, Witness Lee, a servant of the Lord who was instrumental in building up this particular work in Taiwan and in the Far East, did visit Honor Oak after this incident in the summer of 1958. He arrived on July 29 and spoke all the messages during the August 2-4 conference. Here "he made special mention of how God wants to build up His house in every locality, how every saint should be built up in God's life and, in turn, manifest some function. The saints built up locally become the practical expression of Christ's Body, God's dwelling place on earth, and the spiritual house for all God's children."[47] After visiting the continent for more ministry, Witness Lee returned to Kilcreggan, Scotland on August 18 of that same summer and spent two weeks talking with Mr. Sparks. They spent much time discussing the matter of the church and the church ground. These discussions may have added to Mr. Sparks' motivation for writing the editorials on the church appearing later that year in *A Witness and a Testimony*. We have no record from Mr. Sparks' side of the content of their conversation. However, in his *Life-Study of Colossians* Witness Lee relates the following account:

> At our invitation, he [T. Austin-Sparks] came to Taiwan in 1955. We had a wonderful time together as he ministered on Christ. In 1957 he came to Taiwan a second time. On this visit he touched the church ground, the standing of the church, in a negative way. In 1958 I accepted his invitation to visit him in England. During the days we were together, we had many long conversations about the church. However, he could not change my mind, and I could not change his concept. He tried his best to avoid the subject of the church, but my concept was that we must labor for the building up of the churches. His intention was to convince us that we should give up the ground of the church. But I pointed out to him that it was impossible for us to have the church practically without the ground of the church. Brother Sparks tried to assure me that he was not opposed to the church. He went on to tell me that during

the early years of his ministry, he was invited to speak at Edinburgh. When he spoke about Christ, the meeting hall was crowded, and the audience was responsive. But when he spoke about the church, the number of people decreased. This caused him to feel that it was not profitable for him to speak on the church.

I went on to ask Brother Sparks how we could practice the principles we both had seen concerning the Lord's Body. He admitted that these principles could not be put into practice in the denominations. But he would not admit that they could be put into practice only on the proper ground of the church. Instead, he emphasized the fact that the church can be produced only by much prayer and through the Spirit. Then I said to him, "Do you think that so many churches on the island of Taiwan did not all come into existence by prayer and through the Spirit?" I asked him what a group of saints should do after they had prayed regarding the church. Still he would not admit that they would take the standing of the church on the ground of oneness. He simply said that they needed to be assured that any move they made was of the Spirit. This was the conclusion of our conversation about the church.

I tried my best to convince him concerning the church, and he tried his best to avoid the church. Eventually, neither of us would change our position.[48]

Neither Mr. Sparks nor Mr. Lee would change their position regarding the church. Mister Lee felt that the way to practice the church life was through a proper stand of the church on the ground of oneness; there is only one church in one locality or city. Witness Lee, like Watchman Nee, witnessed the Lord plant and build up many churches in China and the Far East in this principle. These two also saw the Lord move and bless many situations where such a church life was established. Even Mr. Sparks, when he saw these churches in Taiwan, could not deny that this "wealthy place" had manifest signs of the Spirit of God working on the basis of the church. However, as we have stated above, Mr. Sparks felt that including the boundary of a locality or city in a stand of the church was to make the heavenly church earthy. He might have feared that this stand could become an empty practice, which could be carried out apart from the genuine, subjective experience of Christ.   To Mr. Sparks the church was Christ, nothing more and nothing less. Therefore, he did not emphasize this matter, but simply stressed that the church should seek the highest measure of Christ.

It should be noted that both Witness Lee and Watchman Nee were also very clear, just as Mr. Sparks was, that the church must be a product of the believers' experience of Christ. They would agree that simply declaring a stand on the proper church ground, if carried out in a dead and lifeless way apart from Christ, does not produce the church.

In the end, it seems there was no animosity between Mr. Lee and Mr. Sparks. There was merely a difference in view between these two servants of the Lord. Beyond this, they shared great similarities: both had a substantial ministry committed to them by the Lord, both saw many of the same revelations, both underwent great suffering for their ministry, and both faced the greatest opposition to their ministry from fellow believers. Others may have taken these two views and used them as a base for division and active opposition of one against the other. However, these two brothers in the Lord continued to respect and appreciate one another even until Mr. Sparks' death. Throughout his life, Mr. Lee received much help from the ministry of Mr. Sparks and spoke many of the same things that Mr. Sparks had previously spoken. Witness Lee even acknowledged that his understanding of the New Jerusalem was significantly based on Mr. Sparks' writings.[49] At the same time, Mr. Sparks included quite a few of Mr. Lee's messages in *A Witness and a Testimony*, indicating that he felt these messages bore the same testimony that he himself had been led into by Christ.

The Home Base from 1955 to 1958

Throughout these three years, the regular conference schedule at Honor Oak was faithfully continued. We know some of the topics at some of the conferences and we list these below to give the reader a brief picture of what was going on at Honor Oak. The topic of the 1955 Whitsun conference was "The Cross and the Eternal Glory." Mr. Sparks ministered at the 1957 Easter conference on the topic "The Arm of the Lord," which series of messages was published in the 1958 issue of *A Witness and a Testimony*. Mr. Sparks also spoke at the 1957 Whitsun conference on the subject "Let the House be Built." This gathering was not at Honor Oak, but was held at The Livingstone Hall, Broadway, Westminster, London. The location may have been changed to accommodate the large number in attendance. As mentioned above, Witness Lee spoke at the 1958 August conference at Honor Oak. He remarked after his visit that the group of brother and sisters gathered at Honor Oak was in his consideration the most spiritual gathering in England.[50]

In addition to the regular gatherings at Honor Oak, Mr. Sparks held a number of special gatherings and international conferences during these years. For example, in August of 1957, the brothers at Honor Oak hosted an "International Conference," where it was hoped that brothers from East and West would share in the ministry. A full report of this conference was written up in *A Witness and a Testimony*. The gathering was held at Honor Oak and included the largest number of attendees in the history of gatherings at Honor Oak. Brothers and sisters arrived from China, Singapore, India, the United States, Denmark, France, Germany, Holland, Switzerland and the United Kingdom. Six brothers ministered during this international conference gathering. Mr. Sparks opened and gave the message on the Lord's Day morning. Throughout the weekend a variety of scriptural lines were ministered by various brothers including Brother R. Bissell of Ranchi, India; Brother H. W. Nelson of Minneapolis, USA; Brother John Paul of Ranchi, Brother Stephen Kaung; and Brother Bakht Singh of Madras, India.

Other 1957 gatherings described as "International Conferences" were held in the following places at the following dates: Switzerland, July 20-28; Copenhagen, Denmark, August 10-12; Nyborg Strand, Denmark (coordinated by brother Poul Madsen), August 13-19; Kilcreggan, Scotland (Personally invited workers only) August 24 - September 2; Switzerland, Lake of Thun, September 18-26. These gatherings indicate that the Lord was drawing more and more people to the rich ministry and that this ministry was being spoken by more brothers from abroad. The fellowship between Mr. Sparks and various indigenous moves of the Lord throughout the world was advancing and vibrant during this summer. Throughout 1958 the regular conferences were continued and the fellowship was enjoyed by many at the Center at Honor Oak.

"The Bible speaks of the creation of man, of the Lord seeking to have a man-race, a corporate man in whom His own thoughts and features are reproduced in a moral way. The Lord has ever sought Him that man. It was the seeking of such a man that led to the creation. It was the seeking of such a man that led to the incarnation. It is the seeking of such a man which has led to the Church, the 'one new man.' God is all the time in quest of a man to fill His universe; not one man as a unity, but a collective man gathered up into His Son. Paul speaks of this man as '...the church which is His Body, the fullness of Him...' That is the fullness, the measure of the stature of a man in Christ. It is the Church which is there spoken of, not any one individual. God has ever been in quest of a man to fill His universe."

—*Stewardship of the Mystery I*

Alone, yet in Christ
1959-1971

We enter here upon the last section of Mr. Sparks' life. The events that transpired in this time period probably never came up in Mr. Sparks' thoughts, but God's hand was present, giving out year by year exactly what His servant needed. Many times in the past 33 years since the little company moved up the hill to begin meeting at the Fellowship Center Mr. Sparks felt that truly they had arrived at a place where there was no way to go on. Through internal problems resulting in T. Madoc Jeffreys' leaving, and through external pressures like German bombs and the wide dissemination of baseless rumor and calumny, the Lord always made a door so that the ministry deepened and spread in spite of all. Mr. Sparks could so many times echo Paul and say that they were "cast down, but not destroyed," and thereby boast not in his success but simply in his continued existence. The final period of Mr. Sparks' ministry witnessed, among other things, a much greater intensification of Mr. Sparks' sufferings and forced him even further to trust in heaven when no way on earth presented itself. People close to him testified that during this time his ministry and his release of clear riches in the word also became richer as he passed through these events. Although his opportunity for ministering greatly diminished throughout the latter years of his life, the opportunities he did have to speak revealed a mature minister full of light and life. He never retired but sought to be faithful to the ministry committed to him by the Lord.

Rejected by the Fellowship at Honor Oak

After World War II, and especially throughout the 1950's, the fellowship at Honor Oak enjoyed a time of spiritual and numerical expansion and enlargement. The ministry of Mr. Sparks, of those with him at Honor Oak, and of many guests provided a rich spiritual feast for Christians who were seeking something more solid and real of the Christian life in God's purpose. In Addition, toward the end of the 1950's a greater hunger was developing in those at Honor Oak for the experience of a real church life.

This hunger for the church life was instilled in the brothers and sisters by Mr. Sparks himself and through his ministry that so much emphasized the church. As we saw in the last chapter, Mr. Sparks very much concentrated on the matter of the church especially in the latter half of the 1950's. He declared strongly that the unique instrument God will use to fulfill his eternal purpose in this age is the church. Indeed the corporate experience is why he had to depart from laboring in the ministry of Jesse Penn-Lewis, who he felt emphasized too much of the individual experience. The universal church is heavenly, spiritual, and full of wonderful relatedness between all believers. The local church takes its character from the universal. The local church is where relatedness is experienced, where many lessons of the cross are learned, where a wide aspect of Christ as the Body is made real, where gifts are manifested and exercised for the benefit of the whole. In 1959 Mr. Sparks described the experience of a believer after he came in contact with the church: "Just as the confession or salvation of an individual is always with the sense of having come home, a local church should be to the company a coming home, the supply of a deep need, the answer to a deep longing; just 'my spiritual home.'"[1] It was just such a sense that began stirring in many of the participants, new and old, of the Fellowship at Honor Oak.

To answer this growing need, the fellowship took a number of steps in the direction of practicing more of a local church life. The first took place in 1958, when the responsible brothers at Honor Oak brought two young brothers from among the Fellowship to share responsibility. However, these brothers soon found that the customary dominance of the trustees made it impossible for newcomers to have any part in current decisions and directions. Therefore, by the end of 1959, they resigned from this responsibility in frustration. However, the responsible brothers still felt to pursue a greater focus on the church life, in response to what they felt was a growing desire in the brothers and sisters. Additionally and surprisingly, these brothers felt that the main barrier to a further development of the local church life was the constant demand placed upon the company at Honor Oak to support a wider ministry—the ministry of Mr. Sparks. In 1965 Mr. Sparks described how the brothers "felt that the great place occupied by aspects of the wider work and ministry—e.g. magazine, literature, printing department, conferences, etc.—was a limitation to this local expression of the Church and the activities proper to the same."[2]

Apparently, many attempts were made to solve this problem. In 1960 more concrete decisions were made toward the end of producing a suitable atmosphere for the activities of this "local expression" of the church. First, there was a noticeable reduction in interests of the fellowship outside of the Honor Oak Center in London. For example, the freehold property in Mysore State India was sold, effectively ending active participation, although not fellowship, in the spread of the church work in India. Also in 1960, the brothers decided to sell the Kilcreggan retreat center, so often used in the past as a part of Honor Oak's ministry to people all over the world.

Also in 1960, there began a reduction of the number of conferences held at the Center and for that matter held at all. Notices appeared in *A Witness and a Testimony* announcing the cancellation of this year's customary January gathering for workers and the customary October gathering for all the brothers and sisters. The cancellation notice for the October gatherings invites all interested brothers or sisters to visit the Center to join in the regular fellowship and ministry. In 1961 the Whitsun gathering was also cancelled thus reducing the number of conferences at Honor Oak to those held at Easter and over the August bank holiday.

Further adjustments were made in 1962 when the Witness and Testimony editorial office was moved from the basement of the Honor Oak Center to a house formerly used for extra hospitality during conference times. The house provided space for the Witness and Testimony editorial equipment and residence for two secretaries Miss Read and Miss Guy who, along with Mr. Clifford Ogden and Mr. Sparks, were responsible for all literature production and distribution. In a brief history of Honor Oak written by Angus Kinnear in 1995, this move was described as follows. "The well-worn printing presses had by now been passed to other Christian charities (MV Logos and GLS Bombay). To ease his [Mr. Sparks] editorial work further the remaining staff and offices of the book-publishing program were now moved closer to his home."[3] Mr. Sparks wrote of the move, "The releasing of the rooms at the Center will also provide for the development of the work of the local assembly which development is a burden on the hearts of the responsible brethren."[4] Also in 1962, the finances of the assembly were separated from those of Witness and Testimony trust in order to give the local assembly even more freedom in its operation.

In 1963 all the conferences, including the ones at Easter and over the August bank holiday, at Honor Oak were cancelled. This notice appears as a "P.S." in the January 1963 editor's letter. "I should be very grateful for special prayer guidance in these coming months. It would seem that ministry at Honor Oak can now be fully assumed by other brothers and that my own way would be further afield, if the Lord still needs this voice. Another period in the United States seems probable in the immediate future."[5] A year later a further development of the life of the assembly is described by Angus Kinnear. In 1964 "two senior trustees, commissioned by the Founder to do so, gave the congregation its own initial group of eight locally resident elders to oversee its spiritual life and the running of its programs. The church's life continued from there with some development, but with an inevitable drop in numbers."[6]

At the end of 1964, notices in *A Witness and a Testimony* inviting people to visit the Center and reside in the guest house were discontinued. The familiar line, published for so many years at the end of the magazine "The guest house exists for the accommodation of those of the Lord's people who desire to come for the value of the spiritual ministry at the Center"[7] was now no longer included. This was a further indication of the path the company at Honor Oak was taking and of the separation that was continuing to widen between their stand and that of the original vision of the founder.

From 1963 onward Mr. Sparks continued to reside near Honor Oak and never ceased attending its gatherings.

But he rarely spoke to the assembly there. Not until 1970, the year before his death, does a notice appear in *A Witness and a Testimony* announcing one day of ministry by Mr. Sparks on 'Good Friday' of that year. Concerning his speaking, Angus Kinnear writes, "He declined invitations to preach again at the Center."[6]

All these developments were a striking blow to Mr. Sparks. First of all, they went against the initial vision that he had for the Center, when he led that little group out from Honor Oak Baptist. This little company was initially committed with a vision of becoming a sign to all Christians of a testimony of Christ to meet the needs of the entire world. In the January 1963 editorial Mr. Sparks writes the following concerning Honor Oak.

> We began with a vision. We believe that it was a God-given vision. This belief has been supported by many evidences, seeing that we have never made any effort at propaganda or advertisement. The vision was of a ministry in and through a Center to which and from which the Lord's people of all the world could come and go with a fuller knowledge and enrichment of Himself. Into this vision the Lord brought others who had gone to many parts carrying—not another's ministry or vision, but—what the Lord has shown to them and led them into. We have steadfastly endeavored to keep this ministry available to all the Lord's people, and avoid anything that is in the nature of exclusiveness, separation or sectarianism. With the advance of years, changes in personnel, understanding, and apprehension are inevitable, but, so far as this paper is concerned, we hope to main-

tain its original purpose; but, we trust, with
growing richness, until its mission is terminated. We pray that it may ever be bread
for the hungry; life in the battle with death;
light for those who seek it; and—in all—a
contribution to that one heart-purpose of
the Father, the fullness of His Son, our
Lord Jesus.[8]

We see from this comment that Mr. Sparks no
longer regarded the Center at Honor Oak as continuing in
its original, what he believed to be, God given vision.
Now, Mr. Sparks looked to the magazine as the only instrument remaining that could still fulfill that original vision. The magazine, then, was the only thing that could
continue to fulfill his commitment from the Lord.

In addition to turning against his original vision,
this new set of circumstances left Mr. Sparks conspicu-
ously alone in his later years. Often in the past did he
write and boast that rich ministry was fulfilled and testimony was borne in his absence. This he stated as proof
that he was not standing as a one-man ministry. He was
standing with a group of brothers in one vision for this
one testimony. Now, he was alone, utterly alone. The
senior trustees who appointed elders at Honor Oak did not
stand with him by standing true to the original vision.
Most of the brothers and sisters in the fellowship did not
stand with him in this way. Most of those who had been
raised up by him and who had seen many spiritual things
because of his ministry did not stand with him. His base
was gone. His home audience was gone. And his co-
workers were gone. Only faithful Harry Foster continued
to work with him and to contribute to *A Witness and a
Testimony*. At the end of 1963, after the brothers took so
many steps towards enriching their local church life, Mr.
Sparks wrote that his work at Honor Oak was completed.

This breach was never healed in Mr. Sparks' lifetime. In fact, its severity increased even up to very close
to the end of his life. In 1969, when Mr. Sparks was 81, at
a time in human life when many practical concerns should
be made as easy as possible, the premises, housing the
editorial section of Witness and Testimony and Mr.
Sparks' two secretaries, was put up for sale. Mr. Sparks'
first two editor's letters of that year included requests for
prayer, because he did not know where they would relocate. He was unable to find a suitable building nearby because it was in a residential neighborhood. So, he feared
that he would have to relocate outside of London. Finally,
an empty garage was found at the back of the Fellowship
Center at Honor Oak. The garage, once repainted and repaired by "willing hands," became the new home of the
Witness and Testimony editorial section. Mr. Sparks' two
secretaries, Miss Read and Miss Guy found residence in
the neighborhood. Mr. Sparks made the following comment, after the solution was found to this worrisome di-
lemma. "This all has one particular advantage: for these
recent years the element of uncertainty and tentativeness
has kept us in suspense, but now there is a sense of release
from this, and we are hoping that concentration will result."[9] At this mature stage in his life, after he had learned
lessons in the school of Christ for so many years, his being free to apply himself to Bible study and to the study of
spiritual situations could have rendered valuable light to
coming generations. Instead, at this age, he found himself
concerned with office space. He was finally released once
this uncertainty had passed, but that time can never be recovered. All these distractions may have meant great loss
for future generations who might have benefited from
more writings and ministry from this very mature servant
of Lord.

Last Years of Uncertainty

Actually, the remainder of Mr. Sparks' life was in a constant state of uncertainty. He was uncertain where he would minister, what doors the Lord would open up and even whether his ministry would continue at all. In November of 1963 Mr. Sparks writes, "How we are here waiting on the Lord for the next phase, seeing that our personal responsibility for the work at Honor Oak has concluded....The probability is that some changes will come in the near future...."[10] In 1964 he asked for the prayers of his readers that the Lord would make him clear as to His course for the year. He wrote, "Does the Lord really want me to spend this year in 'journeys oft'? The calls are many....But the physical conditions of increased years make it necessary to be very sure of the Lord's will and to know His enablement in a fuller way than ever."[11] Then he revealed what kind of setting he would prefer in his old age, "My own inclination would be toward centers or a center to which the Lord's people might come and return to their location."[11] The ironic thing was that he was residing at Honor Oak Center, but was not able to use it as such for his ministry. Again uncertainty rears its head at the end of 1965, after announcing the retirement of A.G. Taylor from responsibilities at Honor Oak, Mr. Sparks lets his readers know that even the future of the Honor Oak property was now unknown, since the city was considering taking over the property for school development. As to his own ministry he expresses the need for prayerful concern as to whether the Lord would provide him a new base or whether he should be led for an extended period of movement in response to many invitations or whether the Lord was bringing his personal ministry to a close. He also remarked that the magazine still seemed to be a wide open door that was enlarging to this day.[12] At the end of 1966, he includes in another editor's letter the following paragraph. "The whole matter of our future base and sphere is a major issue, and we ask for fellowship in this connection. Our work seems to be finished at Honor Oak and the new orientation does not seem to need our particular ministry and function. We, however, have no intention of moving without definite leading by the Lord. We remain His 'ambassador in bonds.'"[13] In a 1967 editorial Mr. Sparks looks back on the forty years of being at Honor Oak to all that the Lord did and writes, "But only heaven and eternity will show the true measure and values which have to be hidden from our eyes for safety's sake."[14] This shows that he did not see at present any lasting sign on earth of the Lord's move through his ministry at Honor Oak over the last forty years. Only the Lord has the real apprehension. The only channel in which Mr. Sparks saw a sign of the Lord's increase was in the magazine. In spite of all the uncertainty and setbacks, hunger for the solid food in the magazine still grew. This made it even more unsettling when in 1969 so much of his concern was with the existence of suitable premises to house the editorial office that made possible the publication of the magazine. These comments, throughout many years, show that most of the years between 1963 to the end of his life were unsettled and particularly baffling. Instead of being able to concentrate more fully on the riches of the word or on ministry to God's people, Mr. Sparks found himself almost continually concerned over the most basic necessities of his ministry. He was forced to be concerned for his base, his audience, his location, his sphere of work and even for his editorial office space.

One has to ask, "Why did all this happen?" No one will ever know the full reasons with all their complications until that day. We venture a few possibilities, one assigning responsibility to the brothers at Honor Oak, one looking at Mr. Sparks himself and one looking from God's side while seeking to discern His mind.

We first look at the shortfalls of the brothers at Honor Oak, so many of whom were helped and raised up by Mr. Sparks. There was a great breakdown of trust and fellowship on the side of these brothers. By all respects they should have had a deep appreciation for Mr. Sparks' ministry and a realization that it was mainly through his instrumentality that they had seen so much of Christ and had been brought to experience many deep things of God. This is not saying that they should have then followed him blindly, but they should have respected what the Lord did through him. Would not this help received warrant from these brothers a forbearance of any peculiarities possessed by Mr. Sparks or even mistakes made by Mr. Sparks? They could not see through the earthen vessel to the treasure of the Christ within. Where was the practical bearing of the cross by these brothers? They became so very small and shortsighted as to only focus on their fellowship in London. Where was their experience of Christ that would broaden their hearts to see beyond themselves to a world full of the Lord's scattered sheep who were sorely in need of a building-up ministry? Instead of caring for the world with a worldwide ministry, they became introverted and desired to produce a small, common, exclusive, free group that yielded little spiritual help to people and that made little impact in reversing the worldwide situation of spiritual decline.

But there were also matters about Mr. Sparks that one could point to as a cause for such developments. Although Mr. Sparks' ministry was rich, heavenly, and full of spiritual impact, many would say that his handling of practical affairs left much to be desired. Furthermore, his ability to relate to many of his co-workers or fellow brothers and sisters on a personal level was often awkward and strained. This matter of furthering the church life of the fellowship at Honor Oak was an intensely practical question. It required a leadership that was both very practical in its decisions and intimately connected to the current condition of the local brothers and sisters. But these roles and requirements did not fit Mr. Sparks. Angus Gunn writes, "I would be remiss if I failed to point out that TAS shared the weaknesses and experienced failures that are common to fallen humanity. He found it difficult to share responsibility and this often deprived him of the benefits and corrective help both of other evangelical leaders and sometimes even his close colleagues."[15] Others close to him testified how Mr. Sparks conveyed a feeling of distance to those around him. He was not one for small talk. Some even said that they could sit for an hour in his presence and he would not say a word. An outsider looking at this situation would say that he should have addressed the desire for a greater church life, because this was what he himself ministered. But Mr. Sparks was not the right person to do it.

In the earlier days of the Honor Oak Fellowship Center, many of these practical interactions and many of the practical affairs of the fellowship were taken care of by other brothers, first by T. Madoc Jeffreys and then by George Paterson. In both cases Mr. Sparks was more responsible for ministry, both at home and abroad. Mr. Jeffreys focused on taking care of the home base. George Paterson's function was very much the same. He ably took care of many local concerns with diligence and understanding. His tireless energy created a loving sense of the corporate life among the brothers at Honor Oak and the many visitors, while keeping a good fellowship with Mr. Sparks. But after George Paterson died in 1951, no brother was able to rise up and take this place. From then on it was easier for the many seeds of misunderstanding sown by Satan, who hated this ministry, to grow and finally blossom in the early 1960s. Mr. Sparks' personality did not promote personal understanding and cooperation and thus gave these many seeds of mistrust fertile ground to grow. Therefore, he, along with the vision that he believed God had given him, became more and more distant to the brothers around him.

It is interesting to note that many times Mr. Sparks would speak about the masterstroke that the enemy wields against the Body of Christ. Satan's tactic is mainly to sow suspicion, misunderstandings, and friction between brothers. In fact, in his 1960 book *Our Warfare,* Mr. Sparks writes, "a favorite maneuver of our enemy is to get amongst us and make us look at one another and misjudge one another, misinterpret one another, get us mistrusting one another."[16] It was just this cancer that damaged the fellowship and effectiveness of the fellowship at Honor Oak. The seeds were planted, found soil to grow, and resulted in open division, loss of focus and loss of the distinctive testimony that had previously been borne.

Perhaps one could consider many more potential causes in the attitudes and actions of the brothers at Honor Oak or in the character and exercise of Mr. Sparks or even in the many seeds of discontent from Satan incessantly bombarding the brothers. But in the end we must recognize and trust in the absolute sovereignty of God. Only in that day may we know the Lord's full intention for this last decade of Mr. Sparks' life. Now we can only surmise the full implications of the divine thought. According to Mr. Sparks' own teaching, God is the Potter and we are never off His wheel. This last phase of Mr. Sparks' life very well could have been Mr. Sparks' last test. In the School of Christ, Mr. Sparks writes of how our revelation of Christ is bound up in practical situations. "We have to come into New Testament situations to get a revelation of Christ to meet the situation. So that the Holy Spirit's way with us is to bring us into living actual conditions and situations, and needs, in which only some fresh knowledge of the Lord Jesus can be our deliverance, our salvation, our life, and then to give us, not a revelation of truth, but a revelation of the Person, new knowledge of the Person, that we come to see Christ in some way that just meets our need."[17] Mr. Sparks described how truth becomes reality in us by us receiving it, being tested by it, and undergoing a crisis in which only Christ is able to bring us through. Mr. Sparks' life of unusual sufferings seemed never to be out of that cycle. Perhaps this was a similar and more severe crisis. Was he relying on his base, his center, his co-workers or was Christ Himself, who Mr. Sparks portrayed in a way that genuinely conveyed His greatness, truly enough for his service to the Body? During this time, Mr. Sparks wrote a series of articles entitled "Christ our all."[18] Now may have been the test of the reality of that truth in Mr. Sparks. The apostle Paul said, near the end of his life, "All in Asia have left me" and was fully content with having only Christ. Now Mr. Sparks was entering into the same lonely experience, where Christ Himself was to be his all.

As we have said before, not until that day may we fully know the divine mind in arranging these last lessons for Mr. Sparks. We will never know the new depths of secret fellowship with Christ that this situation pressed him to reach. We have no record of his complaints or verbal attacks against any brother. Mister Sparks saw that his situations were not really from the workings of men or from the arrangements of things. He trusted that these were from the loving hand of the Potter who was molding him. From a 1968 conversation between a young brother and Mr. Sparks we can see a bit into Mr. Sparks' feeling. This young brother saw how Mr. Sparks realized he had received something from the Lord and that all these things were merely the sufferings associated with that revelation. He detected no bitterness within Mr. Sparks. In fact, Mr. Sparks had opportunity to change his situation because he had been invited to move to other places where his ministry would be easily and eagerly received. However, he did not feel liberty from the Lord to move. Fearing that his move would cause many at Honor Oak to choose sides, he said, "I would not be the cause of division." Mr. Sparks received a revelation of Christ, lived accordingly, and would not move to lesson the associated suffering. Trusting God, he was not bitter, even at the end.[19]

Serving Faithfully Until the End

All these happenings did not leave Mr. Sparks passive or despairing. Rather they caused him to seek God more for the doors He would keep open and for new doors that He would freshly unveil. First of all, Mr. Sparks felt led to respond to some of the many invitations to travel abroad for ministry. In 1963, he spent over four months in the United States. In the November 1963 editor's letter, Mr. Sparks reviews some small groups and individuals with whom he had opportunity to renew fellowship and ministry during his United States travels. He visited a group of believers in Philadelphia, brother Cressy of Springfield, PA; a company of believers in Louisville; and brother Addison Raws of Keswick Grove, NJ, whom he first met in 1925.[20]

During this trip, Mr. Sparks also spent eight weeks ministering at the Gospel Tabernacle of the Christian Missionary Alliance in New York. This tabernacle was associated with the Christian and Missionary Alliance, founded by the late A. B. Simpson, whom Mr. Sparks greatly admired and respected. Concerning A. B. Simpson, Mr. Sparks writes "spiritual enrichment to the church of God has been exceptional through this vessel."[21] Concerning the Christian and Missionary Alliance, Mr. Sparks writes "There are very few instrumentalities of God since the apostolic times which have ministered spiritual blessing over a large area of the world more than this agency."[21] It was here, in the Gospel Tabernacle of the

CMA that Mr. Sparks ministered for eight weeks in 1963. During his stay, and afterwards, items from the Alliance magazine and from A. W. Tozer and A. B. Simpson frequently appeared in *A Witness and a Testimony*.

In addition to traveling for longer periods of time, Mr. Sparks also gave himself more decidedly to making literature available. This was in response to his very urgent realization of the lack of solid, edifying spiritual food among God's people from Far East to Far West. Near the end of 1963 Mr. Sparks set himself to reprint a number of titles that had been long out of print, to print new titles that had previously only been published as series in the magazine, and to edit brand new books. In the beginning of 1964 Mr. Sparks mentioned again in an editor's letter the continued sense of urgency within him to publish. At that point, twelve books and booklets were at the printer and three new ones were edited and ready for printing. This particular burden continued throughout the 1960s. It was during this time that Mr. Sparks republished his "Stewardship of the Mystery" volume one and rewrote volume two for republication in 1966.

In January of 1964, Mr. Sparks felt led by the Lord to heed a call for ministry from Manila in the Philippines. He had been receiving pressing invitations to make such a visit for the past two years.[22] Now at last, he felt that it was in the Lord's timing to visit. He ministered forty-two meetings in Manila, from January 30 to March 12. Mr. Sparks had visited the Philippines twice before, during the same two visits he was invited to minister on the island of Taiwan. During those times, his visits to the Philippines were part of a wider tour of the assemblies and work associated with his fellow brothers in Taiwan. Now, the brothers from Manila themselves had invited Mr. Sparks. Some of these brothers and sisters in the audience had served the Lord in China with Watchman Nee, before the communist takeover. Mr. Sparks chose as his theme a phrase from the Lord's Prayer in John 17, "That they all may be one, even as we are one." In the letter in which he accepted the brothers' invitation Mr. Sparks wrote the following. "The great enemy does not give up his determination to interrupt fellowship and to spoil the work of the Lord by bringing division among His people. Everywhere this evil work is being pressed with increasing intensity. The enemy is set upon destroying anything that will result in the Lord Jesus coming into His full place. We must stand and withstand and do all in our power to keep this ground from him. It is costly, and it demands that we let go all that is only personal, and that we stand for the glory of our Lord's name and His interests alone."[23] Mister Sparks also included the following line in his letter, concerning more directly and practically the theme of his coming. "I am sure that you will never make me or my ministry a ground for division. There is no need to fight for me; the Lord is on the Throne, and He can order things to His Own will—while we pray and trust Him."[24] The meetings took their text from the parables of the kingdom in Matthew and some portions from the gospel of John. Much of Mr. Sparks speaking was not intended to be a systematic teaching, but rather a description of experience of how he himself had learned some of the ways of the Lord in the school of God.

Mr. and Mrs. Sparks' visit to Manila was unexpectedly cut short because of a sudden tragedy in their family. In an insert in the May 1964 issue of *A Witness and a Testimony* this notice appeared. "Since the note inserted with the last issue of *A Witness and a Testimony*, many more friends have sent us very kind expressions of sympathy and assurances of prayerful fellowship. It is quite impossible to write personal letters to these many friends, but we do want every one to know that, although this seems to be a formal acknowledgement, it is not so. Everyone is in mind for very real gratitude. We are not making this a matter of greater importance than should be. There are many others whose trials and sorrows are as great as, or greater than, ours. We should not have mentioned it only to explain why we returned from the Far East sooner than expected." The author believes that the tragedy calling Mr. and Mrs. Sparks back home was the sudden and unexpected death of one of the Sparks' children. Expressions and love and sympathy poured in from brothers and sisters all over the world.

That visit to the Philippines would be the last visit to the Far East for Mr. Sparks. Afterwards, his travels and his ministering would be limited to the European Continent and America. During the remainder of 1964, Mr. Sparks only ministered one time, at a gathering in Switzerland. It seems that in late 1964 Mr. Sparks attempted to resume ministry gatherings in the United Kingdom. At the end of 1964 an announcement appeared in *A Witness and a Testimony* for a 1965 Easter gathering in "Slavanka" Conference Center, Southbourne, Bournemouth, Hampshire April 16-19. In the next issue of the magazine a notice was included announcing the cancellation of this conference, giving no explanation for the change. In some way, it seems that the Lord did not allow this avenue of ministry, i.e. large conferences in the United Kingdom, to open up again for Mr. Sparks.

The cancellation of this conference may have been due to a lack of brothers and sisters who would stand with him in carrying out the gatherings or it may have been due to the still increasing opposition to his ministry from evangelical Christians in that country. In a 1967 editor's letter Mr. Sparks writes about both the decline of the fellowship at Honor Oak from within and the opposition to his ministry from without. In this letter he first gives a brief history of the Lord's work at Honor Oak. He describes how in a very short time, the stand that they took resulted in this ministry being spread all over the world.

Now, just as the New Testament churches themselves disappeared and only their spiritual value remained, he finds himself in the same place concerning the heavenly measure and value of what happened at Honor Oak. Then he brings up the matter of the current opposition to his ministry. He writes, "It might be thought that after so much battering and toiling a period of respite would be given, but the fact is that this ministry is being more fiercely assailed today than at any time before. By printed and radio opposition, falsehood and calumny are being disseminated against us. No effort is made to ascertain the truth or 'prove all things.' Perhaps, in this, we have to accept what we so often said—that the battle will be fiercest as the end draws near."[25] It might have been the combination of these two things—the decline of the fellowship at Honor Oak and the growing noise from the opposition without—that limited his further ministry in the United Kingdom. No other announcements for conference gatherings in the United Kingdom would be given by Mr. Sparks.

We pause here to note the peculiar variety of sufferings that Mr. Sparks faced during his life, and especially during this last decade of service. Not only was he beset by problems with brothers at Honor Oak, but he also suffered the loss of dear and close family members and bore the brunt of baseless attacks of falsehood and calumny spread by evangelicals of his day. At his funeral, brother Harry Foster included this line in his remembrance of Mr. Sparks. "For various reasons many other sufferings came into his life, but this was consistent with his own teaching that in the School of Christ one learns more by suffering than by study or listening to messages."[26] We see that Mr. Sparks' life was full of suffering and also full of learning. In his editor's letters written during this decade, when so many countries of the world were closing up to the gospel and persecuting the Christians within their borders, Mr. Sparks would often ask who can give these believers real spiritual food that would enable them to stand? It may have been that the Lord gave Mr. Sparks such peculiar sufferings in his life that his ministry could deepen and be true bread to the many others suffering in their own countries. It was not his teaching that so often brought people closer to the presence of Christ. Rather, it was his experience and the conveying of that experience that brought people into the real experience of Christ for themselves and thus rendered them the real, solid food that could bring them on to maturity. Mr. Sparks' life experience was consistent with his teaching: from his sufferings and from finding Christ in his sufferings came the riches for his ministry.

In addition to accepting a few invitations for extended ministry visits and applying increased effort to make literature available, Mr. Sparks maintained one regular ministry gathering in Switzerland throughout the 1960s and added one regular ministry gathering in America in the latter half of the 60s decade. Through his faithfulness to these gatherings, we see that Mr. Sparks faithfully walked through the small doors that the Lord opened, or kept open.

Mr. Sparks continued to minister at an annual September conference in Switzerland that had been gathering consistently since 1958. In 1965, this ten-day gathering proved to be the only outlet for his ministering. As far as we know, this gathering was not sponsored by any specific group in Switzerland. Possibly some small group of readers provided an initial invitation, but all the particulars of the conference were handled by the conference secretary at Honor Oak. Surely though, a large proportion of the attendees was made up of interested readers of *A Witness and a Testimony*. This was to become an annual source of rich, spiritual food for this small, but growing group of seekers. It was also to become a gathering place, not unlike the conferences at Honor Oak once were, for seekers from many different countries to come for ministry and fellowship. The setting for this conference was a hotel in Aeschi, which was beautifully situated in the Burnese Oberland. Below the hotel, in full view, sat the beautiful Lake of Thun stretching off to Interlaken. Above, on either side, towered the mighty mountains of the Oberland, with year round snowy peaks and green valleys. In this beautiful setting many seekers of God sought His presence, ministry and fellowship.

Looking at the themes of Mr. Sparks' messages during these conferences is like looking at the books that emerged from his ministry in the 1960s. This conference became a focal point of release for the riches the Lord gave him throughout the year. In his November editor's letters from 1963 onward (except 1969) Mr. Sparks included a report of the Switzerland conference and many times remarked how the gathering was a time of great blessing and an outstanding ministry of that particular year. Later in the 1960s Mr. Sparks would remind his readers early in the year to pray for this September gathering in Switzerland.[27] As we review these conferences, we ask the readers to follow the topics ministered by Mr. Sparks and consider them a picture of his spiritual considerations throughout these remaining years of his life.

In 1962, Mr. Sparks shared the messages that were later to become a book entitled *Discipleship in the School of Christ*. In 1963, his message series became another book entitled *The On-High Calling*. In 1964 Mr. Sparks spoke on the theme entitled, "Into the Mind of God." He shared the ministry with Mr. Lambert and Mr. Warke. In attendance were brothers and sisters mostly from France, but also from ten or eleven different countries, . Three were baptized during this year's blessed gathering. In 1965, Mr. Sparks took as his theme, "The Greatness and Glory of Jesus Christ." Mr. Lambert and Mr. Warke shared in morning prayers. Representatives hailed from France, Switzerland, Germany, Belgium, Holland, India, Congo, Singapore, Yugoslavia, United States, and the United Kingdom. A good number of young people were present. Three were definitely brought to know the Lord. In 1966 Mr. Sparks spoke from the last two chapters of Revelation messages entitled, "The Holy City, New Jerusalem." Mr. Lambert of Richmond, and Mr. Thomson of Bombay shared in morning prayers. Six were baptized. The gathering in 1967 was a time of "spiritual strength and blessing." Mr. Sparks shared on the theme, "The Work in the Groaning of Creation." 1968 saw quite a contingent of young people present at the conference, including some brothers and sisters from Czechoslovakia. Mr. Sparks spoke on "The Mission, the Meaning and the Message of Jesus Christ." In 1969 Mr. Sparks spoke on a series of messages called "God's New Israel." 1970 saw the last gathering of Mr. Sparks' life. He reported in his description of the time that many considered this gathering the best of all his conferences. It was held in a different, bigger hotel, to accommodate the growing number of guests. The guests hailed from Europe, Africa, Asia, and North America. Mr. Poul Madsen, Mr. Roger Forster, Mr. W. E. Thompson and Mr. Sparks all shared in the Ministry. Mr. Sparks spoke on the theme, "The Holy Spirit's Biography of Christ."

In addition to the Switzerland gatherings, in 1966 Mr. Sparks began a regular series of conferences in America. In July of this year he first visited Wabanna Camp, Maryland, to minister at an annual conference of believers who gathered there from many regions in North America. He was 78 years old when he first visited and he continued faithfully to minister there every July for the next four years. In 1966 Mr. Sparks reported, "The conference at Wabanna Camp, Maryland, was one of great blessing."[28] People gathered there from over a wide area from Florida to Canada and from the Eastern and Western states. Many were *Witness and Testimony* readers. The ministry was shared by Mr. DeVern Fromke, Mr. Stephen Kuang, and Mr. Sparks. That summer Mr. Sparks went on to share for four days in Indianapolis, Indiana and then visited a gathering in Jamaica, New York. In 1967, Mr. Sparks returned again to Wabanna Camp and Indianapolis. He shared the ministry at Camp Wabanna with Mr. DeVern Fromke and Mr. Stephen Kuang. In 1968 Mr. Sparks lists the ministry at Wabanna Camp as an outstanding ministry and indicates that more people came, including some from California and Canada. Mr. Sparks also ministered at this gathering in the summer of 1969 and in 1970 with Mr. Roger Forster accompanying him.

In addition to the Wabanna Camp gatherings and other ministry opportunities in North America, Mr. Sparks ministered in Denmark on two occasions during the last years of his life. In 1966 and again in 1970, he visited Nyborg Strand, Denmark for ministry. On both occasions particulars could be received from Mr. Poul Madsen who lived in Copenhagen, Denmark. Furthermore, in 1970 he ministered for one day, "Good Friday," March 27, at Honor Oak.

The continuation of these ministry gatherings became a demonstration that Mr. Sparks still struggled and sought to fulfill his ministry in his last days. He was now in his 70s and had lived out a very full life and a very prolific service to the Lord. By many standards he could have retired peacefully to spend much of his time considering how the Lord had worked through him in his blessed and colorful past. But Mr. Sparks had no thought of retiring. Indeed he intended to continue to fight to serve the Lord until he was no longer physically able. In *Recovering the Lord's Testimony in Fullness*, spoken in 1953, Mr. Sparks gives the following testimony about retiring. "How many times recently have people said to me, 'When are you going to retire. So-and-so has retired and So-and-so is retiring'—yes, ministers of the Gospel. There is no discharge in this warfare, no day for retiring, brothers and sisters. I am sorry for you! You are not going to be pensioned off down here and spend the rest of your life vegetating. You have to go on to the last breath, with battle and cost to the end. There is a cost bound up with the full purpose of God, and in many ways we know it. But oh, the answer! The Lord is taking note; He is putting it down, and He is saying, 'That tithe, that freewill offering people, shall be My peculiar treasure in that day that I do make.'"[29] Now, more than 10 or 15 years after Mr. Sparks spoke this word he was still struggling to fulfill it. He did not cease making plans. He did not strive to loose himself from the battle. He was still keenly aware of what the Lord committed him with and was still struggling to fulfill it.

Mr. Sparks did not allow his old age or his uncertainty about his future ministry or even the thought of the Lord's imminent return to diminish his service to the Lord. He continued to fight for the Lord's interests with whatever the Lord gave him and through whatever door the Lord would open. In fact, the continuation of the Switzerland conference demonstrated that he was still fighting to fulfill the commission that he had received from the Lord. In March of 1966, at the age of 78, he includes this inspiring comment in his editor's letter. "In times of uncertainty like these, one of the difficult things to do is to foresee the future and arrange accordingly. There will be many plans and arrangements which will never have been carried out when the Lord comes, and it would be easy for those who look for His soon return to stop making plans, especially as to His work and ministries. But He has definitely told us not to let go, slacken our hands, or fail to 'occupy till I come': and so, leaving issues to Him, we seek to *complete* our testimony and re-

linquish none of the trust. This has a particular bearing—
in our case—upon a further conference in Switzerland this
year."[30] It was at this gathering that Mr. Sparks unveiled
so much about the holy city, New Jerusalem.

In addition to Mr. Sparks' continued ministry, we
can see his attitude of pressing on till the end from a few
quotes from some of his last editor's letters. These letters
also reveal the intense battle and warfare he was involved
with up until the very end. In July of 1966, Mr. Sparks
wrote, "We do not know how much longer the ministry of
this instrument will go on, perhaps for only a short time,
but God will have other instruments for what He needs.
We are concerned, however, that 'our bow may abide in
strength' until it is laid down, and we need your prayers
that it may do so."[31] In September of 1968, Mr. Sparks
writes, "we are much exercised about the continuance of
this ministry, when the present personal channels are
called to 'higher service,' and we would ask your prayers
concerning this. He takes His workers, but carries on His
work."[32] In 1969, Mr. Sparks writes, "We are much burdened for the many hungry sheep.... The first sermon I
ever preached as a young man was on Acts 26:17b-18, and
I feel that burden more than ever now. You ask the Lord
to raise up men who have seen, and have that commission
and anointing."[33] Concerning the battle he was in, Mr.
Sparks writes in his last editor's letter, "Now, with this
issue of the paper we complete another year. It is truly of
the Lord's grace that we have done so, for it has been a
year of unusual pressure and difficulty. There have been
times when we have wondered whether our ministry was
not drawing to a close."[34]

Before his death in April of 1971, announcements
appeared in *A Witness and a Testimony* for the 1971 Switzerland conference in September and a 1971 American
conference in July. His death prohibited him from attending these times. But the announcement of these gather-

ings shows that he was still making plans to serve the Lord. For Mr. Sparks there was no retiring. For this faithfulness, we trust the Lord was counting Mr. Sparks as "His peculiar treasure."

Late Period Editor's Letters

Throughout these later years, Mr. Sparks' editor's letters became more frequent and more personal. While many misunderstandings plagued his fellowship at Honor Oak, his readers continued to be willing receivers and continued to grow in number throughout this time period. This gave Mr. Sparks more incentive to open personal feelings and spiritual observations of current situations to his willing listeners. As a result, these letters contain many personal references and opinions that make them very instructive to review.

Below we present a survey of his letters and direct the reader to use this survey to gain some specific impressions of Mr. Sparks' ministry, observations, and practical helps. We place his letters from this period into the following four categories and explore each category chronologically by presenting a brief synopsis of each letter along with the month and year it was written. The categories are 1) letters defining the purpose and aim of his ministry 2) letters denoting spiritual principles that frustrate or enhance God's move throughout history 3) letters commenting on the current political, cultural or spiritual situation 4) letters providing help on personal Christian life. These letters contain Mr. Sparks' personal observation and his own learning before the Lord. There is little doubt that the content of each letter was influenced by Mr. Sparks' present walk and recent history with the Lord. We will not seek to draw conclusions relating his recent history with particular topic of that letter. We leave this to the reader and also encourage the reader to use these let-

ters to gain more insight into Mr. Sparks' ministry and
personal views.

Letters Concerning the Purpose of Mr. Sparks' Ministry

We begin with letters concerning the purpose and
aim of his ministry. This indeed was Mr. Sparks' original
and stated purpose of writing editor's letters. They were
included from time to time to remind or introduce readers
to the character of Mr. Sparks' ministry and to state more
specifically what he would like to see accomplished by his
ministry.

In September of 1959 Mr. Sparks begins this category of letters by quoting Acts 2:25, "I beheld the Lord
always before my face"[35] and reminds readers of what the
nature and object of his ministry is and is not. It is "not to
propagate a teaching as such; not to constitute a new community; not to support a particular 'movement'; but truly
and solely to bring and keep the Lord Jesus in view in
ever-growing fullness: that is its object. It seeks to be occupied with the far-reaching purpose of God concerning
His Son, Jesus our Lord."[35] The rest of the letter is occupied with showing the utter importance of seeing Christ
from the beginning of our Christian life until "we shall see
Him even as He is." The tragedy is that so often Christians see men, people, ministries, or Christian work and
fail to see the Lord Jesus as their focal point. With Him as
our focal point, our ministry becomes open to all believers
and there is hope for the rest of the Lord's work to go on.

In November of 1959, Mr. Sparks comments on
the relatively small number of believers who read his
magazine, compared with the number of believers in the
world. But he realizes that this magazine is a test of spiritual hunger, because its message is neither light, nor superficial. In this context the hunger among some for solid
food is an encouraging sign. Giving believers solid food

is the aim of his ministry.

In May of 1961, Mr. Sparks again addresses the food question. His ministry, and the ministry of this little paper, is full of "fairly solid food" and "only the really hungry will appreciate it."[36] This, he feels is his particular calling. Other food is available in wide varieties from other sources. These provisions have their place and value, but believers may come to a certain stage when the other food ceases to satisfy. That is when the solid food, although maybe less tasty, will be what is necessary to bring these believers on towards full growth. For these advancing ones, "The great need is that spiritual life and spiritual truth keep in step as demand and supply."[36] It is this balance that this ministry seeks to keep for those who are hungering after more.

In January of 1962 Mr. Sparks asks, what is the function of "this little and unpretentious paper?"[37] He answers, "It is the revelation of the significance of Jesus Christ in God's universe. The context speaks of, 'God, who said, let there be light.' Just as the sun is the center of the solar system and the source of all its light, life, and energy, so Christ is the divine Center of the spiritual universe, governing all things and giving light, life, power and purpose to all in that sphere. Yes, it is the absolute ascendancy and victory of Christ, and His filling of all things which is 'this ministry.'"[37]

In November of 1962, Mr. Sparks speaks of how God's ways are balanced—there is length, breadth, height and depth—but man so often only emphasizes two dimensions—breadth and height. These symbolize acceptance and prominence in the Christian life. His ministry seeks to bring in a balance again by emphasizing length—endurance—and depth—substance. Mr. Sparks writes of depth, "While never meaning or thinking to overstress this one dimension, we are particularly concerned and burdened to restore it to its equal place. Depth does matter, dear friends, for the storms and adversities will find out the roots and the foundations. The ministry of spiritual depth is the least popular, and only a comparatively few will want it, but it is the ministry of the long-term."[38]

In November of 1963, Mr. Sparks again reminds his readers that the purpose of this ministry is to give God's people solid food. He writes "we feel also that there is a need for that which will meet the Lord's people at and from the point where a greater measure of Christ is called for."[39]

In the January 1965 letter Mr. Sparks briefly reviews the history of this ministry. Through the Lord's help and through the faithful prayers of so many friends, this ministry has stood and even grown in spite of so much opposition throughout the years. He states that he does not feel that this ministry is unique or more important than other ministries. It simply has its place. "It is complimentary and auxiliary."[40] And does not seek to form its own groups but rather seeks to be a ministry to all Christians. If groups do form, by the intrinsic nature of the life, then that will be the Lord's doing. However, Mr. Sparks has seen so much loss due to an "inadequate foundation and edification"[40] among Christians and Christian workers. His ministry seeks to fill up this lack. Only then will believers be able to stand the test in which much "wood, hay and stubble," has already gone up in smoke. In January of 1966, Mr. Sparks simply states concerning his ministry, "We have—what we believe to be—a God given burden for 'the perfecting of the saints' and 'the building up of the Body of Christ.'"[41]

In July 1966, Mr. Sparks describes more specifically the growing light he has received concerning "the greatness and fullness of Jesus Christ, the Son of God and the Son of Man."[42] It should be noted that he would not claim this light as a "new revelation," beyond the New Testament, or beyond foundational Christian doctrine.

Rather he views light as a new seeing that brings in fresh impact and fresh application of the age-old truths. Here he states concerning the greatness of Christ, "this greatness has been centered and unfolded in (1) His Person; (2) The immensity of God's eternal purpose as centered in and exclusively related to Him; (3) The greatness of His Cross as basic and essential to the greatness of His Person and work both *for* and *in* believers; (4) The greatness of the Church which is His Body as essential *to*, and chosen *for*, His ultimate Self-Manifestation in fullness and government in the new heavens and the new earth; (5) The necessity that all the people of God should know, not only of salvation, but of the immense *purpose* of salvation in the eternal council of God, being brought to 'full growth' by the supply of Jesus Christ in ample measure."[42] Mr. Sparks felt that the New Testament contained a tremendous urgency in the matter of the believers seeing and experiencing the greatness of Christ in these aspects. The Apostle Paul summed up such urgency when he spoke of "admonishing every man and teaching every man...that we may present every man full-grown in Christ." This aim, Mr. Sparks believes, is what "all the sovereign activities of the Holy Spirit are directed to and dictated by."[42] And it is this aim that his ministry sought to further in many believers. This was the solid food that Mr. Sparks referred to so many times.

In January 1967 Mr. Sparks emphasizes again that this ministry is complimentary and auxiliary and its purpose is for the building up of the Body of Christ. "It is not the thing and superior to other ministries, but just to supplement them."[43] He appreciates the preaching of the gospel to the unsaved. "But the Lord has held this ministry to the purpose of maturing those who are being saved."[43]

In the November 1967 editor's letter, Mr. Sparks gives a succinct summary of the ministry the Lord committed to him. This was to be the last summary of his ministry and therefore the one where he apprehends things from the most mature position. He lists four points and we quote them in their entirety.

> 1. The eternal counsels of God, firstly in relation to His Son, who became Jesus Christ, the Christ, our Lord. The superlative and transcendent place and greatness of God's Son in the eternal counsels of God from everlasting to everlasting. We have been extended far beyond our ability in seeking to convey to our readers the greatness of Christ, and to indicate His significance in God's universe.
>
> 2. The greatness of man in those thoughts of God. "What is man?" has remained an unanswered question as to its fullness in God's purpose concerning him. With all his "fall" and depravity; his ruin and evil propensities, he still remains a conception of God for glory, honor, and dominion over 'the inhabited earth to come.' This is not 'humanism,' the antichrist counterfeit of God's thought.
>
> 3. The greatness of the church; the 'one new man,' the counterpart of Christ. We have given much time and space to trying to show the true nature, vocation of this elect Body of Christ; its present out-calling and preparation, and its glorious destiny and function in the ages to come. What the word calls, 'a glorious church.'
>
> 4. The greatness of the cross, by which Christ gains His preeminence of victory. By which alone man—redeemed man—can reach his purposed nature, glory, honor,

and dominion. By which the church can
attain to its 'eternal purpose.'[44]

To these four points Mr. Sparks added another feature
which was the great warfare and struggle involved in carrying out these items. "If these are the realities of God's
eternal counsels, and if ministry concerning this has—in a
small way—been entrusted to us, it is not to be wondered
at if this adversary has done a good deal to discredit, injure, limit, and malign both ministry and its instruments."[44] This was to be the last summary Mr. Sparks
ever wrote concerning his ministry.

In March of 1969, after reporting briefly on the
uncertain future of the Witness and Testimony editorial
office, Mr. Sparks again remarked about how much he
was burdened for the "many hungry and scattered
sheep."[45] He repeated that "there is a great need that the
saved shall be instructed and fed. This is evidenced by the
fact that so much of the New Testament is occupied with
the concern for believers and the 'building up of the Body
of Christ.'"[45]

By reading all of these descriptions we receive a
fairly comprehensive view of the content of Mr. Sparks'
ministry, the nature of his ministry, the way he sought to
fulfill it, and the effect that he desired to see.

Letters Concerning Principles of God's Move Throughout History

We now proceed to Mr. Sparks' letters concerning
the principles that either frustrate or enhance God's move
through a certain vessel, either an individual or a corporate vessel. We have to thank the Lord for these five insights from Mr. Sparks, who had extensively studied the
Bible and Christian history, and who had lived through
almost a century's worth of Christian moves and efforts.

We also appreciate that his view and his contact with Christian groups was not merely limited to those in Britain. For nearly 50 years he had been traveling all over the world and had come into contact with many of the Lord's servants and movements of that time.

In January 1960, Mr. Sparks began this category of letters by quoting Jeremiah 18:4; speaking about the potter and a marred vessel, it says, "He made it again." Mr. Sparks then looked at the situation among the children of Israel at that time to see why God would consider them a marred vessel. These principles apply to tendencies among God's people at all times, even today. Sparks hypothesized that the potter might have said this about the marred vessel: I chose you in sovereign grace and brought you into relation with my great purpose, but this was never meant to "exonerate you from being a responsible and cooperative substance."[46] My mercy to you and the immense glory to which you were called were meant to instill in you my own nature of grace and selflessness, but instead you viewed it all objectively. I have given you much light and truth that you received and continue to receive, but you do not walk in it nor have it in your inward parts. Furthermore, all the light I've given you has only made you spiritually proud, conceited, and superior. I wanted a vessel for my use, which would result in a ministry to the entire world, but you have fed your own souls. The potter's solution to all these problems is to throw the vessel away and remake it. But for this to happen there needs to be recognition, repentance, remorse, and yielding on the side of the marred vessel. "As we move into this new year 1960, and maybe are all aware of how we have failed and disappointed earlier hopes and expectations, let us focus upon—not "it was marred in the hand of the potter," but—"He made it again, another vessel, as seemed good to the potter to make it." The end of all God's work is, 'It is very good.'"[46]

In March 1961, Mr. Sparks began his editor's letter with "The history of Christianity from the latter days of the apostles is the history of prisons. Not literal, material prisons, though there have been not a few of these, but prisons which are the result of man's inveterate habit of taking hold and bringing into bondage. How many times has the Spirit broken loose and moved in a new and free way, only to have that way brought under the control of man and crystallized into another 'form,' creed, organization, denomination, sect, 'order,' community, etc."[47] Mr. Sparks then describes how the Spirit begins something new, then what the Spirit began is taken as *the* unique way and crystallized as such. After this, every seeming departure from that way is viewed with great suspicion and cast out. Soon, what began as the energy from the Spirit producing a "living organism expressing what God really wanted," becomes something that "the next generation has to sustain and work hard to keep going."[48] The answer to this problem comes by facing costly questions, like, "Did I enter into this objectively?" or "Did the Spirit open the eyes of my heart, and give me a heavenly vision?" If we entered into something objectively then we will become prisoners of a system instead of bondslaves of Christ. "The Spirit must have initiated our course and position. The Spirit must be referred to and deferred to all along the way. The Spirit will be a rebel in anything in which He may have His liberties limited; and if He is in us, He will make us such rebels. This does not for a moment mean that all rebellion and bid for what is called 'liberty' is of the Spirit. It just means that we are broken people in the realm of nature, and robbed of power to fight for our own conceptions."[48]

In July of 1962, Mr. Sparks continues this line of thought in an editorial called "The curse of the earth touch."[49] From Genesis we know that the earth is cursed and this curse affects many things in the world, in Christendom in general, and even in the realm we call "evangelical." In the world we have confusion, in Christianity we have weakness and inability to hold the things of Christ, and in evangelical circles we have criticism, suspicion and distrust to anything that is new, even towards the things that may be new of the Spirit. "Why is it that so many things which have greatly served the purpose of God have eventually fallen apart; broken up; and have little more than a great past to live upon?"[49] It is because of the earth touch. Initially these moves of the Lord were characterized by a separation between earthly and heavenly. However, at least two features came in to bring what was of God down to earth. They were 1) the first ones sought to crystallize their history into a form or framework for others. "They presented or imposed a set form instead of keeping in full view the meaning of 'Christ crucified' and *travailing for the crisis* in others."[49] 2) Others came in and sought the blessing of the move of the Spirit without paying the cost, namely letting go of former mentalities, ambition, traditions and natural judgments. Thus, they brought much of the fresh move of the Spirit down to earth. "Oh, this earth touch! How deadly it is! When will the Lord's people understand the essential meaning of their union with Christ *in Heaven*?"[49]

In May of 1963, Mr. Sparks warns about extremes in exclusiveness or inclusiveness, both of which can be a frustration and dilution of God's move. Extreme exclusiveness finds its fullest picture in the Judaizers described in the New Testament, who had their base in Jerusalem and tentacles extending throughout the earth. Corinth showed a subtler form of exclusiveness in preferring the ministry of a certain brother over that of others. From this we learn that our fellowship cannot be based on who holds our particular interpretation of the truth, or who conducts meetings as we do. Rather, "the base of our fellowship is thus determined as being the acknowledgment, accepted, and declared Lordship of Jesus Christ."[50] Anything more narrow than this is more exclusive that Jesus Christ. God's move can also be frustrated by extreme inclusiveness. Extreme inclusiveness presents the danger of making Christ more inclusive than He is. "There are two irreconcilable spiritual systems in this universe, the very nature of which are positively inimical and hostile to each other, emanating from two utterly contrary sources."[50] These two systems are that of Christ and that of the world. When these two mix together, then that which is of Christ loses its distinctiveness. Many times a particular ministry is raised up to make up a specific lack among Christians. When the world mixes with this ministry, it may grow as a cancer to become abnormally large in the Body. Or it may lose its distinctiveness and become impotent in effecting that for which it was raise up. Both results are the dangers of extreme inclusiveness. Mr. Sparks concludes, "The two great needs of our time are, on the one hand, salvation from man-made fences around the Lord Jesus by which He is made smaller than He really is; and, on the other hand, the recovery and consolidation of the outstanding distinctiveness and unmistakableness of what is really Christ, without mixture."[51]

Mr. Sparks' final commentary on the principles of God's move is entitled "The Lord is Risen Indeed."[52] This was the second to last editorial Mr. Sparks wrote before he died. He begins this letter by recounting the dynamic spread of the gospel in Acts. He quotes Dr. Fairborn, "in the year 33 A. D. a few Galilean fishermen were seeking liberty of speech in Jerusalem, and were hardly handled as men poor and ignorant. In the year that Paul died, how did the matter stand? There were churches in Jerusalem, Nazareth, Caesarea, in all Syria, Antioch, Ephesus, Galatia, Sardis, Laodicea, in all the towns on the west coast throughout lesser Asia, in Philippi, Thessalonica, Athens, Corinth, Rome, Alexandria, in the chief cities of the islands and the mainland of Greece, and the western Roman colonies."[52] The Lord is Risen Indeed! The apostles labored under certain principles and witnessed this phenomenal expression of the glorious truth of the risen Lord. Whenever these same principles have been honored, there has been a fresh move of the Lord. These first Apostles did not consider that they brought a new teaching, a new religion or that they had to make plans and arrangements for a new movement. Rather, they simply affirmed a fact—"The universal sovereignty and Lordship of Jesus Christ as the Son of God established and vindicated by His resurrection from the dead."[52] This was their testimony, not their creed. We see these principles and corresponding fresh moves of the Lord throughout Christian history. We see this with the Moravian missions, who experienced a deep work of the cross and the unique exaltation of the Holy Spirit and were able to send out more missionaries in 20 years than all Protestants had ever sent. We see this principle with Hudson Taylor and the China Inland Mission. Mr. Taylor did not advertise for people to go to China as missionaries. Instead he spoke about the believers' union with Christ and through prayer effected a "deepening of the spiritual life of the church, so that men should be unable to stay at home."[52] We see this principle with A. B. Simpson and the Christian and Missionary Alliance, who together have ministered great spiritual blessings to a large part of the world. We also note the same spiritual principle with Dr. Andrew Murray and the original Keswick Convention. "The evidence is overwhelming that God moves by way of a deep and full knowledge of Christ; it is not just theory or academic knowledge, but a knowledge born out of a deep work of the cross in spiritual history with God."[52] Mr. Sparks ends his letter by giving the following testimony showing the condition of so many Christian workers today. "In speaking to the most responsible man in one of these 'missions' about the decline in spiritual power since their beginning, he fully agreed, and then asked, 'But what can we do?' When I said that perhaps much recovery would take place if all the responsible leaders were called together for two weeks of prayer, heart-searching, and consideration of the spiritual principles of their beginning, he said, 'Yes, I believe that would be of great value, but it cannot be; all our men are too busy.' Too busy to recover the full impact of 'The Lord is Risen Indeed.'"[52]

These five observations—the Lord's remaking, freedom from imprisoning the Spirit, avoidance of the earth touch, being as exclusive and as inclusive as Christ, and exalting the risen Christ—are all lessons we can learn today as we follow the Lord. When we look at today's situation in light of these items, we feel a deep need for God's mercy that in this age also He could do something new.

Letters Helping Believers Live the Christian Life

Mr. Sparks wrote five letters containing practical points on living the Christian life during this time period, three during 1960, one in 1965 and another in 1970. We summarize them below.

In March of 1960 Mr. Sparks talks about perils faced by believers who have begun to walk on the pathway of God's eternal purpose. So many of the Lord's people, who begin their Christian lives with the intent of going right through with the Lord become side-tracked to some thing less than God's eternal purpose. This may not involve sin or the world, but may be something that gives them a great deal of gratification. Today, God is at work "seeking to secure a maximum of eternal value in accordance with eternal purpose in His elect. His discipline is to sift out the perishable in favor of the imperishable." The danger for us is that we would choose a way according to our own disposition and temperament and not according to the supreme purpose of God. "We shall have, ever and always, to be governed by principle, and not by feelings, preferences, arguments, or natural appeal. Intellectual palliatives, emotional ecstasies, activity-gratifications must be suspected or challenged. The one question must be paramount—where does this lead? Does it essentially and intrinsically relate to the one supreme purpose of God?"[53] As an example, Mr. Sparks illustrates how the doctrine of predestination can be a peril or a help. If this doctrine becomes an end in itself and we relax with the thought that it mainly refers to our salvation then it is a peril that can lead us from the path of God's eternal purpose. However, if we see in the Bible the many instances where predestination, foreordination and election are used in the context of God's eternal purpose—our being conformed to the image of Christ—then this teaching becomes a help and encouragement to the believers to press on to the fuller purpose of God.

Later that year, in the May 1960 editor's letter, Mr. Sparks speaks about the importance of "spiritual punctuation"[54] in a believer's walk with Christ. Just as many people have problems with punctuation in reading and writing, many Christians have problems with the subtleties of punctuation in their Christian life. The comma symbolizes a brief pause or a little break in which we commune with heaven before we continue with affairs of this life. How many times does such a brief pause, "the simple spiritual comma" save us from confusion and give meaning to a moment. "There is a very great value in the periodic pause in which, amidst the pressure of work, perplexity, sorrow, and care, we take a spiritual breath of heaven."[54] A semicolon or colon is a "sufficient pause and let-down to provide for a fresh start before the present phase is finished."[54] Mr. Sparks likened these pauses to be "not only the private withdrawal for a small space of time, but the prayer or fellowship gathering."[54] The full period symbolizes our rest in the full Sabbath of God, which is His Son. In His Son God enters into His rest and in His Son we enter into God's rest. "God has written this law, the law of the 'period,' deep in human life. Some of us have had to learn deep lessons by painful ways in this matter. We cannot—even in what we call service to God—violate this law of the rest period, without having to pay heavily for it in lost values, maybe lost days or months, vitiated energies, and frustrated labors. It is never lost time to take rest when there is conscientiousness in work. Satan is all against rest. To drive, harass, and keep too busy is a part of his strategy to mar the new creation life."[54] Mister Sparks concluded this description of spiritual punctuation with the following. "So meaning, intelligence, value, and effectiveness are bound up with spiritual punctuation, from the comma to the full period."[54]

In July of 1960, Mr. Sparks included another editorial of this category entitled "Do it yourself."[55] Mr. Sparks asks "Is it not true that a vast amount of our Christianity is secondhand, in a wrong sense?"[55] Of course in the matter of redemption we have no part, but our substance or form of Christianity should not be based on tradition, history or a crystallized system, but should be original, deep heart relatedness. How much of what we have is really our own? We should be able to say, "This is my very life." Now there is a lot of falsehood and misrepresenting in Christianity. This is because so much of Christianity is secondhand. "If Christianity, rather than being a mere 'religion,' were really a life—that is, Christ as an indwelling reality checking us up on our behavior, conduct, manners, speech, appearances, influence, courtesies or discourtesies—would He not be saved from the hands of many who want a case against Him and find it too easily in those who bear His name."[55] Mr. Sparks took this matter one step further to address the many suspicions and misrepresentations that circulate among believers about other believers. Before we simply take them as truth, we should seek out the matters to find out if they are true. Then we will not be cheated with cheap wares, but we "in the matter of being sure and 'knowing the truth'— 'Do it ourselves.'"[55]

In the final two editorials of this category Mr. Sparks quotes extensively from other sources. In September 1965 he includes a report of the committee on prayer that appeared in the Alliance Magazine. This was a call for the more fervent prayer of warfare for revival. In March of 1970, Mr. Sparks appeals to his readers to respect the presence of the Lord, for where two or three are gathered He is there in their midst. To this effect he relays a 'dream' conveyed by A.J. Gordon of Boston, a servant of the Lord from whom Mr. Sparks received much help. The dream was "How Christ came to church,"[56] and concerned how the Lord Himself was present in the congregation. Mr. Sparks recounted this dream as an encouragement and appeal to his readers to respect the presence of the Lord, not only "on one day a week when we 'go to church,'" but as "we ask for His presence always."[56]

Letters on Current Political and Spiritual Situations

We come now to the final category of editor's letters—Mr. Sparks' comments on current political, cultural or spiritual situations in light of what he felt the Lord was doing or speaking at that time. Much of what Mr. Sparks saw became an encouragement for believers to watch and be ready for the near return of the Lord, although Mr. Sparks himself would never make predictions, even in the most catastrophic of world events. During these last years, Mr. Sparks made six such observations of the times; two of them concern current political and cultural trends and four concern the spiritual situation among

God's people.

The decade of the 1960s presented a world engulfed in tension and uncertainty. The Cuban missile crisis underscored the tenuous grasp on peace and the real
potential for total world destruction by mankind himself.
Blacks were fighting for civil rights. The Vietnam War
was causing protests. Unrest was rampant in young people. Anti-Establishment became the norm as the new generation threw off the old things in search of itself. The old
system of Christianity was looked at with disdain by the
young generation. "Is God Dead?" appeared on the April
8, 1966 cover of Time Magazine. Unrest, violence and
questioning characterized much of humanity throughout
the world.

In November 1961 Mr. Sparks writes an editorial
on the coming again of the Lord and what trends in the
world will be present when He returns. Mr. Sparks never
made specific prophecies concerning the time or setting in
which the Lord may come, because he had seen too many
predictions not come to pass. Instead, he realized that the
prospect of His coming was a real encouragement for
watchfulness, preparation, faithfulness and purity. Concerning world events and the hope of the Lord's coming
he writes, "It is true that world conditions have always
been the occasion for the strengthening and renewing of
this hope and expectation."[57] With this in view Mr. Sparks
summarized his view of the condition of the world in
preparation for Christ's return in one word: intensification. He lists many areas that are currently being
"intensified." These include the intensification of the following: 1) spiritual antagonism, pressure and conflict; 2)
outward difficulties in Christian life and work; 3) satanic
deception; 4)'religion' that does not give Christ His true
and real place, a 'Christianity' without Christ in truth; 5)
human sufficiency, importance, and independence 6) war-
fever and anxiety and a temporary respite in which men

cry 'Peace and safety' and are put off their guard so that 'sudden destruction' comes 'as a thief in the night'; 7) alternatives to the truth, false prophets; 8) knowledge; 9) nature, human life, spiritual realms, phenomena, and particular ungodliness. Everything in this setting will make it easy for God's people to lose heart and feel helpless or worn out. May his coming be an encouragement to us to remain watchful, faithful and pure.

In March 1963 Mr. Sparks made another keen observation on the state of the world, as compared with things in the beginning of the century. He sees now 'the deadening hand of mediocrity."[58] Mediocrity is the middle ground, the moderate degree, middling. "In no realms are there the outstanding leaders, teachers, preachers, artists, singers, politicians, etc., of the last century. Only here and there is there a man who is a little above his fellows and a bit more outstanding as a leader, preacher, or teacher, than what is general. How ordinary has almost everything become. We call to mind the Piersons, Gordons, Simpsons, Moules, Webb-Peploes, Meyers, Hudson Taylors, Spurgeons, Parkers, and the whole galaxy of spiritual giants in the realm of Christianity, and we say, 'Where are there such today?' There seems to be no voice which rings out so that the whole church can hear God's distinctive word to His people today. No specific testimony is given a chance. Where there is a big quest for God to do a new thing, God must be careful not to upset tradition or interfere with the set and established order or system."[58] Mr. Sparks closes by appealing to the Lord to save this ministry from the trend of mediocrity. "The note has been struck and to it all that follows in the ministry of this little paper is tuned. The Lord, in faithfulness, keep us from falling a prey to this historic enemy—mediocrity, the middle measure, loss of distinctiveness of testimony, definiteness of vision and purpose. We have an immense Christ; a superlative calling; and unsearchable riches of resource."[58]

In July 1964, Mr. Sparks observes a fundamental lack in the spiritual condition of God's people. The pre-eminent thing that stood out to Mr. Sparks through his extensive travels in the Far East to the Far West is the matter of a lack of real, solid, edifying spiritual food. Many Christians are caught in the trap of work, where work has become so important that they neglect the quality of the food they are eating and serving. Real food will create a change in the life of the eater. Such a changed life is the real test of the food a believer is eating.

In November 1966, Mr. Sparks made another comment on two trends that he saw among believers of that time. The first was a move toward union (not unity) where leaders from different denominations were gathering and were considering how to put differences aside and unite. The second trend was a growing dissatisfaction with the established system of churches and institutions. Mr. Sparks feared that these two trends might result in the formation of another undenominational or interdenominational denomination, which would still fall far short of what God desired. He cautioned people not to try and form something, but rather to start with "organic growth, from a living illumination, a revolutionary encounter with an unveiling of the true nature of the church."[59] He felt that in the current situation among Christians God must do a new thing. When God began His new move in Acts, He started with a nucleus of deeply disciplined men who had been broken by the cross and reunited by the resurrection. A move with these principles is the only positive way that a new thing can emerge. It won't merely be a negative reaction to the situation, but would be something that the Lord could use to have spiritual impact on the world.

In September of 1968 Mr. Sparks remarks that at the end times the Spirit's move will be "a concentration and intensification of focus on Christ."[60] He felt that this very thing is the deepest movement of the Spirit today. Today many Christians do not want forms, teachings, techniques but they want reality; they want to see Christ. At the same time, "the non-Christian world is turning out and repudiating Christianity as a system, but it cannot turn Christ out where He is a life and a spiritual power." Both of these trends require a fuller presentation and a fuller seeing of who Christ is. "If it is true that 'Christianity is Christ,' and that the church is Christ in corporate expansion, then, not from without, by forms and organization, by human efforts, but by a Holy Spirit work of inward eye-opening and inward revelation of Christ will Christianity be what it really is in the mind of God. We cannot do this, but our labors may, and must, be to provide the Holy Spirit ground to work upon by seeking to 'present' Christ in His greater fullness to the Lord's people in these serious times. This we will do, by His grace and enabling. So help us, Lord!"[60]

In May 1969, Mr. Sparks wrote of the severe lack of spiritual discernment that he observed among Christians. The general situation was seemingly hopeless and encouraged the thought that it is impossible to see a pure expression of the church as it is revealed in God's Word. At that time the main problem among Christians was that so many of the leaders and of those responsible did not see, therefore they entered into many foolish and unwise things that created even more complications and confusion. There was a great need for an eye-opening ministry and for prayer that a "spirit of wisdom and revelation"[61] may be given.

In his last editor's letter, four months before his call home, Mr. Sparks fittingly longs for the Lord's return and points to the present situation as an encouragement that His coming was near. We reproduce the last paragraph below, as Mr. Sparks' final observation of the current world situation and of his calling for the Lord Jesus to come.

"It is not easy to believe that things can go on much longer as they are in the world. Much easier is it to believe that His coming is drawing very near. Amongst the various 'signs' in the national, international, political, industrial, phenomenal, etc., the moral degeneration has always been a very clear pointer to an intervention on God's part; what the Bible calls 'the cup of iniquity.' Surely this cup is fast filling up. In Noah's time it was said that 'every imagination of man's heart was evil.' The Pilgrim church longs for home. Nature groans within itself. Iniquity cries in the streets. We all say, 'Come, Lord Jesus, come quickly!" But the urge is upon us to take from the Lord's hand all that He is prepared to give us to feed the hungry sheep. Pray that the strength needed may be given, and that we may still 'bring forth fruit (even) in old age.'"[62] For Mr. Sparks, his cry of "Come, Lord Jesus" was met by his soon departure to Him.

Leaving this Earth Trusting that God's Work Would Continue

In January of 1971 Mr. Sparks gave his last message to a group of London City missionaries.[62] At the end of the month he became sick and was henceforth confined to bed for the last months of his life. At this point he was unable to carry the things of his ministry any further. Over the past decade he had seen many of his close co-workers pass from this earth to be with the Lord. In 1959 Brother K. P. Oliphant, who had been with him from the beginning at Honor Oak Baptist, went to be with the Lord. In 1967 Brother C.J.B. Harrison died; this brother had carried much of the ministry at Honor Oak in the early days and had spent nearly a decade laboring at the ministry station at Westmoreland Chapel in California. January 1968 saw the call home of Lady Ogle, who had been associated with this ministry for over 40 years and whose prayer ministry upheld so much of the Lord's work. In July of that same year was the home call of Madame Ducommun, who Mr. Sparks had first met in Paris while he was traveling there to minister at conferences of 'White Russian' refugees. She was instrumental in translating many books of Mr. Sparks into French thus allowing his ministry to reach a good portion of the French speaking world.

Now, after witnessing the passing of so many co-workers, after struggling to the end with fresh charge from the Lord, after being fully engaged in the battle till his last days, it was Mr. Sparks' turn to depart and be with Christ. He left no organization to propagate his written ministry or his many tapes. He left no group, groups or movement that bore his name or had particular commission to carry on his teaching. If he would have a legacy on this earth it would be through the Lord's own doing. As for him, he 'cast his bread upon the waters' at the end of his life. He was one who served his own generation. In an editor's letter he mentioned that the Lord's workers cease but the Lord's work goes on. He trusted in this principle and trusted that, if it was His will, God would carry on the very same ministry that had been committed to him.

Perhaps, while we consider the end of Mr. Sparks' life, it is fitting to quote from a comment that Brother Watchman Nee made concerning King David, who served his own generation.

> David, after he had in his own generation served the counsel of God, fell to sleep, and was laid unto his fathers" (Acts 13:36): David served in one generation, his own. He could not serve in two! Where today we seek to perpetuate our work by setting up an organization or society or system, the Old Testament saints served their

own day and passed on. This is an important principle of life. Wheat is sown, grows
ears, is reaped, and then the whole plant,
even to the root, is ploughed out. God's
work is spiritual to the point of having no
earthly roots, no smell of earth on it at all.
Men pass on, but the Lord remains. Everything to do with the Church must be up-to-
date and living, meeting the present—one
could even say the passing—needs of the
hour. Never must it become fixed, earth-
bound, static. God Himself takes away His
workers, but He gives others. Our work
suffers, but His never does. Nothing
touches Him. He is still God.[64]

Theodore Austin-Sparks served his own generation and
passed on, trusting that God would call other faithful ones
to labor in His field. Indeed, he trusted that the Lord
would raise up other ministers to meet the pressing need
among God's people that his ministry had attempted to
meet for so many years. God takes His workers but carries on His work.

The following note from his wife, Florence Austin-Sparks, appeared in an insert to the 1971 March issue
of *A Witness and a Testimony.*

To Our Readers:

Greetings in the Name of the Lord
Jesus! Towards the end of January my husband, Mr. Austin-Sparks, the Editor of this
paper, was taken quite ill with pleurisy. He
spent some time being nursed at home before going into Hospital. On his return we
hoped he would have made progress towards full recovery, but although all was

done that could be, humanly speaking, the Lord called him into His presence on April 13th, quite peacefully after a time of prolonged weakness. For the present we are expecting the paper to be published as usual until the Lord makes the pattern clear.

Yours in His Service
F. Austin-Sparks[65]

Harry Foster wrote an appreciation of T. Austin-Sparks in the next issue of *A Witness and a Testimony*. He reviewed his life and thankfully acknowledged many aspects of his ministry through which help was received. A memorial service was held at Honor Oak on May 1, 1971. Mr. C. Fischbacher read the scripture, Mr. Paul Wolff from Strasborg led the prayers. Letters were read from the Atlantic States Christian Convention in the USA and from the elders of *Jehovah Shammah* at Madras India. Mr. John Paterson, son of George Paterson, Mr. Sparks' closest colleague, gave some reminiscences. Harry Foster spoke about Mr. Sparks' past ministry, pointed out the need to face the future and then introduced two of the younger generation—Mr. Roger Forster and Mr. Alan Barrow. Mr. Forster had first met Mr. Sparks 13 years ago and gave a brief message stressing the need for having singleness of purpose represented by the phrase "this one thing" from Phil. 3:13. Mr. Alan Barrow then brought the meeting to a close with a prayer of rededication to "this one thing"—the eternal purpose of God.

Publication of *A Witness and a Testimony* was continued until the end of 1971. Before Mr. Sparks' death, Harry Foster resigned from duties at Honor Oak and moved away to Somerset. After, Mr. Sparks' passing, he took up the work of editing a magazine called *Toward the Mark*, which was intended to continue along the same purpose as *A Witness and a Testimony*. This magazine was published and distributed free of charge, supported by gifts from its readers, until its last issue in 1989.

Impressions of Theodore Austin-Sparks

In addition to leaving his written and oral ministry to the next generation, Mr. Sparks also left impressions of his life on many who personally knew him. We have collected stories from seven different people who had personal interaction with Mr. Sparks.[66] Some we collected from writings and others from personal interviews. Many of these various sources relate matters with striking similarities. We will try to put them all together to leave the reader with an impression, not only of Mr. Sparks' teaching, but of his character and person.

First impressions of Mr. Sparks were of a tall, commanding figure, an almost majestic appearance, with a warm and friendly smile. As people got closer to him, they began to realize an intense and almost constant inward drive. There seemed to be a fire burning in this man. Intensity was seen in his Bible reading, in his service, and in his interaction with the believers around him. He had a very careful way of studying the Bible, going over an interpretation again and again to make sure of its balance and correctness. The same intensity was almost always present with other things concerning the Spirit. Mr. Sparks would treat every gathering and every fellowship with great importance. After he had fellowship with a young man who was about to minister to a small gathering of a few young people, he ended their time with prayer for the ministry of this young man. He prayed as if this upcoming message to the young people was the most important time of ministry. When only two or three were present at a prayer gathering, he would still minister in the same careful and profound way as if many were present. He seemed to live every moment intensely, with the realization that this moment has importance in light of God's eternal purpose.

Mr. Sparks' very presence was many times enough to convey a sense of the Lord Jesus. He was a man who knew the Lord and knew men. Some believers felt that the first time they met Mr. Sparks his gaze was able to pierce right through to their inner motives and feelings. Others felt that simply by being in his presence they could sense a nearness to Christ. One man testified that rarely did he leave fellowship with Mr. Sparks without sensing how small he was and how great was the Lord Jesus.

Getting closer to Mr. Sparks, people would soon find out that he was not for small talk. One could sit for a long time in his presence while he would not say a word and was seemingly oblivious to the conversations going on around him. He could give the impression to many who sought his fellowship that he was aloof, distant, and cold. In this sense he was a very lonely man. One brother testified how the Lord was working to make Mr. Sparks more approachable in his old age.

Despite his aloof characteristics, those who could sense the Lord's presence appreciated that the cross had worked in Mr. Sparks to bring out his spirit. Watchman Nee writes, "We often say that we have to deal with our natural life. But what should be the extent of the cross's dealing? The cross must operate to the point that our spirit is released. Let me tell you a little story about Brother T. Austin-Sparks. He is not a skillful host at all. If you ask him to be a host, you have found the wrong person. He does not speak much, and if you sit down with him for half an hour or even an hour and a half, you may only hear the ticking of the clock on the wall. Although you cannot hear anything from his mouth, you can sense his spirit and feel the presence of the Lord."[67]

Mr. Sparks was a person with an extremely strong character. He was strong-willed and strong-minded and could not be easily influenced by the opinions of others. Concerning this Watchman Nee writes, "Brother T. Austin-Sparks is robust in his mind, calm in his emotion, and strong in his will. He is strong and steady. But when you touch him, you do not touch his mind, emotion or will, but his spirit."[68] On the one hand, these strong characteristics enabled Mr. Sparks to stand with what the Lord had given him, even when such a word or revelation was unpopular. On the other hand, this character trait often made it difficult for him to share responsibility or receive helpful corrections from others.

What was most outstanding about Mr. Sparks was his continual hunger before the Lord and his continual desire to press on to further reaches. One of his favorite songs was a hymn written by Pastor John Robinson with the refrain, "The Lord Has Yet More Light and Truth to Break forth From His Word." This significantly characterized his life and one could not know him without being impressed by his continual drive and hunger for more and more of the Lord Jesus. Mr. Sparks was not satisfied with position, success, past revelations, or past work. He was always seeking something more of the Lord. When people touched him, they felt there is a great deal more of Christ that has yet to be explored.

In a sense Mr. Sparks' life was a very poetic picture of a life with the heavenly Christ. Saved in 1905, he faithfully pursued the Lord until the day he died. He was given many fresh revelations of the greatness of Christ, of God's eternal purpose, of the church, and of the cross. He faithfully conveyed not only the teaching of what he saw, but the experience that made those heavenly things his own reality. His ministry helped thousands find a deeper meaning in Christ and also brought him into much suffering at the hands of those in opposition to his ministry. In spite of his faults, he was faithful to the end. And in the end he left nothing but his words and his effect on those who received his ministry. He established no society, group, movement, or system. He left this earth, having served his own generation, being faithful to what God gave him, and trusting that God would provide others after him to carry on the labor in God's own field.

"We have to recognize that there are two sets of things. On the one side there is fundamental truth, about which we are never flexible and from which we never depart. There can be no question of giving up fundamental truth, or of changing our foundations. They remain: on that we are—or should be—inflexible. We ought to be immovable, too, on the matter of the all-governing object of God: as to that, we are set, and nothing will move us...But, on the other side, we have to recognize that God changes His methods. While He does not change His truths and His foundations and His object, He changes His methods. He has in His own sovereign right the prerogative to do as He will, and to do a new thing that was never heard of before. But that is something that Christianity today, for the greater part, just will not allow! It will not even allow God Almighty to do something that He has never done before."

—*Our Warfare*

Summaries of Some Works of T. Austin-Sparks

Recorded here are summaries of twenty four books of T. Austin-Sparks. I hope these summaries help more Jesus seekers read the actual books. In summarizing, I freely use many quotes and, where I don't quote, I attempt to use the same phraseology as Mr. Sparks. By doing this I hope to capture his unique utterance and the key spiritual revelation conveyed in each work. Although any summary is an imperfect representation, I hope that by a quick pass through the following pages, the reader may gain an overall view of Mr. Sparks' key revelations and emphases throughout his ministry. Indeed by reading these summaries along with the dates of when the messages either appeared in *A Witness and a Testimony* or were spoken, the reader can see the progress of Mr. Sparks' ministry from 1926 to 1970. The reader may notice that most of the main revelation of his ministry appears in seed form in the 1926 series *Incorporation into Christ*. This revelation becomes richer, more applicable, and more practical throughout his life. In the 1930s the revelation was profoundly and clearly defined; in the 1940s and 1950s the way believers enter and live a life according to this revelation becomes clearer; in the 1960s Mr. Sparks' words and illustrations become very simple, yet convey a great depth of revelation and a ready door for entrance. May these imperfect summaries help bring to mind afresh the depths of sight of this servant of the Lord.

Incorporation into Christ
1926

The phrase "in Christ" with its variations in form and translation occurs more than two hundred times in the New Testament. God has summed up all things in Christ and nothing outside of Him has any place in God's purpose. The implication of this is that "No man can live the Christian life; there is only One who can live that life and that is Christ Himself. We must have such an experimental incorporation into Him that He lives His life through us as members of His one Body, so that 'For me to live is Christ' and 'It is no longer I, but Christ.'"

The presence of Christ in the world was firstly to manifest the "nature, method, means, laws, purpose, and power" that would be realized after the days of His flesh and secondly to make this life possible by the work of the cross. By the cross, the Lord enabled men to be transferred into the same realm He was in and then "changed the separate and individual presence for the corporate and universal. Thus 'the church which is His Body' was brought into being as the abiding instrument of His world-incarnation." When Christ was on earth in the flesh, He made a great emphasis that His words and His works were not out from Himself, but were out from the Father. Furthermore, He declared that He abode in the Father and prayed that in the future His disciples would abide in Him, as the unique way to carry out an effective and fruitful life and service. "For the practical purposes of God in this age Christ is the One Body holding the Head, and the business of every member is to realize more and more fully the meaning of this incorporation and oneness of identity." Tests and hardships will prove whether or not such union with Him is real.

Only that which proceeds out from God is truly recognized by God. Anything out of Satan, the flesh (even when it may take a religious form), or the world has no acceptance with God. Today God does not move through our own ideas or independent schemes. Rather, He moves only through those who have been baptized in one Spirit into the one Body and are thus incorporated with Christ. Just as the Son lived by the Father and was in the Father, so also we are placed in that position. Just as the Father was head of the Son, so also the Son is head of the Body. As those who can enjoy such a position we must not be led by anything from within our natural life or from our outside circumstances until we determine that it is of the Spirit.

We are incorporated into Christ in His death, resurrection and ascension. The death of Christ has a twofold aspect: substitutionarily His death is isolated and conclusively secures our redemption; representatively His death includes us in the fallen nature of Adam. "Our sin is dealt with in the substitutionary; ourselves are dealt with in the representative." Both aspects are crucial, but the latter is emphasized for our living the Christ-life and fulfilling the Christ-purpose. If we are progressive in our spiritual life, after enjoying justification by faith and all that is involved with the substitutionary work of Christ, we will begin to learn about the large gap "between the old creation and the new, between the natural and the spiritual." We will realize our deep need to be more fully incorporated into the representative death of Christ. The only kind of service that God accepts is that which is from the new man, with a new life, mind, spirit, capacity, consciousness. As we accept by faith God's word and judg-

ment concerning the cross, God proceeds to work out this
death in us so that we grow to refuse to move on anything
that is not of the Spirit. As we grow further in the incorporation into the death of Christ, our old man becomes
nullified and we live the life of the new man.

   "All things which are of God have their new beginning and vital value since 'the fall' in and by the representative and inclusive resurrection of Jesus from the
dead." This is not speaking of the future resurrection of
the body, but of its immediate spiritual significance to the
believer. God desires a testimony of the resurrection of
Christ, so even something that has its origin in God, must
"pass into death in order that by resurrection it may have
its supreme divine seal and attestation." In our experience, we come to live increasingly by the divine life
through more and more drastic cycles of death and resurrection. These may occur in relation to a truth God is
showing us or to a relationship that must show more
marks of the divine in resurrection. Resurrection is a life
that cannot know death. Through new birth, we have become partakers of the life of God, and through cycles of
death and resurrection we come to live more and more
supremely by this life. The immediate issue of Christ's
resurrection was described by the declaration of the Father, "Thou art My Son; this day have I begotten Thee."
In this He became the representative "First begotten from
the dead" and was ushered into a specific and peculiar
kind of sonship. "This life is the life of the whole corporate Body, and the individual member can only have it in
relation thereto." The victory that Christ began on the
cross will be completed, through His Body in resurrection.
"In His cross Christ drew on Himself the whole hierarchy
of evil...stripped off the principalities and powers, broke
through and rose their conqueror, and in resurrection far
above all rule and authority was the first begotten from the
dead—the first and inclusive one of all that should be

identified with Him. We now see that the final triumph of His Body will be the consummation of Revelation 12:11, victory over the system and its power by reason of the life of the Risen Lord indwelling."

"When the Lord Jesus ascended up on high and was 'received up,' it was representative and relative just as was His death and resurrection." This truth can be described by two words that are two halves of one truth: ascension and translation. "Ascension is an act, conclusive and definite. Translation is a process culminating in a climax." In His representative and relative ascension, the source of our spiritual life was transferred from earth to heaven and a principle of God's people was established: "We must come into every divine thing as out from above, and not from the earth level." Ascension causes our source to be heavenly and our earthly walk to be a pilgrim's walk. Only those in ascension union with Christ can serve Him effectively, not out of the earth but out of a heavenly position with Him. This also is a corporate matter, where His Body shares His position in ascension. The process is described as follows. "If it is true that Christ has taken our humanity, redeemed, purged, sanctified, into the very throne of God, and is reproducing this corporate union of Himself with us and of ourselves with Himself in His Body—the church, then ascension union means that we now have a place in the place of His sovereignty to have dominion in Him over principalities and powers." Translation is a process that climaxes in the appearing of our Lord Jesus. Faith, the principle of translation, is being wrought into us in a progressive series of steps and leads us progressively from relying on earth-bound sources to relying on heavenly sources. "It is corporate faith in the whole Body of Christ, proving it to be what it really is—a heavenly Body—that will bring about the advent of Christ." All these aspects, His death, His resurrection and His ascension are relative to us as we are being incorporated into Christ.

God's Reactions
1929

In all God's fresh activities and revelations He is constantly working toward attaining His original position and His eternal purpose. From man's standpoint this means that God is always doing a new thing, but from God's standpoint it is not new at all. God knows to the greatest detail exactly what He wants. He desires to see this brought into reality and He will not stop until He attains His purpose in full in every detail. Whenever there is a deviation from or a falling away from this line, there will be a "Divine Reaction" and God will start over somewhere, somehow with the same goal of attaining His desired end. We see this throughout Scripture in the picture of Abel, Enoch, Noah, Abraham, Isaac, Jacob, Israel, Ezra, Nehemiah, Haggai, Zechariah, Mary, Anna, Simeon, and finally in the calling of the overcomers out of the degraded churches in Revelation.

What God needs is a new cruse, or vessel, as spoken of in 2 Kings 2:19-22 to contain the healing salt, which stands for recovery, preservation and permanence. This new vessel must have the presence of something which makes it alive and superlative: the resurrection life. In the New Testament, the Lord Jesus Himself produced this atmosphere of spirit and life. "The Lord Jesus had been glorified and the Holy Spirit had come as the Spirit of the glorified Lord to glorify Him on earth." When the Holy Spirit glorifies the Lord Jesus in the believers' hearts then this vessel of life is produced. Today God needs such a vessel that stands absolutely on the New Testament, that has been eradicated of personal interests and resources through the cross, that yields fully to the absolute government by the Spirit, that recognizes the utter Lordship of Jesus Christ, that sees all things—wisdom, power and grace—are in Christ, and that selflessly seeks only the glory of the Lord Jesus. God will make such a vessel the instrument for the restoration and preservation of His testimony on the earth. This vessel cannot be separated from the Body of Christ; it cannot be exclusive or iconoclastic. It must be relative, related to the entire Body of Christ in an attitude of seeking fellowship, and representative, standing for the testimony of the entire Body on the earth.

Such a cruse is composed of what the Bible calls overcomers. These overcomers are not moved by discontent, difference of opinion or personal dislike, but by a divine sense from God that God's testimony must appear on earth according to every detail of God's mind and thought. The overcomers are thus occupied with the same thing God desires, which is the realization of His purpose from times eternal. Such a purpose can be summed up as the procurement of the house of God and the city of God. The house and the city are for "the glory of God in Christ and His universal worship." The nature of the worship and the way of glory are represented by the cross, which forms the basis for the overcomers' testimony. The blood *shed* on the cross was for the remission of sin and the securing of the basis for salvation. This blood, representing the very life of God, is also *sprinkled* indicating that it brings believers into a living vocational fellowship with God. The two-fold aspect of the blood provides a strong base for the overcomers' testimony.

Throughout the history of the church, divine reactions moved to attain this testimony, typified by the lampstand all of gold. The reformation was such a reaction, where justification by faith was recovered. But men pulled it down and formed the protestant churches. The Moravian Brethren were used to recover the church's responsibility for the testimony of Jesus in all the nations. But human hands molded this move into a 'church' with all its religious orders. Another reaction was seen in

Whitefield and the Wesley's with the recovering of soul saving evangelism and practical holiness. Yet another reaction was seen with the Plymouth brethren recovering the exclusive place of the Lord Jesus and the vision of the Body of Christ. "It will be seen that each fresh movement was an advance upon those that preceded it in the matter of truth recovered: from the divine standpoint it was a movement nearer to the original position." Today God still has a movement, which may not be something that can be 'joined,' but definitely is a matter of deep inward exercise where believers enter into a common spiritual travail that will move the testimony yet nearer to God's original thought. Near the end times, such a testimony will be by those to whom the Lord is everything and to whom He is all in all. These must gather together, not as an organization, but rather as a spontaneous thing of life, united by the Holy Spirit in mutual love. They will gather unto Christ, in a prayer fellowship, to eat spiritual food, and to engage in ministry raised up to meet the need of the testimony at the end time.

The Body of Christ
1932

The whole church was included together in the resurrection of the Lord Jesus . Now, in spite of the many divisions seen here on earth the church is still one corporate whole. All the differences do not touch the ultimate fact that there is a realm in which there is a togetherness, oneness, and a corporate life. This unity exists; our business is to apprehend it, not make it. Our disagreements mean that we suffer loss, but it makes no difference to the fact of our oneness in the Lord Jesus. If we yield to the movements of the Spirit in us, we will be recovered to the oneness, because the fact of the oneness remains.

The feasts in the Old Testament represent the corporate life of the people of God, the corporate life of the church. During these holy convocations all that which is departmental is abandoned and the people are found as one. The Passover represents a covenant by life in blood. The Passover is just that we have come into an experimental, living, active union with one another in Christ in the power of His blood in that covenant. That is the oneness of the church, the Body of Christ.

The feast of the unleavened bread represents a perfect spiritual period throughout which all that is of the flesh is eliminated and ruled out, for the leaven is the ferment of the flesh, the work of the flesh, the potent element of the flesh which is corrupt. The oneness of the church the Body of Christ demands that not only our sins should have been put away, but that we should have been put away in the flesh.

The feast of the first-fruits represents the great truth of the representative resurrection of the Lord Jesus. We have been buried with Him, that is, the old man put away; now we are raised with Him. The real oneness of the members of Christ, the oneness of the Body of Christ is found in its living testimony to resurrection union with the Lord Jesus.

The Day of Atonement represents the fact that in the atoning work of the Lord Jesus His blood was sprinkled on the mercy seat, right in the presence of God. God has found an answer to all His desires and requirements and has come to His rest, full satisfaction in His Son. When we arrive at the full apprehension of the perfect work of the Lord Jesus in His atonement we ought to come to rest. The element of unrest, ferment, dissatisfaction goes out, and we have peace with God and harmony.

The feast of tabernacles is the means of perpetuating the memory of Exodus. The people came out of earthly, stone houses of Egypt into the wilderness where everything was heavenly. What God is doing now is building a heavenly church, a Body in the heavens. The church of God is not a thing seen, it is a thing unseen, a secret people, spiritual. That is fundamental to our oneness. When there is a tendency to establish a standard here on earth, you will inevitably produce divisions.

Concerning the nature of the Body of Christ we must see that there are local churches or local assemblies, but there is no such thing as a local Body. Rather the Lord's mind is that every local company shall be a living representation of the whole Body, a microcosm of the whole Body of Christ. In the thought of God everything to do with His church is universal, relative and interdependent. Furthermore the Church as the Body is the complement and fullness and completion of Christ. It is associated with Him as Head over all things. As such, the Body is for the display of Christ. Just as a man expresses himself through his body, so Christ expresses Himself through His Body.

The unifying factor of the Body of Christ is the Holy Spirit, not mutual acceptance, nor doctrinal agreement. The Body of Christ has only one Spirit and that is the factor which makes the Body one. When each member gives the Spirit His full place, then there is not only the fact of oneness in the Body but also a function in oneness. Thus each member must not live by his natural man, which by nature upsets the sovereignty of the Spirit. Only the unrestricted liberty of the Holy Spirit can produce a right representation and a right functioning and activity of the Body.

The Holy Spirit is the spiritual nervous system of the whole Body, linking all with the Head, and by the Head all the members are related. The Holy Spirit is the consciousness of the Body. He brings us to a realm where if one member spiritually suffers the whole Body is involved in that suffering. This shows that the Body is a

heavenly thing and its relationships are not natural, because the Spirit operates in this way apart from the natural
consciousness. All the relationships of the believers are to
be on the principle of the one Body. Relativity, that is being related to all the members of the Body, is holding fast
the Head and is the law of the Body of Christ. Let us be-
ware of trying to maintain the Body in its oneness along
the horizontal line. You cannot do it. It is a hopeless
thing and we shall always be running round and making
apologies. On the horizontal we cannot do it, but if we
hold fast the Head, we shall find our gravitation is together.

This Body has no place for a system, which ap-
points officers and workers in a kind of mechanical way.
Workers must grow up by a spiritual process. Such ministry is expressed, grows up, out of the inner life. It is not
official, it is organic. The Body is spiritual, heavenly and
illimitable.

In Touch with the Throne
1934

The incense and the anointing oil of the Old Testament tabernacle indicate to us that the ground of all acceptable prayer is that of the moral excellencies and glories and graces and virtues and merits and worthiness of
the Lord Jesus. Once that is settled, we can list five aspects of prayer. Firstly prayer is communion, fellowship,
a loving opening of the heart to God. Prayer as communion is in the spiritual life what respiration is in the physical. Communion with God is a sustained thing, a thing
like breathing, which goes on or should go on. Secondly,
prayer is an active submission to the will of God. It
means getting into line with the divine mind. Thirdly,
prayer is petition or request or asking. Fourthly, prayer is
co-operation with God. We get life and power when

prayer is entered into as cooperation with God. Prayer should bring us into the divine plan, the divine method, the divine time and the divine Spirit, or disposition.

Fifthly, prayer is warfare. But the kind of warfare referred to here is not just the general warfare of the Christian life involving vices, wrongs, and human conditions which should be otherwise. Rather, it is that warfare which is especially connected with and related to the full testimony of the Lord Jesus. If you come as a believer to a revelation of the fullness of Christ in His personal sovereignty and lordship, in the greatness of the work of His cross in every realm, and then into the light of the Church which is His Body, you enter immediately into a new realm of conflict. The battle changes its character, and a consciousness begins to grow in you that you are up against something far more sinister, far more intelligently evil than those wrongs that abound in the world. The battle ground of this warfare is prayer and the focal point of all the enemy's attention and strategy is our prayer life. One of the devil's tactics is to promote our occupation with many things, even things for the Lord, if he can thereby crowd out our prayer. He will try to prevent our prayer and, if this is not possible, he will try to interrupt our prayer times and our regular schedule of prayer. He will try to isolate the members of the Body so as to divide and weaken their prayer. Because of this, a major occasion for prayer conflict is the Church and the glory which Christ can gain through the church, which is His Body. Our defense is to set a watch. We need to watch our prayer time and also watch that no device of the enemy can intrude on our fellowship with other believers in the Body and thus limit our prayer.

Many people ask if there is a contradiction between submitting to a situation and continuing to ask God concerning that situation. In other words, does not submission take the driving force out of your knocking? The solution is seeing that God is interested in certain moral elements *in us*, which many times are the reason these situations arose in the first place. We continue to ask but with a particular set of aims. Firstly, our prayer can lead us to deliberately and persistently apprehend the moral virtues and glories of the Lord Jesus, which we so often lack. It also opens the way for those excellencies and virtues to be wrought in our own souls by the Holy Spirit. Secondly, prayer brings in a fuller knowledge and understanding, which cannot come from books, but must come from our experience. This is a life process; first of all there must be conception, which is an inward thing; then there must be formation; and then there must be travail leading to birth. Third, prayer has a collective aspect, where we realize and experience relatedness to all the other members of the Body and thus can take responsibility in prayer.

Watch unto prayer! Watching and praying in this sense is watching that you may pray, and watching against things that would stop you praying. A great help in our watching is to join God's word with our prayer. The word gives us a place of strength, because we stand on God's promises. May the Lord gain His group of overcomers, related to the rest of the Body and fighting in prayer.

We Beheld His Glory (on John 14-17)
1935

John 14: This whole chapter gathers around one word—"abide." Jesus' words about the Father's house and the abiding places in His house refer to our position now, not in the distant future. When Jesus, referring to being in the believers, says "that day," He is referring to the day after the cross, resurrection, ascension and the Spirit's descent. When Jesus departed from this world, He went to the Father. Our way today is through present personal association with Christ and through a progressive inward revelation of Christ by the Holy Spirit. Nothing natural can go this way, for this is a way of abiding in Christ. Abiding is the ground for our assurance of peace, our heart not being troubled and our rest. Knowing Him after the Spirit in such a way that we abide in Him is far superior to any other kind of knowing.

John 15: Christ is the true vine who exists only for the glory, pleasure and satisfaction of God. Glory is defined as "the divine nature satisfied in seeing His purpose realized: His very nature in its peculiar requirements satisfied." It is for this reason that the vine corporately exists. The Father being the husbandman indicates that the Father is more than merely an owner. The Father is inwardly related to the vine and the vine is something begotten of God. We are the branches indicates that "coming to the Lord Jesus makes us an organic part of Him." Only the Son can satisfy the Father, so only through such an identity of life of the Son can a corporate instrument fulfill this purpose. The purpose of the vine's existence is to bear fruit to glorify the Father. Fruit is the evidence of the life of Christ, which life is essentially and spontaneously fruitful. Thus, our union with Christ is a spontaneous service to God expressed by fruit. "To express Christ, to live Christ, to manifest Christ, to let everything around feel Christ and be touched by Christ through our presence— that certainly is to the glory of God and the satisfaction of His heart, and that is service." The pruning knife comes to all the fruitful branches to cut out anything that would limit the richness and quality of the fruit, so that the fruit may express the essential qualities of Christ.

John 16: Chapter sixteen presents a great turning point of dispensations, from the dispensation of the law to the dispensation of the Spirit. The coming of Jesus saw the law have its perfect fulfillment in man. Now man is imminently going to the Father and announces the coming of the Spirit as an essential part of the course of things. Christ's physical presence was outward, objective, limited to one place at one time and of short duration. The Spirit would be within, subjective, immanent, omnipresent, and would abide forever. In His physical presence Christ accomplished eternal redemption through His cross. The Holy Spirit would convict men all over the world on the basis of that work. The followers of the physical Jesus witnessed failures and contradictions while trying to follow His outward commands. Afterwards, the believers would become spiritual men, having the Spirit of Christ within them. The Holy Spirit would come and work in relation to Christ towards both the believers and towards the world. Towards the believers, "He would be to and in them the Spirit of revelation" to make the knowledge of Christ "a power, a life, a revolution, not just a system of doctrine." Towards the world, He would convict them of sin, righteousness and judgment. "Thus the Spirit has as His ground the person and work of Christ, in their respective meanings to the believer and the world."

John 17: This chapter can be called "The High Priest in the Holy of Holies." In the Son's prayer to the Father we see "the intimate breathings of His heart in the most solemn communion of the nearest place to God." The predominate words in the prayer concern "1) the glory of the Father and the Son, and that glory imparted to the disciples 2) the oneness of the Father and the Son; of the disciples and the Son and the Father; and of the disciples themselves 3) the world." The meaning of these three can be combined in the statement "The glorifying of the Father and the Son, and the effectual testimony of the Church to the world, will be by the reality of unity or oneness in that Body." This chapter shows that "the glorifying of the Father and the Son is in resurrection." When applied to believers, the glorifying of the Father requires resurrection and oneness. Thus, "the ground of resurrection is the ground of oneness." In our experience it follows that "there is no oneness, no unity (of the kind for which Christ prayed), until those concerned have entered experimentally and actually into the meaning of the cross—substitutionally and representatively—and into the power and life of the risen Lord." This oneness is organic, not organized or arranged or produced out of man-made associations, and is completely a matter of another life—"the unity of John 17 is the unity of one life." Only Christ's life, with its nature and energy, could put away the natural man and live "as another order of man in God's pleasure." This life is the secret of our unity. The lesson we can take from this chapter is "let Christ be our only and utter interest. Be prepared to put our 'Christian' things aside if they should in the slightest degree threaten the glory. Thus, and only thus, will the church register a convincing impact upon the world."

The Centrality of Jesus Christ
1936

The Lord Jesus is, by divine appointment, at the center of everything in this universe and He is its explanation. Additionally, everything about the Lord Jesus, from His incarnation, through His works, to His present activity and His coming again is marked by universal features, things which reach out to the very bounds of the universe and embrace all realms. This One has been put into our hearts; He is "Christ in you." God makes this Christ the centrality of the believer by working within the believer in five aspects: the revelation of Christ within, the living of Christ within, the forming of Christ within, the home-making of Christ within and the consummation of Christ within. The revelation of Christ within is what constitutes our lives as children of God. All that we are and do in relation to Christ rests upon inward revelation Everything that the church testifies of Christ must be based on inward revelation and not on activity, organization, movement, teaching or systematized doctrine. The living of Christ within denotes the living in us of the person of Christ who has fulfilled the law of God and who satisfies the Father in all that He is in His person and work. When He lives such a life in us by faith, then we also live. The forming of Christ within us results in the features of Christ being defined and delineated clearly within us; formation means Christly faculties are definitely developed within us. Christ home-making within us denotes that Christ makes more than a lodging, but a home; a home gives Him ample time to speak to us and to see our responses to His new unveilings. Christ being glorified within denotes not only the objective Christ coming in glory but the subjective Christ manifested in us in glory.

Christ is also central and supreme to the church, which is His Body. Christ is Head of the believer, and this one Head leads the believers into a life related to other believers in the unity of the one Body. The Body, produced out of and with the resurrection of Christ, reverses the innate spirit of independence in all fallen human beings. In this sense, the Body represents a tremendous victory of Christ, because it reverses Satan's devices of schism, division and disintegration. An independent life for the Christian is contrary to God's will, it is a taking of the Lord's glory for self glory. The remedy for this is the Body of Christ applied practically where, as a member, one has to defer, refer, consult, submit, let go in order to have this Body life. The Body is necessary for our full apprehension of Christ and for full growth in Christ. We need the members who are differently constituted to make possible the varied aspect of apprehension of Christ. It is also the Body that grows up and that builds itself up to the full measure of the stature of a man in Christ. This Body is also required for the full manifestation of Christ in the

ages to come. From all these aspects we see that the Lord
Jesus, as Head of the Body, brings us to enjoy all that He
is as the Head in relation to the saints and in fellowship
with the saints.

Christ is also central and supreme as Head of all
principalities and powers. Christ is absolutely supreme;
His order is far above every other order and there is no
other like Him. The great Colossian error describes a fascinating philosophy that is a mix of Judaism and spurious
Christian elements. Yes, this philosophy does lead people
to worship Christ and to adopt an attitude of reverence and
humility. But it denies the absolute supremacy of Christ
and lowers Christ from the absoluteness of His place in
the Godhead. We are thus robbed of a fuller apprehension
of Christ, which is the only way of victory. The Holy
Spirit will never move in us to make us a better person
through such a philosophy. He will only lead us to a
greater apprehension of Christ as our perfection and as our
salvation—"Not what I am, O Lord, but what Thou art."
May the Lord give us a new joy in Christ who is supreme
in every realm.

The Stewardship of the Mystery Volume I
1937

Divine revelation, not any human self-reliance,
confidence in the flesh, or pride of advance, is the only
way for us to see the tremendous meaning, value, and content found in God's realm. Our revelation, like Paul's,
should be a continual and ever-growing unveiling, which
leads us to discover more of Christ, from now even
throughout eternity. Paul's experience on the Damascus
road lifted Christ out of time and unveiled the eternal purpose of God in His Son. In God's *purpose* there was no
fall and no redemption; it was a straight and uninterrupted
and unbroken line from eternity to eternity. Redemption

is something more than saving men from sin; it involves the ultimate ranges of the universe and is a linking up of eternity past with eternity yet to be.

God's eternal purpose concerns His Son and involves man collectively in a progressive, ever increasing apprehension and expression of Christ. There is thus a movement in this universe which brings man into an ever greater fullness of God. Such a purpose shows the central place man holds in God's thoughts. Man is an expression of divine thought, an image and likeness of something conceived in the mind of God. God desires that man would be a living embodiment of God's heart. Man is to be in a moral-spiritual sense the image of God. He is not to share Deity, but to have the moral nature of God; the spiritual nature of God in mind, and heart, and will is to be reproduced in man. This is where God's thought rested, and this is God's purpose. God intended that man would be a created corporate race as an expression of that which is in essence God. This is not in the sense of Deity, but in a moral essence. This man would have the kinds of thoughts God thinks, the kinds of desires God desires, the kind of will God wills. God intended a created corporate race as an expression of Himself in this sense.

We see this in Christ and we see this in the believers, whose destiny is to be conformed to the image of God's Son. Christ will be corporately expressed. The question of Deity apart, the moral and spiritual essence of Christ will utterly govern every other unit in the universe. It will be Christ in that sense; one great universal, collective, corporate Christ. This can only come about when people receive eternal life, which refers not only to duration of life but to the very life of God Himself. It cannot come about by man's natural life, which tries to grasp hold on the work of God. Nor can it come about by the fallen flesh of man, nor by the old man, who is still in the race of the corporate, collective Adam. God's purpose can only come about exclusively in the New Man, Christ. Nothing but what is of Christ is allowed by God in the ultimate issue.

Eternal life by the Holy Spirit is the base upon which God will gain His purpose. It is by Christ who, beginning on resurrection ground as the last Adam, became the life-giving Spirit. As the last Adam, the life-giving Spirit, Christ breathes upon the believers infusing eternal life into the new creation. After being infused with eternal life, believers can walk in the Spirit. If we are walking in the Spirit, our lives will automatically be ordered according to the word of God. Our lives, like that of Jesus, will be a continuous and spontaneous fulfilling of the Word of God.

In accordance with His word, Jesus, the heavenly Man, gains a corporate expression of Himself. The Lord Himself now continues His own life and work through His Body. All the members of the Body must thus be filled with the Spirit and share the one eternal Life of God through the Holy Spirit. This results in members of Christ's Body living an inter-related and inter-dependent life, as members one of another. The corporate expression contains the blessings of the gifts, given by the Heavenly Man, for the progressive realization and expression of Himself as the corporate Heavenly Man. The apostles manifest the authority of Christ, the prophets reveal the mind of God in Christ, the evangelists show the heart of God in Christ and the pastors and teachers apply the resources of God in Christ for building up. All these gifts are given in order that the corporate, heavenly Man, deriving the values of these functions, shall itself minister to its mutual building up; for the making complete of the saints unto the work of the ministry, unto the building up of the Body of Christ. Thus the eternal purpose of God is fulfilled.

The Stewardship of the Mystery, Volume II
1938

God's purpose is that a corporate Man would become an ever fuller expression of God Himself. The instrument and vessel of this purpose is "The church, which is His Body." The eternal counsels of the Godhead are bound up with the church, the love and labor of the divine Trinity are focused on the church and the redemption of Christ is for the corporate Body, the church. The Apostle Paul uniquely spoke concerning the Body and showed a concern not merely for the foundation of the church, but for its "superstructure," for its increase in the measure of Christ.

The church cannot be only heavenly and spiritual. It demands a vehicle of expression and representation. An assembly of physical believers constituted by the Holy Spirit on the principles of the Body of Christ is an essential thing to the spiritual increase of all His members. The local church is going to bring its impact upon all the details of the lives of the believers; it will touch every Christian's home and will involve every Christian's domestic relationships. It is essential that the local church would take its character and meaning from the heavenly, universal church of which it is an expression. This local church cannot be an institution or an organization. It cannot be national, international, denominational, interdenominational or undenominational. The practical values and outworkings of the corporate nature of this church are derived only because Christ is present in the whole spiritual and cosmic realm as a personal living presence in this spiritual organism.

If the church is an expression of Christ here on the earth and if it is governed entirely by one supreme goal— the fullness of Christ, then the measure of Christ becomes a ruling factor. All that should matter to us is how this end may be best reached, and we should be willing to make any sacrifice to get into this way. God has only one end in view: the fullness of Christ *in the church*. All ministries are for the increase of the measure of Christ in the church. If any exercise of ministry does not have the church as its basis and object, it falls far short of God's divine purpose.

How should a local church be formed? It should not be formed as a result of a dispute or disagreement; or as a policy of any movement, enterprise or organization; nor on the basis of any particular teaching or interpretation; nor because of any discontent or mere disaffection. Rather the local assembly should come into being in the same way as the heavenly, universal Body came into being. There must be a revelation to the heart of the believers and a deep work of the Holy Spirit by which the Church as His Body is seen. The constituting of assemblies should be brought about only on the gravitating together in a living way of those who have received such a revelation of the church.

What the One Body is in the divine thought is Christ in His corporate expression; this should be seen in the life, function, order and testimony of each separate assembly. The assembly life has as its objects the building up of believers by instruction, mutual edification and fellowship; corporate action in the spiritual realm by prayer; and the making known of Christ through its members in widening circles. The measure of Christ is the thing which determines whether an assembly is justified in its continued existence. The law which governs their continued existence is the fullness of Christ.

Baptism, the Lord's Table and the laying on of hands are all testimonies of the spiritual realities experienced by believers. The laying on of hands is a testimony of the believers' identification with Christ as the Head and with His One Body. The elders laid hands on Paul and

Barnabas as a testimony that Paul's work and ministry had the church as its basis and object. It is as though the church said, "This ministry is ours." The laying on of hands is also a way of bestowing spiritual gifts upon members that would result in a further building up of the Body. The laying on of hands also indicates that the church shares one, corporate anointing, because it is attached to one anointed Head, Christ.

The corporate anointing brings all believers into an organic oneness—oneness in life. When all the members have a full tide of divine life flowing uninterrupted and unhindered, then you get a mighty corporate movement, with the Holy Spirit Himself as the one intelligence in the one Body. Fullness in organic life results in an organism being produced with function, order, and fruit issuing from the law of life within. Ministers should grow from the inside solely upon the basis of spiritual life and value, rather than being appointed or elected from without. The organic life by the One Spirit has a great many aspects, and it touches the whole nature and order of the Church, universal and local. To have divine fullness we must have divine grounds.

What is Man?
1939

Man, according to God's mind and according to a dim and intangible sense in himself, is of a universal character, with universal interests. But something occurred, which, on the one hand, makes the realization of God's intentions impossible in man as he now is, and on the other hand, causes man to persist in a vain effort to achieve such realization. The main reason for this is that in general man does not make a distinction between his soul and his spirit. According to philosophers and psychologists there are two parts of man, soul and body. But according to the New Testament, man is made of three parts: spirit, soul and body. The spirit makes man unique in all of God's creation. The soul relates to man in his own conscious life here in this world; his good or evil; his power to do, to achieve, to enjoy, to profit, to know and acquire what is of this world, and to live as a responsible, self-conscious being, answering to God for himself and his life. The spirit is that by which—given the necessary renewing—man is directly related to things divine. He is thereby constituted to be capable of relationships with spiritual beings and spiritual things. It is only in the spirit that man is an offspring of God and it is only man's spirit which can worship God, who is Spirit. To fulfill all these divine intentions, man's spirit must be kept in living union with God.

Before the fall, although Adam was sinless and innocent, he was not perfect as God intended him to be. Rather his human spirit carried with it a potentiality or a possibility of having a perfect link with God through his partaking of the tree of life. However, Adam did not attain to that life. Rather, he fell and became a being that was a different species than what God created. When Adam fell, death entered and resulted in a severance in spiritual union with God. This does not mean man ceased to have a spirit, but that the ascendancy of the spirit was surrendered to the soul. Adam became a soul-man instead of a spirit-man preeminently. Thus, the entire world fell into the realm of the soul, having all things based upon desire, emotion, feeling, reason, argument, will, choice, and determination. It is not the case that the soul, as such, is a wrong thing and that it therefore should be destroyed. However, this soul of man has been poisoned with self-directive interest, and has become allied with the powers which are opposed to God.

New birth is the reception of an entirely new and different life, required to be generated from above by a specific act of divine impregnation—a quite new and original endowment which has never been in our human life, and which remains an altogether other life that is not in us by nature, but a unique and miraculous generation—as Christ is. When man asserted himself in favor of the body and not of the spirit he became a sinful soul. Now he must be saved from himself. This is accomplished in two ways. Firstly, the power of Christ's death is wrought and established in the soul-consciousness of man. Secondly, the resurrection of Christ is also a mighty power in man's spirit, and by its introduction via the Holy Spirit into man's inner being, he is made a spiritual man, as over against a merely natural. Let the soul surrender to the body and all is lost. Let it surrender to the spirit and all is well.

The spirit that is quickened, raised, indwelt and united with Christ is set to be the organ of divine government over the rest of man, soul and body. The rightful place of the soul, which is a trinity of reason, affection and volition, is to be an organ that can be used by the spirit as a very fruitful and useful servant and instrument. It is the organ to interpret, translate and make intelligible to other humans the divine things apprehended by the spirit. It is also the organ by which we can appreciate and apprehend everything of this world which can be brought to the spirit for consideration and enlightenment as to God's divine standards. A soulish person is simply a person in whom the soul predominates. A spiritual person is one in whom the spirit is given preeminence.

To learn to walk in the spirit is a life lesson of the New Man. The spirit is a trinity of conscience, communion (worship) and intuition. The conscience accuses or excuses and serves to maintain a God consciousness, even in the unregenerate. Intuition is that faculty of spiritual intelligence by which all spiritual beings work. It is very different from natural reasoning. Men who had a close walk with God many times received intuitively a leading which was not approved by natural reason, but usually had all such reason in opposition. Intuition is a leading by revelation, as the Apostle Paul so many times referred to. God desires that we learn to walk in this spirit and that our spirit will come to have absolute ascendancy over our whole being.

In the end, our body, which will have been sown a soulish body, will be raised a spiritual body. By the Spirit, we were first quickened and made spiritually alive. By the Spirit of life, were we made free from the law of sin and death. So, by the Spirit of life, is the consummation brought about when what is mortal, our body, is swallowed up by life.

The Law of the Spirit of Life in Christ Jesus
1940

"The supreme issue which governs everything between God and man is life." Romans 8:2 tells us that life is a law in the hands of the Holy Spirit: "the law of the Spirit of life." "A law is a fixed and established principle. It has potentialities. It means that, if you are adjusted to it and governed by it, certain results are inevitable; that the potentialities which it contains will most certainly find expression when that law is established." If a law is established, accepted and recognized then it works out in a specific way. "That outworking is perfectly spontaneous, perfectly natural; we might say it is automatic." When we, as born again believers, allow this law to govern us, it regulates us and results in Jesus living His life over again in us. If you look at the human life that Jesus lived "You will see a divinely governed life, in word, in movement, in act, marvelously governed; and He is living that over again in us." As Christians, we do not need someone to adjust us outwardly in our actions, words or attitudes. If we are sensitive, the life within will direct us increasingly to completely live out the life of Jesus. "If only we have life and that life is allowed to have its way, we are going to reach God's full end. It is not an abstract thing, it is a divine Person resident within; Christ, who is the life, governing from within by the Holy Spirit, the Spirit of life."

To know life we must know Christ Jesus, and we must understand Him. "To know Him truly is to know life. Thus, in keeping with this whole truth, it becomes the work of the Holy Spirit, as the Spirit of life, to reveal Christ Jesus, to make Him known, to lead us into Him as the life." This book looks at seven men in Genesis "each of whom brings Christ into view in some specific aspect of life." In looking at these seven men, we see seven aspects of the life and we begin to realize how life works out from its beginning to its consummation. So we proceed from the first man Adam, through Abel, Noah, Abraham, Isaac and Jacob until we arrive at Joseph, one who represents the reigning aspect of life, the very fullness of life.

In Adam we see a type of Christ who is to come and the first aspect of the law of life: utter dependence upon God. With Adam, the law of life is represented by the tree of life in the Garden of Eden. Adam was intended to take this tree and thus to show forth the way of life. However, he acted independently from God and failed. Not until the last Adam, Christ, came was this first aspect of the law of life fully displayed. When Christ lived as a man on this earth, He did not do anything from Himself, but was utterly dependent upon the Father. This is the first aspect of the law of life.

In Abel we see a life that recognized sin and "saw that the sinful soul must be poured out unto death, not offered to God, neither it nor its works or fruits." Abel is in contrast to Cain, who offered something to God for worship out of his own natural life. Cain sought to be accepted before God on the ground of what his soul deemed to be its own good.

Like Abel, Noah represents another aspect of not serving God by the natural life. But Noah represents the positive side. He built the ark, indicating that he repudiated everything of the natural life and the mixture of the world. After the flood, he positively walked with God in resurrection. His life shows us that the way to a life in resurrection is to be occupied with that which is not of this world, "out of what is here, out of nature, out of this world, and out of ourselves."

Abraham shows forth a life of faith, which is a life in Christ. He demonstrates that from start to finish the Lord Himself must be everything. God was going to fulfill His promise to Abraham in God's time and way. This pushed Abraham to learn to walk by faith "with God alone and for God's own sake."

Isaac, the son of Abraham, represents sonship. In New Testament terms sonship is described thus: "The human spirit becomes the vessel of the divine seed, the vessel in which something that is of God Himself is begotten, and the presence of that something constitutes the one in whom the deposit is a different kind of being from all other beings in God's universe....There is that within the child of God upon which the eye of God rests as something belonging to Himself, which has come out from Him and is part of Him, and His eye is upon that as upon a cherished child."

Jacob represents one who sees the value of the birthright and who is serving God in the house of God, Bethel. From him we see that all true service to God must be bound up with the house of God and it is truly inseparable from the house of God.

In Joseph we see the final consummation of the working of the law of life, a life on the throne, reigning with Christ. This is the final fullness of life and the consummation of the working of the divine life within us. In the hands of the Holy Spirit this life is worked out in us as the law of the spirit of life.

God's Spiritual House
1941

God's spiritual house exists for the purpose of proclaiming the exaltation of God's Son and for rejoicing in this fact. A very blessed fact about His exaltation is that He is our kinsman, our brother. He is the firstborn who is leading us as many sons into glory. "The exaltation of our Kinsman means the family is coming to glory." This is the house of God, where Christ as the Son over the house is being continually enlarged in us. God can find true rest and satisfaction only in His Son, because His Son satisfies all that He morally and spiritually requires. Thus God's house, which is Christ Himself corporately, in you and in me, is the place of God's rest and satisfaction. The presence of God's house is the focus of satanic antagonism, because the vocation of God's house is mainly to intercede on behalf of God's people for their deliverance and life. The life of the people of God is the enormous trust committed to the church and it is for this reason that the house of God and the interceding life of the house become such a focus for Satan's attacks.

The spiritual house of God is the representation of Christ in every place. "The church is Christ as distributed, though not divided." We can see the special importance of the local corporate expression of Christ when we consider that Paul, while addressing the local company of believers in Corinth, says, "You are the body of Christ." "It is remarkable that local churches in the New Testament are always viewed in the light of the whole Body." The purpose and function of a local expression is three fold. Firstly, it is to be the meeting place between God and

man. All who come into such a realm where Christ is corporately expressed should realize that God is in their
midst. Secondly, the local expression is the embodiment
and expression of God's thoughts. "There should be there
a disclosing of God's thoughts in a very blessed way, a
coming to know the mind of the Lord for His people, a
rich unveiling of what is in the heart of God concerning
His own." Thirdly, the local expression should be the
sphere of divine government and authority. Matthew 18
reveals to us that we should tell it to the church and let the
church decide what the mind of the Lord is. From these
three functions, we see that a "corporate company, liv-
ingly constituted according to Christ," is of a very real and
practical consequence as the representation of Christ in
every place. Many children of God are yearning for this
practical representation in their place. Brother Nee, during his time at Honor Oak, testified of how this yearning
was in the hearts of some believers and how through
prayer and waiting on God, the Lord eventually formed
just such a representation of Christ in their neighborhood.

From this example we can see that three hin-
drances to the fulfillment of God's purpose regarding His
church are: individualism; the prevailing static, routine
church system; and an over emphasis on "the gospel mission" to the exclusion of the deeper things of the Christian
life.

As a law, life and spirituality govern all matters in
the house of God. The exaltation of the Lord, the ministry
of the house of God to God's elect, and the corporate life
of the house of God as a representation of Christ in every
place are all marked in the believers by life and spirituality. Concerning life, the ultimate end or aim of the church,
the house of God, is the manifestation of sons in the corporate sense. We begin as children of God by generation
when we received the Spirit. Then we grow in this life as
Sons of God until one day we will reach Sonship, which

literally in the Bible is "the placing of Sons." We are all in this school of Sonship unto adoption and when we graduate we will manifest sonship brought to completion, represented by the manchild in Revelation 12. This is the end of the house of God—full Sonship. "It will be Christ corporate who will come to take the kingdom of this world in the coming ages, and it is unto that—the fullness of Christ—that God is working pre-eminently in our experience."

The School of Christ
1942

"Ye did not so learn Christ!" (Eph. 4:20) It is to the school of Christ that every born again believer is brought. Here the Holy Spirit, the Teacher and Interpreter, shows us the great object of our education—Christ Himself. "The mark of a life governed by the Holy Spirit is that such a life is continually ever more and more occupied with Christ, that Christ is becoming greater and greater as time goes on." It is as if the Holy Spirit brings us to shore of a mighty ocean, which is Christ, and impresses us with the sense that even if we could spend our entire life exploring Him, our quest would merely touch the fringe of His vast fullness.

The first thing the Holy Spirit makes clear in our education is the complete "other-ness" of Christ. He is altogether different from us. His thoughts, feelings, desires, ways, motives, doings, nature, are entirely other than ours. "The difference is such that we move in two altogether opposite worlds." Christ is the model that God set up as His own perfect concept of man. And we must be completely impressed with the utter impossibility of our being that model in ourselves or by any means out of ourselves. Once we see our inability, the Holy Spirit can begin to show us His power to conform us to the image of

God's Son. We finally say, "Not what I am, O Lord, but what Thou art, that alone, can be my soul's true rest."

Christ, the supreme object of our education, is the truth, the house of God and the light of life. Christ said "I am the truth." Christ being the truth means we do not learn truth as doctrine but we learn truth as Christ Himself—a living Person. Only by knowing Christ as a living person who is truth can we "know the truth" and experience "the truth shall set you free." In this day of spiritual declension, God's "way of recovery" is not to bring us into a new church practice, but to bring into view Christ as the truth in a fuller and richer way. The only way such seeing will affect us is if our seeing is by an inward revelation. Such living revelation is utterly bound up with our practical situations, where we realize the Holy Spirit has arranged our environment such that only a fresh, living revelation of Jesus Christ can be our salvation, life and deliverance. In this context we do not learn doctrines, but we learn the experience of Christ as the truth.

Christ is also the house of God, which is not merely an individual house but a corporate house of God composed of believers who are in Christ. We learn that when we are in Christ we are in the house of God and we are the house of God. We have all entered this house via the altar, the death of Christ symbolized by baptism and we live in this house via the anointing, symbolized by the laying on of hands. Christ death takes care of our sins and ends our natural life. The anointing means that the Holy Spirit is taking His rightful place as Lord in us. And when we all stand under this anointing, allowing the Spirit to take His place as absolute Lord, we touch the reality of the house of God. Here is a living knowledge of what it means to be under the headship of Christ. When people enter such a place, they will say "The Lord is in this place."

Christ is also the light of life. "God's purpose is that there shall come a time when He has a vessel in which and through which His glory shines forth to this universe." Thus, as we proceed in the school of Christ, the Holy Spirit will lead us into increasing light. In Old Testament times God's light was made known through the shining of the Shekinah glory of the most holy place. In this place, where God directly communed with man, there was no room for the natural life. Likewise, we can only have such a shining by coming to a crisis where there is death to our own life, our life apart from Him. Practically, such a process may look like a difficult situation in our home, our business or in our relationships. Here, as the grain of wheat, we fall into the dark earth to die with Christ. Union with Him in such death causes us to experience a transmission of His life through us. Thus, space in our being is being made for Christ who is the light of life. It is in this way of the cross that God's purpose of gaining light and glory in and through us is accomplished. We become people living in the era of the Spirit under an opened heaven. Here we are given an entirely new set of faculties and the Spirit Himself proceeds to make our living under the reality of an opened heaven where all the values of Christ are made real in us.

We see from these examples that the nature of the school of Christ is not the objective teaching of things, but "an inward making of Christ a part of us by experience." Here we learn, under the anointing of the Holy Spirit and by our sense of the divine life. The meaning of the anointing is that the Holy Spirit takes His place as absolute Lord. This implies that all other lordships have to be set aside; the anointing can never be enjoyed except this has taken place. Even the Lord Jesus had to be baptized, taking the place of man in representation in order that, from that point on, He was "not to be under the government of His own life in any respect as He worked out the

will of God, but to be wholly and utterly subject to the
Spirit of God in every detail." For us, such subjection
means that Christ has preeminence; and we "come after
Him and take all our value from Him." We know whether
we are under the Lordship of Christ by sensing and dis-
cerning life, the divine life and the Spirit of life. Life is
the Spirit's instrument in the school for teaching us Christ.
"The mark of a Spirit-governed, Spirit-anointed, man or
woman is that they move in life, and that they minister
life, and that what comes from them means life."

The school of Christ ends with God gaining His
glory, which is a governing principle for the operation of
God's love toward us. The only glory that God recognizes comes from His Son. In the school of Christ we
learn that we contribute nothing to God's glory through
who we are or through what we do. "All that He can use
is His Son, and the measure of our ultimate glory will be
the measure of Christ in us." Throughout our lives in this
school, we learn that we must begin from a zero point and
"that the glory of life depends entirely upon our faith apprehension, appropriation and appreciation of Christ."

The Centrality and Universality of the Cross
1943

Picture a wheel with four spokes labeled "the Person of Christ", "the Holy Spirit", "the so great salvation"
and "the coming again of the Lord". At the center of this
wheel, at its very hub, lies the cross of Christ. The cross
"gathers up in itself everything, and it makes possible everything." In fact, there is not a theme in the Bible related
to God's eternal purpose that is not governed by the cross
of the Lord Jesus. When we say cross we do not merely
mean the crucifixion of Christ. It includes "the death, the
burial, the resurrection, the ascension to the throne, and
the sovereign relationship vested now in Christ there for

us." All this is by way of the cross. The cross then is not just a line of teaching, a theme or a "department of truth." Rather it is the "all-comprehending, all-explaining center of the universe." These four spokes, which are moving from the hub and ever coming back to it are related to the cross of Christ.

The Person of Christ: The preeminent thing for which Christ stands in the entire revelation of Scripture is union with God. This very thing is what humanity is seeking after, but to no avail because of man's fall. Now mankind is constituted with lies, full of enmity toward God and other men and full of death, which is a separation from the source of true life. In the incarnation of Christ we have the "very God joining Himself with the very man" producing a new humanity, a man "all-together other than ourselves." Our union with God must always and can only be in Christ. By the cross, His humanity, the humanity in union with God, can be shared with us to the extent that what is true about Christ's relationship with the Father and the Father's relationship with Him can also become true in us in an inward way. To accomplish this, Christ went to the cross and fell into the ground as a grain of wheat that He would become many grains. When this One died, all died that now we may live unto Him. Thus, to really know who Christ is in His preeminent characteristic of union with God we must know the cross in an experimental way, that we would know His death as ours and also know a risen life in Him. We see that the cross brings us into a living union and oneness with God.

The Holy Spirit: Whenever God moves to further His purpose, He does so by agency of the Holy Spirit. What God is doing now is "to project and constitute and consummate a new ordered spiritual system, a spiritual cosmos, an entirely spiritual nature of things," a new spiritual creation. The pattern of this spiritual order or system is Christ. Christ's Person is the "embodiment of this vast, this comprehensive, system of divine thoughts, of divine elements, of divine laws, divine principles and divine nature." Christ is a "universe of spiritual laws, of spiritual principles, of spiritual forces." The work of the Holy Spirit now is to "lead us into this vast universe which Christ is." For example, Christ is all the relationships and interdependencies in this universe. By the operation of the Spirit, the church will be "the reproduction of what Christ is," so no member of the body can say to another member, "I have no need of you." In the realm of the Spirit this sort of thing is going on. Now, the cross is basic to this work of the Spirit in us. Man is under a curse but on the cross Christ redeemed us out of the curse of the law that we might receive the promise of the Spirit (Gal 3:13-14). To continue in the Spirit is only possible by the cross removing the curse. When we positively follow the Spirit as it leads us into this universe which Christ is, the Spirit will attend to the application of the cross to us in our experience. We will then experience the implications of the cross ending our old man, delivering us from our natural or soulish man, freeing us from legalism and outward practices to realize that the Spirit should be Lord within, and delivering us from earthly things such as differences of class and nationality. Finally, the cross will free us from any high mindedness and allow us to be emptied that we might allow Christ to have His rightful place on the throne. We see that "the Spirit always works through the cross, and the cross always leads on to the Spirit."

The So Great Salvation: The work of the cross results in man experiencing a "so great salvation." The many sidedness of this salvation can be represented by eight words: substitution, representation, redemption, justification, reconciliation, regeneration, sonship, sanctification, and glorification. Substitution speaks to the fact that man is judged and condemned and must die, which is a state of being consciously forsaken by God, but that God provided Christ to be our substitute in order to take our place in being "made sin on our behalf" and in being forsaken by God on the cross. Whereas substitution means that Christ died for us, representation means that Christ died as us. Representation does not just take away our sin, but ourselves: "One died for all, therefore all died." Redemption indicates that man, who sold himself to Satan and sin, is now redeemed unto God; Satan's rights have been undercut and disposed of. Justification is the believer's standing or position when the three previous steps have taken place; substitution solved the sin problem, representation solved the old creation problem, and redemption destroyed the link with Satan. Now we are fully justified. Reconciliation brings us, who once were at enmity with God, near to God and into a "blessed fellowship of a new life and a new spirit." "By regeneration something is present which was not there before, a life from God which only the born-again possess, an indwelling of the Holy Spirit which is not true of any others." Sonship represents growth unto fullness and is the grand climax of the new creation. Sanctification and consecration are synonymous terms firstly meaning being set apart unto God. The process of sanctification is the working of the cross in us to nullify our old nature and to bring in an ever increasing fullness of Christ. It is to cause us to arrive experientially at the position to which we are placed by the grace of God. Glorification is the "spontaneous issue of the working in us of that divine life, the incorruptible life of God." Glorification begins in the spirit, proceeds as the soul—our reason, desire, volition—is brought into subjection to the spirit and consummates with our body, "the redemption of our body." This is the final outworking of regeneration. It is the sanctification of spirit, soul and body with the final issue being glorification. Through these eight steps, we see the greatness of our salvation and we appreciate the extent of our salvation that God has accomplished "in the Person of His Son and in the work of His cross."

The Lord's coming again: The Lord's coming again is not merely a matter of signs of the times, but it is also very much a matter of inward spiritual preparedness. The Lord will return to a people who are separated from the world, freed from Satan's authority, joined to Christ and living on heavenly ground. The working of the cross is to prepare a spiritual people as such. It is in this way that the cross is central to the coming again of the Lord.

It should be noted that only in the church do these four spokes take their meaning and value. The meaning of the person of Christ is in the church, the Holy Spirit's work expresses its value in the church, the church is constituted with those who experience the so-great salvation, and the coming again of Christ has its primary meaning in the church, because it is primarily for the church that the Lord comes back. Thus all these spokes have an organic, corporate aspect to their experience. Here the cross, by nullifying our natural life, which denies the church and the sovereign headship of Christ, makes possible an expression of the heavenly spiritual church that can truly match who God is. The working of the cross allows the church to be "Christ in corporate expression." This expression is full of divine life, which is energetic, reproductive, and filled with light and love. The church, which is a crucified company of believers, is a testimony to the nations of what Christ is. All authority has been given to Christ. Those who have been "incorporated into Christ in death, burial, resurrection, ascension and reign" will share His authority as His body and will thus assail the satanic kingdom and manifest the wisdom and grace of God to the entire universe.

Four Greatnesses of Divine Revelation
1946

Most of the problems among Christians are due to one simple fact: smallness. Pettiness, smallness or lack of spiritual greatness is a root malady of most Christians today. The need of our hour echoes Paul's "full-hearted outburst" to the problem ridden Corinthians: "Be ye also enlarged." *Four Greatnesses of Divine Revelation* uses the portrait of King Solomon to depict the New Testament greatness of four "pillars of the faith": Christ, the cross, the church and the word. If we truly apprehend more of the greatness of these four, we will be brought to a new horizon, a new sense of greatness, and we'll be enlarged according to the Lord's standard. Such enlargement and greatness are surely needed among the Lord's people today if the spiritual condition of the church is to return to the standard shown typically with the glorious picture of Solomon in the Old Testament.

Christ is great in three aspects. He is great as King, He is great in His possessions and He is great as a Son. Christ as King is the Son of God, which is a position that has no higher place in the divine thought. He is King because He's kingly in His moral and spiritual features, which are the elements that support the divine throne. He is also King because He is beloved by God and was installed by God as King by sovereign grace. Christ is great in His possessions, which are for the glory of God and for the enrichment of the people of God and for the distribution by God's people. Christ's possessions include abundant spiritual food for the satisfaction and maturity of God's people, and wisdom, which discloses divine principles and apprehends divine secrets. As Son, Christ is great because He is an eternal Son. And as Son, He possesses a heavenly and thus exercises His sovereignty over the entire universe, turning even Satan's schemes to the advancement of God's purpose. As Son of Man, He is our redeeming kinsman, the one who joined our race, entered into a vital relationship with man and thus fully redeemed us.

The greatness of the cross transcends time and reaches to the ends of the universe; it is "super-historical and extra-terrestrial." Christ on the cross was one perfect sacrifice that fully satisfied God forever. In this sacrifice God overcame the heavenly powers of evil and redeemed all of His creation from vanity and corruption. In the Cross, God Himself was vindicated as the creator of all things and as the one who chose Israel to be the blessing of all the nations. Furthermore, the greatness of the cross lies in our relationship with Christ. The greatness of Christ is not merely something to be admired as if we were observing someone outside our universe. His revelation is intended to show us His close association with us. God's thought in eternity past was that we would be perfected in His Son. The only way to realize this divine thought is through the cross. "The cross is the bridge through all time between the eternities, to take up the purpose on the one hand, and to secure it as a realization on the other hand." Through the cross, the Lord Jesus, the man God intended there to be, entered into resurrection. And this man became a new order of man in resurrection, "the perfect specimen of all the divine thought in man's creation." When we are born again, we receive "the embryonic life of that new order." Throughout our life, we are changed into the same image, transformed until one day "we will be like Him." This is the greatness of the cross. Through the cross, the death of Christ enables us to one day be like Him. Through the cross, the Church becomes the expression of the risen and exalted Christ. And through the cross, the Lord gains His rightful place on the throne among God's people. From His enthronement comes rest and wealth for God's people, victory over

God's enemies and the enlargement of the kingdom of God. This is the greatness of the cross.

The greatness of the church stems from the fact that the church takes up the greatness of Christ and the greatness of the cross. "They give the church its real character." The church takes its character from Christ's eternal being, heavenliness, divine Person and forward looking vocation. The Word of God is great because it is the divine Person: "the Word was God." It is the unique language of God, which is not Greek nor Hebrew, but something that comes from God Himself and thus can only be apprehended by a heavenly faculty given at our new birth. As such, the Word of God is not merely letters; it is God's act. Thus, when we receive God's word, which is spirit, we must be changed. For example, we were begotten by the Word of God and the Word of God must maintain us today. The Word requires divine, not human, interpretation and it therefore must be accompanied by faith. "What is really needed today is a recovery of the Word of God in its essential, intrinsic greatness, and of the fact that the Word *is* God, with a personal impact upon us." If we would truly apprehend these greatnesses, we would be enlarged and the spiritual condition of the church could be recovered to the glorious state shown typically in the portraits of Solomon.

Prophetic Ministry
1948

"The function of a prophet has almost invariably been that of recovery." Something related to God's full satisfaction was lost. The prophet, sounding a note of dissatisfaction, speaks of the costly way to recover God's full thought concerning His people. In contrast to many of today's mission societies, where great resources of men and money are used for little impact, we see examples in

China and in India where living, spiritual churches have sprung up over wide regions. The factors involved in these moves are a throwing off of old traditions and practices, heavenliness and spirituality, openness and the negation of exclusiveness, and the Lordship of Christ operating by the sovereignty of the Spirit. We see that prophets today bring into full view God's eternal purpose, which is the full significance of Jesus Christ. A throwing off of the set established system is the natural result of a fresh and living revelation of the significance and realities of Jesus Christ.

Prophetic ministry is much larger than predicting; it is a holding forth of God's full, original and ultimate purpose. It is often declared as a reaction to the present course and drift of things. Within the prophet, the anointing operates to make known the laws and principles governing the purpose of God. Such knowledge comes by revelation and makes the message of the prophet more than mere teaching. Rather, with genuine prophets, the minister becomes the ministry itself. "The identity of the vessel with its ministry is the very heart of divine thought....The vessel itself is the ministry." The message of the prophet is inwrought by experience so that prophetic ministry becomes a life, not merely a teaching.

The prophet's vision, which is a unifying vision, is needed by all children of God and results in growth, definiteness, ascendancy, and purpose to the Christian life. Such vision, not teaching or knowledge of facts, defines the vocation of a servant of God. For example, Israel's vocation was to *be* as God in the midst of the nations, not merely to say things about God. Similarly, the church's vocation is to be a "corporate representation of the lordship of His Son," not merely to preach about this. When you come into touch with a nucleus of men who are such before God you will come in touch with reality. This is prophetic ministry.

However, many do not hear the prophet's message, or receive the benefits of the prophet's message, because of the offense of the cross. On the negative side, the cross outwardly implies a suffering Messiah and inwardly implies death to our self life, an utter self-emptying. But on the positive side the cross brings us to know the Lord's resurrection. As such, the cross is the way for us to come to a fuller knowledge of the Lord Himself, which knowledge is the only way we will be made useful to the Lord. It is impossible to have this knowledge without definite transactions with the Lord Himself.

In the Bible we see that the prophets prophesied mainly about the Kingdom, which is a new life (the heavenly life), a new relationship (a relationship in life with God where we call him "Father"), a new constitution (not laws and regulations but new capacities derived from the new life), a new vocation (we begin living for divine ends), a new gravitation (to heaven not earth). Entrance into this kingdom is through violence, which is desperation not to be sidetracked by Satan, any man, any man-made system or even any good thing.

This kingdom is of the new dispensation—the dispensation of the Spirit. "The words 'dispensation' and 'stewardship' mean an economy, an order; how things are done in this regime. We find that in this dispensation, when the Holy Spirit came, He began to change things, because He was in charge." In the old dispensation men were of the letter and tended toward a fixed position and organizational limits. The danger for us is that a prophet may see a vision, then an organization or a church is built upon that vision and finally the principle concern of the church becomes sustaining itself as an organization. In the new dispensation, for the fulfillment of divine Purpose, the Holy Spirit must always be in charge at all times, so that He has the freedom to bring us into a vast realm of what God may reveal. Our responsibility is to yield to the Spirit. In the Bible, the Spirit is seen to have a double operation, coming 'upon' and coming 'in' believers. This is to carry out two purposes. "He came 'upon' to possess for the purpose of God, and He came 'within' to see that everything in the inner life corresponded with that purpose."

Finally, the Spirit of life in this new kingdom, which is of the new dispensation, requires that everything be constituted according to God's heavenly pattern, Christ Himself. "As that Spirit of life was allowed to work, things took a certain course and a certain form, and that form was Christ." The nature of Christ is holiness. Any un-holiness that is known by us and not dealt with by us can arrest the move of the Spirit of God. Thus God's people need to clear up any controversy with the Lord in order for the Spirit to have a way to produce the testimony of the Lord, which is the form of Christ. This process brings us closer to the fullness of the divine thought for man. May we listen to the prophets and bear this testimony of God's kingdom in this age.

The Work of God at the End-Time
1951

"An end-time is transition from a lot that has to do with Christ to Christ Himself, transition from frameworks to the essential and the intrinsic, transition from all the works and things related to Christ to that which is known of Him personally." At an end-time the work of God takes on a particular nature. We see this illustrated with Simeon, Anna and the infant Lord Jesus. The aged man with a babe in his arms represents "an end handed on to a beginning, a beginning taking up all the fullness represented by the old." This was a crisis and a turning point. God was turning from the earthy, temporal, and outward and beginning to constitute a "new and spiritually inclusive dispensation." We learn from the picture of Simeon, that the work of God has abiding value; what He is doing in us today will be for the good of the coming ages.

At an end-time there is a sense of disintegration of what exists presently and of the ushering in of something new. In this situation vision is of tremendous importance. The effect of vision is to keep us alive, to keep us linked with God's purpose, to keep us walking with God, to encourage us to have a strong prayer life and to keep us accountable in the things of God. God needs people who exercise according to such vision.

In such a transition, Simeon was a picture of service. Real service is "the bringing in of Christ in fullness." This servant was prepared through pressure, was tested by God's hidden working, and was reduced to be a small vessel unto refinement and effectiveness. He offered himself as an absolute servant of his Lord, he meant business with the Lord, served Christ alone as his only master, and was not satisfied with anything short of the divine intention. This is a picture of the Lord's dealing with His individual or corporate instrument in preparation for the bringing in of Christ in fullness.

What Simeon prophesied concerning the Lord Jesus revealed that the deep meaning of Christ was wrought into him. The only way to comprehend the greatness of divine things is to have this wrought into us. This is illustrated by the phrase, "the fellowship of His sufferings," which possesses three aspects. "The first [is] cooperation with Him in His work of delivering souls from a jealous and bitterly hostile enemy; the second, the discipline and purifying which makes for Christlikeness; the third, the enlarging capacity, and developing of faculties for apprehending and understanding the greatness of divine things, particularly the knowledge of Christ." A person with such a vision will see that Christ determines destiny. He will see that Christ is a sign spoken against, which means that

His presence was a challenge that measured things and provoked people, His manner of life that held to inner principles repudiated mere formalities and customs, and His cross represented the final 'No' to all of mankind to leave room for only Christ. Finally, His suffering will cause a sword to pierce through the souls of many. Simeon represented the remnant clinging to the heavenly vision in the midst of a setting where things of God had become merely traditional and formal. He realized the tremendous significance of Christ and brought in Christ in His fullness to usher in the new dispensation of God. Today we are in a similar setting and God needs a similar vessel to bring in Christ in fullness. How much we can learn from this picture of God's work at the end-time.

Union with Christ
1952

"Union with Christ is the heart and center of all that has been revealed of God's thought concerning man and of man's relationship to God." Before we see our union with Christ, we must look at the greatness of the Christ with whom we are united. Christ is not the title of His essential Godhead, but a title that carries the significance of a mission. Christ's greatness is seen in His relationship with God, because He is the image of the invisible God. In relation to creation His greatness is seen because He is the meaning of all things, the heir of all things the idea of all things and the final test of all things. Such a great Christ was prophesied in the Old Testament. He is loved by the Father, opposed by God's enemies and demanded by the Father to be honored. His greatness is spiritual because of His relationship to the Father and moral because of His perfect separation from the whole earthly realm. His greatness is seen in His satisfaction to the Father, His redemptive work and in the Spirit's operations to ensure Christ's Lordship in us.

Now we can look at our union with Christ, which has many aspects, each with its own significance and value. Eternal union concerns God's choosing, foreordination, and foreknowledge of man in eternity past. It transcends the fall of man and is enhanced by the redemption of man. The Holy Spirit enacts our eternal union with Christ. When we receive the Holy Spirit we are joined to Christ, joined with God's purpose concerning Christ and linked with eternity. "The presence of the Holy Spirit within at once links us with timelessness, and in that timelessness with the eternal purpose of God concerning His Son, and in that purpose with the Son Himself."

God's pattern for His entire creation was a man, Christ. Becoming a Christian ushers us into creational and racial union with Christ. Whoever is in Christ is a new creation. We were made with a capacity for divine relationship; in Christ our human spirit is quickened and restored to its proper place to bring us into spiritual union with God. The growth of this spiritual union results in our maturing to receive the full inheritance of Christ; this is not primarily an individual thing, but has its fulfillment corporately in the church, "which is to be the vehicle and vessel of His universal dominion."

Our marital union with Christ has two sides. Legally we enter into marital union when we are born anew; spiritually we grow into the consummate union through fellowship and companionship. God said of Adam "It is not good for man to be alone," which applies to Christ's longing for companionship. "The church has been created by God because of this very prompting of interest in and desire for companionship for His Son." Through fellowship, which is "identity of life and purpose," the church becomes the complement of Christ. The church is the fullness of Christ. "It seems marvelous that the church could give something to Christ to make Him complete."

The ultimate spiritual union is seen in the marriage supper of the Lamb. This is where the legal union has grown to fullness through a process where the two "are growing into one another. The fellowship is dependent, the mutual contribution is increasing. One is becoming ever more to the other and the other to the one."

Vocational union emphasizes the fact that through our union with Christ the house of God has been established. God's house is his dwelling place where His presence can be found and where God can be known. It is also His household that hold God's name and exists as God's family. It is a family by life: "We know that we have passed out of death into life because we love the brethren." God's house is also His temple, where His rightful worship is established. Finally God's house is where His stewardship is exercised, where He establishes His order and where the Holy Spirit works in the members to make them realize their stewardship, "where everyone ought to be a steward of the manifold grace of God."

Functional union emphasizes the inclusive function of the Body, to express its personality—Christ. "Christ is not merged into something called His Body and His own personality lost. He remains the personality of His Body." The Body functions to locate the person and to express its personality. "The Body of Christ is the fellowship of believers, in the Holy Spirit, in a very definite, conscious relatedness, involving an inward registration and recognition that we are related to all the Lord's people." The interrelatedness and interdependence of the members, where there is a mutual consideration and need of one another is crucial for the full expression of this union with Christ. In this union every member, "by the Holy Spirit, is in some way constituted with a function." The key to this expression is Christ's headship of each member.

All believers enter into a vital and organic union

with Christ. The seed, which is the word of God, enters into us and contains within itself "all the wonderful possibilities, potentialities, of what is of God, of what God is like, and of God's nature, of God's mind, of God's features, of all the dimensions to which God would bring life; the very shape of the life which God would produce." Begetting is the imparting of this seed into us, birth is the first manifestation of the life of this new thing, new life, divine organism. Growth takes place as Christ is imparted into us, Christ is assimilated into us, and Christ is known by us.

Our union with Christ is consummated when we are conformed to the body of His glory in the final glorification of our body. Corporately this is when the church becomes a "glorious church, not having spot or wrinkle or any such thing." Glory is not only a future hope of Christians, it "bears present evidence of its full reality." As the Lord brings us through crises, we return to Him and realize more life, more of the Lord and more glory than ever before. Finally, Christ will return to be glorified *in* His saints. This will be the final consummation of our union with Christ.

The Recovering of the Lord's Testimony in Fullness
1953

"God is concerned with the accomplishment of something worthy of Himself." As men who follow God, we need to pick up the same concern as God and be moved to cooperate with Him, though it may involve very real conflict and cost. The book of Nehemiah illustrates this; in it we see three things: the wall as the object, the work of rebuilding, and the warfare or conflict. God was moving to recover His testimony, symbolized by the wall. Nehemiah had the same concern as God and entered into the same travail and thus became a vessel through whom

God could recover His testimony.

The wall firstly signifies a definition—"a clear defining of what Christ is and what is not Christ," as is true of the wall of the New Jerusalem. Secondly it represents a demarcation, a distinction. There is no mixture because of the wall; it says only what is of Christ can be within. Thirdly, the wall represents a defense. "It was responsible to protect the Lord's interests and the Lord's people from that which would invade, which would attack, which would corrupt, which would change the character." Finally, the wall represents Christ from two sides: the Christ that the world sees from without and the Christ that God's people see from within. The Lord called Nehemiah to repair this wall, not build it. Spiritually, the Lord laid this wall in the book of Acts, now in our age it needs to be repaired.

Why was the wall broken down? The main reason was idolatry, which takes many subtle forms, and which in essence involves "heart communion with anything that takes God's place, that gets in God's way." Very often this could be tradition, dead history, names, titles etc. The broken wall symbolized the condition of God's people, which in essence involved the matter of worship. Jerusalem, which was defined by the wall, speaks comprehensively about the matter of worship. Worship means that things are redeemed to God, recovered to God and brought back to God. The wall was broken because the self-life came into the people's worship of God.

In the history of God's move of recovery we see a cycle: man falls away from God's original thought and intention, then God comes in to make progress towards recovering the fullness that He intended from the beginning. After a time man again falls away and God must start again. Every fresh move of God is marked firstly by intrinsic fullness, where the potential to attain the whole exists, and secondly by an advance upon the previous moves of the Lord. To enact a move of recovery, the Lord first must raise up a vessel marked by vision and passion and one who has undergone a peculiar treatment by the Lord in preparation for such a recovery.

When God moved to recover His testimony, as in Nehemiah, His way was in resurrection, which is the unique province of God and which marks every true move of God. We see this in the book of Acts, where God recovered His testimony on the day of Pentecost. However, decline soon came in. Now, the Spirit is working to create a corporate relatedness in resurrection for the rebuilding of this testimony. Just as in Nehemiah's time, when people of many different trades worked on the wall together, today, we are standing together, putting aside our preference of who we like to associate with, for the sake of rebuilding God's testimony.

Nehemiah's enemies typify the peculiar warfare connected with the Lord's purpose, which is beyond the warfare connected with the struggle for salvation or for living the Christian life. The enemies were close to God but had no living relationship with Him; they were superstitious and carnal and fleshly men. Nehemiah faced many forms of opposition including grief, scorn and ridicule, wrath, subterfuge, misrepresentation, intimidation and tiredness. All these demand watchful, intelligent prayer from those who rebuild the Lord's testimony.

Nehemiah closes with a tithe of people who chose to live in Jerusalem. These are special to the Lord, because they have persisted with God and have chosen to make a sacrifice and live at the heart of the Lord's testimony. These are firstfruits, those who have willingly chosen to live and suffer for the Lord's testimony. Their reward is to become the Lord's peculiar treasure in that day.

Pioneers of the Heavenly Way
1953

"If we are children of God our whole education and history is related to heaven...We are related to the kingdom of the heavens by birth, by sustenance, and by eternal vocation." From the beginning the divine intention was to have His presence here on earth just as He is in heaven. This is His testimony. "The whole history of divinely apprehended instruments for that testimony, whether they be individual or corporate, is the history of spiritual pioneering in relation to heaven." Features of such pioneering include a center of gravity transferred from earth to heaven, the feeling that this heavenly realm is altogether different and unexplored, and finally that this way is fraught with cost and conflict. This journey is summed up in the meaning of the name "Hebrew," which means "a person from beyond." On this earth, we are pilgrims, "pilgrims of the beyond."

Heaven is not satisfied with the world as it is; therefore there is a great conflict between heaven and earth. The need of our time is that the church would come into its true heavenly vision, position and vocation. Today, an instrument is needed to lead the church in the principle of death and resurrection from the current state of failure to the full realization of the heavenly thought of God.

From Abraham to Joshua we see examples of pioneers of the heavenly way. Abraham was a great pioneer, within whom heaven operated to give a deep, inborn sense of destiny. He fought the conflict between the spiritual and temporal (his travels down to Egypt) and between the spiritual and the carnal (Lot). The proofs that he had the reality of heavenly vision were seen because he had faith in the God of the impossible, he had a capacity for adjustment when he made mistakes, and his faith showed that he

had the working of the heavenly power within. Moses'
life demonstrates that the heavens govern in spite of his
failures. Moses became restless in his high position in
Egypt, killed an Egyptian while attempting to free God's
people and was forced to spend forty years in the wilderness. He then underwent the ordeal of emancipation
through the rod, symbolizing the word of the cross, and
his leprous hand, symbolizing the futility of his own
fleshly strength and the sufficiency of God alone. The
whole nation of Israel was then called by God into this
long conflict between heaven and earth, in which they
failed many times.

A transition came when Israel crossed the Jordan.
The object of crossing the river is the land, which symbolizes a life in resurrection and heavenly union with Christ.
The Jordan represents the transfer from the authority of
darkness to the authority of Christ and from desolation
and barrenness into the fruitfulness of life in the Spirit.
The ark typifies Christ as the great Pioneer who entered
death alone for God's people to enter the land. Just as
twelve stones were buried in the river and twelve more
were placed on the side of the Jordan, we are identified
with Christ by faith and by testimony. Then "we shall
have found the land flowing with milk and honey, we
shall have found the riches of Christ, we shall have found
the opened heaven." This is a heavenly life of spiritual
fullness.

Such a full expression of what is heavenly is the
end of God's ways. For this end, God chooses vessels,
individual or collective, and "brings them in a peculiar
way sovereignly into relationship with His full end, and
then does that in them which He means for a much larger
company than themselves." God deals with this representative vessel to make it a living representation of His fuller
thought by establishing essential and intrinsic values in it.
Thus the vessel has "spontaneous ministry"—it only has

to *be* and it happens. God first lays hold of individuals and then of companies through which He gives people "a peculiar kind of discipline and training which belongs to corporate life." These have spontaneous ministry because of what God has done in them. We must realize that conversion is not an end in itself and assembly life is not an end in itself. Rather, God wants the full expression of what is heavenly. The ways these vessels grow are not by official appointment, but by having a humble, servant spirit, by God's sovereign grace and by having the natural man ruled out.

We take possession of the heavenly land by the Lordship of the Holy Spirit, who is an earnest of our inheritance and who is committed to God's purpose. This is symbolized by the man, the "prince of the host of the Lord," seen by Joshua. Joshua bowed, symbolizing the work of the cross, and then put himself under the Lordship of the Holy Spirit. Thus, the way to heavenly fullness was opened. The prince has a drawn sword and proceeds to lead Joshua into conflict, symbolizing that every bit of spiritual increase is accompanied by conflict. However, the battles are the Lord's and, like that of Jericho, are won with no carnal or human weapons.

In the Old Testament picture we see that the Levites have no inheritance on earth. They therefore represent God's *heavenly* thought. In their heavenly function they bore the ark through the Jordan. The Lord must have those who separate themselves from the earth, who are "standing wholly, utterly, at all costs, for His full heavenly thought concerning His Son and concerning His Church." These have headquarters in heaven and not in any earthly place, as Jerusalem became in the New Testament times. The divine idea is "to have companies of the Lord's people, planted here and there and everywhere, as a corporate Levitical ministry, to keep heaven near, and to keep things near heaven."

The Spiritual Meaning of Service
1955

The Lord's people are called into a vocation to be a priestly people. In that function they are precious to the Lord, just as the serving Levites in the Old Testament were precious to God. When the Lord Jesus began His priestly ministry, the Father showed His affection by saying, "Thou art My beloved Son; in Thee I am well pleased." As priests, we can be brought into that same belovedness. God is pleased with service that corresponds to the Lord Jesus, that is under an open heaven indicating that there is no shadow, cloud or interruption between us and God. The marks of such ministry are that life is ministered, not merely truth or intellectual knowledge, and that peace is brought in, where God is satisfied and man's heart is at rest. Satan is utterly opposed to such ministry, while God is jealous over it and chastens His people to produce it in them.

The Bible describes the service of God in terms of the priesthood. All of God's people are called into such service. Essentially, this service brings "God and man together in one," preserves "the ground of God's presence with man," takes as its central object the testimony of God as symbolized by the ark, and embodies or sets forth "in representation God's full thought concerning all His people." Service is related to the whole matter of life, so that people go away more living than when they came, and it takes life, not position or office, as its only principle of continuity. A great warfare rages against such ministry; many times opposition even appears from within the people of God themselves.

We can learn lessons about service from Zacharias. He ministered as a priest according to the situation that God ordained. However, when God came in to do a new thing, beyond the tradition of the people, an obstruc-

tion arose even within Zacharias himself. This shows that
what God desires has no natural ground upon which to
rest itself and is obstructed so easily by pride and convention. "The greatest things that God will ever do will always be beyond us—beyond our power of understanding
and beyond our attainment in knowledge." God's way
can never be realized through what is natural. Not until
we make adjustments to God's new thing will His living
testimony have a way through us.

Just as the priest's robe was all of blue, God's servants must be fully in harmony with heaven. Such harmony can be achieved through a simple belief and acceptance of the atoning and redeeming work of Christ. God's
people then have another life, a heavenly life, which
makes them distinct from all other people and which
gravitates them to live in a heavenly way. They belong to
another world, they have another goal, they are united by
virtue of the one life they share, and they have the same
interests, which are "the interests of Jesus Christ and the
glory of Jesus Christ."

In the Old Testament, God's people were officially
divided into three realms: the priests, the Levites and the
main body of Israel. In the New Testament, these divisions are not formal or official, but they are spiritual. The
great mass of the Lord's people remain in the objective
realm, where they partake of salvation by virtue of the one
great offering of Christ. The Levite realm represents
those who have advanced to a more inward, subjective
experience with Christ. What Christ has done has become
a "powerful, working reality, so that it is in their very being." These, then have a basis upon which to minister to
others. Ministry is not formal or ecclesiastical, but "is
based on an inward knowledge of the Lord." Both of
these groups are still the Lord's people, but the Levite
group has subjective, inward experience. Such experience
came about through a deep application of the cross to de-

pose the selfhood that Christ may have His place. This experience also came through an application of the blood of Christ make alive, that service may be of another life, the divine life. This experience also comes through the Spirit of life that leads us into the realm where the Spirit within is truly governing. Such a spiritual person is under the government of the Holy Spirit, where this person spontaneously fulfills the word of God and unconsciously or consciously does not do anything to violate the word of God. These ministers have an anointed ear, symbolizing spiritual perception and sensitivity to God, an anointed thumb, symbolizing the things they handle are handled under the government of the Spirit, and an anointed big toe, symbolizing their character is under the government of the Spirit.

Such service to God will be princely service and will thus take its character from the Lord Jesus. Princely character is noble, fine, big, great, honorable, and dignified. It has spiritual stature, spiritual wealth, and appreciates the experience of the cross. "The cross, rightly apprehended, is a wonderful delivering power from all littleness—from our poor, miserable, contemptible little selves." A minister with princely character is not interested calling attention to himself but has a genuine meekness and humility accompanying an absolute outpouring for the Lord. The Lord is seeking such a great and princely people to serve Him in His sanctuary.

The Israel of God
1957

"We have before us a very full, deep and far-reaching matter: nothing less than the producing, securing, training and using of a spiritual seed—a new spiritual Israel." In producing such a seed God never departs from His principle of travail, which implies that something is costly. God is travailing for a seed and we also enter into that travail. In the Bible all the divine initiations, enlargements and consummations are effected through travail. The travail of the cross had universal significance. God has two Israels today; one is according to the flesh and the other is spiritual, what Paul calls "the Israel of God." The Israel of God is created entirely according to the principle of travail.

While these two Israels are in vastly different realms, lessons from the first can be applied to the second. First God called a people from beyond the river through Abraham the Hebrew. Now God's real Israel is spiritual, inward; it is "Christ in you." Like the first Israel, the true has certain unmistakable features that declare this is a child of God. The first Israel is different from other nations. It is united, eats a unique diet, and hopes for the coming Messiah. Likewise, the divine birth of the new Israel causes it to be essentially different and separate from the things on this earth, drives all the members to be one, gives it discrimination in diet, and bestows it with a governing hope of His coming again. This unique stand is made in the realm of intense conflict, because Satan will oppose the securing of such a heavenly people "whose life is not composed of outward things at all, but whose life is the corporate expression of God's Son."

The supreme characteristic of this divine seed— the Israel of God—is faith. Without faith it is impossible to be well pleasing to God. All the divine virtues, like love, joy, peace, meekness, rest upon the foundation of faith. The focal point of faith will always be the very character of God. The spiritual counterpart of Israel after the flesh apprehends the promises of the covenant, the seed, and the land by faith. No Christian truly likes to live in this principle of faith, because it involves not merely believing what God can do, but in what God is. However, this is the supreme characteristic of the divine seed; All those who are of faith, these are sons of Abraham.

The dinner described in Luke 14 where people have no appreciation for God's invitation, no appetite for the feast being offered and no desire for fellowship with fellow feasters shows that man's choice can cause God's invitation to be missed. God desires that He would be man's only joy and that there would be oneness among the children of the kingdom. May we all have a heart to tell the Lord we are ready now.

John chapter 3 displays the great transition from the Israel of the flesh to the Israel of God; it is through the new birth. In this chapter the "Pharisees represented the very essence, the intrinsic meaning of the 'Israel after the flesh.'" There is a necessity of a birth by water and the Spirit. This illustrates the principle of death and resurrection as the only way to be "put on the ground of Christ," the unique ground of the Israel of God. The new birth constitutes the child of God with a new nature. The essential nature of the Israel of God is Christ; "its very constitution is Christ." This new constitution brings with it a faculty for a new knowledge (spiritual understanding, discernment and perception) and a new power that proves itself superior to even the best human strengths and abilities.

The Israel of God is the object of God's travail. As such, it has infinite value to Him. We hardly realize the infinite preciousness and value that His seed, His people, we who have believed unto eternal life hold in God's estimation. Christ has infinite love for His own. Furthermore, the church has infinite importance to Him. What this means on our side is that there is an infinite motive for our response to God. Surely when we first responded to God there was an infinite motive that led to our new birth. Afterwards, there remains infinite motive for our response, service, obedience, and giving everything to

God. God will come back again and again until He has
gained His full purpose and acquired that which He has
set His heart on—His seed that will express His Son.

Discipleship in the School of Christ
1962

A disciple of Christ is a learner of Christ. In the
New Testament, "The disciples were people who learned
and then put into practice what they learned." As a disciple, our teacher is the Lord Jesus, whose unique subject is
Himself. He says, "I am the way," "I am the resurrection," "I am the true bread." He is His own subject. Additionally, in the New Testament, His teaching was usually accompanied by His acts.

The gospel of John portrays the teacher, Jesus, in
the way of life; "All the teaching and works of the Lord
Jesus related to this thing that He called life." Here, the
existence of life in the Lord Jesus was proven by miracles
or signs. We must see that our possession of this life is
the basis for all of God's work in us. In the gospel of
John we see a progression involving signs, belief and life.
The signs were instruments; belief was the reaction; and
life was the result. This life is different from animal life
and human life because it is the divine life of God.
"Every kind of life has its own nature, and divine life has
divine nature in it. Peter speaks about being made
'partakers of the divine nature,' and with this life the very
nature of God is implanted into us." For us, this life
brings in a new consciousness of God, just as Jesus was
continually conscious of His union with the Father. Additionally this life has the power to grow, which is a sure
sign that we have it.

The meaning of this life is unveiled in seven signs
recorded in the gospel of John. As we consider these
signs, we must remember that in our experience this life

can never be separated from the person of Jesus Christ. The seven signs along with what these signs reveal are listed below.

Turning water into wine reveals the quality of the divine life, which is better than any other. "We may be naturally poor wine. But when the Lord Jesus comes in with His life, it will be the best wine." The healing of the nobleman's son unveils that this divine life is unlimited by time and space. The raising of the impotent man by the pool of Bethesda unveils how this life brings deliverance from bondage to sin and death. The feeding of the five thousand reveals that this divine life, Jesus as the true bread, is all-sufficient and inexhaustible. Walking on the water reveals that the divine life is triumphant over natural forces. The raging of the sea is likened to turbulence among nations and troubling situations. "Wholly committed people are not saved from trouble, but they are made ascendant over it, or they are kept through it by His power." Giving sight to the man born blind unveils that this life brings with it real spiritual sight. "This life which we receive in Christ has a simple beginning, but it is a progressive life, and the progressive nature of the life is a fuller and fuller discovery of the Lord Jesus." The final sign, the raising of Lazarus from the dead, shows that this life overcomes death in its fullness. Lazarus represents the gathering together of all forms of death resulting in a complete end of our ability to do anything. Here Jesus shows that only He is the resurrection and the life. As disciples, we are learning the full meaning of the life that is the Person of the Lord Jesus. These things make up the true Christian life. "We must, every one, ask the Lord to teach us what this means and to bring us into the reality of this great life."

The Holy City, New Jerusalem
1967

Note: The following summary draws on material from Mr. Sparks' 1967 conference message on the New Jerusalem and an earlier writing by Mr. Sparks published in a 1972 issue of *Toward the Mark*.

In Revelation 21 and 22 we see a marvelous vision of a great city, the New Jerusalem. From its very position in the Bible we can see that it is God's goal and that it should be the goal of every believer.

But what does this city mean? Are we to aim at one day living in an enormous physical city of pure, clear gold, which has a golden street, pearl gates, a wall of precious stones, a throne, a river and a tree? This, in fact, is most Christian's concept of "going to heaven." But according to the book of Revelation, this city is not a literal city. Revelation is a book of signs, and this city is also a sign. The sign of this city is used to portray the consummation of God's plan. Such a thought is quite revolutionary to many Christians who look forward to entering pearly gates and living in mansions on a golden street. This city is a "symbolic representation of Jesus Christ and His church." It also represents the end to which God is working. Mr. Sparks writes of the symbolic representation of this city:

It can all be gathered into a few words: the Lord is trying to show us what is the great end toward which He is moving in the lives of His people, and that end is the expression of His own divine nature in them. That divine nature has been brought to us in His Son, Jesus Christ, and the Holy Spirit has come to reproduce Jesus Christ in the Church, so that when God's work is done in His people there will be a manifestation in His universe of the divine nature in a people. God is not doing two things, but one thing. Evangelism is just the gathering of the people, the adding of believers to the Lord Jesus. From that time it is the work of the Holy Spirit to conform those believers to the image of God's Son, and the end of the work of the Holy Spirit is the manifestation of Christ in and through the Church.

The Christian's life is progression in the increase of Christ. That explains all the dealings of the Holy Spirit with us, for His one object is to bring the Church to the fullness of Christ. If you want to know what the fullness of Christ is, then you have it in the symbolic representation of the holy city, New Jerusalem. Every aspect of this city represents some spiritual feature of the Lord Jesus, that is, it represents some feature of the divine nature which is to be reproduced in the Church, the people of God.

Some features of this city and what they represent are the following.

Gold: "Pure gold is the dominating presentation of this city, and we have seen that in the Bible gold is always the symbol of divine character, especially love."

Jasper: "Jasper, as a symbol of clearness, is mentioned in all the main connections of this book of the Revelation....he saw, "a door opened in heaven...a throne set in heaven...and he that sat was to look upon like a jasper stone." (Rev. 4:1-3) The churches have been judged, and now all the world, and everything else, is going to be

judged, for the throne means judgment. It is the governing of everything from heaven, and everything is going to
be judged in the light of the jasper stone, that is, according
to the divine nature which is absolutely clear.

The wall: "The wall represents a boundary. It determines what is of God and what is not of God....and
when you examine this wall and see what its foundations
are 'all manner of precious stones' then you are seeing, in
a symbolic way, the character of God in its many aspects."
The wall is a testimony of God, "firstly, the testimony to
what God is like, and then the testimony that only that
which is like God can come into the church."

Precious Stones: "All these stones set forth the
many-sided riches of God's grace brought to us in Jesus
Christ."

Pearl gates: "Pearls are a parable of the preciousness which results from suffering, since they are formed
as a result of the agony of the host creature. These pearls
are the only gates. There is no other way into the city than
by suffering love, for the elect people who are to reign
with Christ are those who have first shared something of
His sufferings."

The street with the river: "The one street has one
river which means that from the inner realm of fellowship
with Christ there is an outflow of life."

Oneness: "The single street is central; a river runs
down the middle of the street, and the tree of life grows on
either side of the river. Nothing is in plural...At the end,
however, everything is gathered into absolute unity: one
city, one street, one river, one tree. It is a symbolic reminder that at the last all will be summed up into a perfect
oneness, the oneness of Christ....The city is being spiritually formed now...if the church is to be God's metropolis
with an eternal vocation at the center of the universe, then
here and now it must learn oneness with and in Christ."

The tree of life: "Now you see that the tree is not just a tree, it is a person, and that person is Jesus Christ, the Son of God."

The throne: "The city is the seat of government, and you notice that the river of the water of life flows from out of the throne, so it is the throne that produces everything....In a word it means the absolute Lordship of Jesus Christ.

Adorned as a bride for her husband: "What the Lord is doing in us now as daily we learn new lessons of grace and humility, will be manifested in that day, and although this may bring gratification to us and joy to others, it is primarily meant for the pleasure of Christ. The Church's spiritual adornment is to be the reward to our Bridegroom-Redeemer for all His patient, suffering love."

The New Jerusalem is not merely a city that we look forward to reaching at the end of our Christian life. Rather, *today* we can experience many aspects of the New Jerusalem in our Christian Lives. This experience began at our regeneration, "If you are really a born-again child of God, you are a part of the city which God is now building. God is now building something and this building is going on inside of us—or it ought to be! God is, by His Spirit, building His Son into us. Christ is being built up in us, and we are being built up in Him." It continues as we take grace according to our specific situations. "On the foundations were the names of the twelve apostles of the Lamb. Now this means much more than I am going to say, but I am quite sure that it means this one thing....The riches of His grace are at last manifested in them. Peter needs grace in one way—I don't know whether he corresponds to the jasper—and John needs grace in another way—perhaps he corresponds to the sapphire. But they all needed some form of divine grace in a special way. And that is true of us all. My nature needs divine grace in a special way, and everyone here needs the grace of God in some particular way. But the grace of God in Jesus Christ can meet every one of us in our particular way, and right at last...we will be in the city." Our corporate experiences help us greatly to be built up as the New Jerusalem. "When we are born again the Holy Spirit gets hold of these pieces of rough stone—and what poor bits of humanity we are! What poor pieces of material we are for a heavenly city! We have a lot of corners like a piece of stone so the Holy Spirit says, 'We will knock off some of those corners'....We are very awkward and do not fit anywhere, so we have to be made to fit this heavenly city. You see this heavenly city is very practical....The symbolism may be very wonderful, but the actuality is through suffering. But when the work is finished we will say: 'God has done a wonderful thing in me. What a difficult person I was! How difficult it was for me to fit in with others...But God has done His work faithfully.' All the awkward corners have gone and Jerusalem is a city that has been 'compacted together'....We just do not get on smoothly together, and then the Holy Spirit takes the sandpaper to smooth us down. But, oh no, he does not take a piece of paper and rub us smooth—He puts us up against someone else who is not smooth, or He puts us into a situation in life which is not smooth....We shall never have a smooth time until we are smooth—and do you know what makes us smooth? It is the grace of God in suffering."

The vision of this city shows us that "What God is doing in the small fragment of time in our lives is going to be revealed to His glory for eternity." May we all live and enjoy His grace in the light of that Holy City, New Jerusalem.

The Holy Spirit's Biography of Christ
1970

"The Holy Spirit is writing a biography of Jesus Christ, and it is a spiritual biography, written in the spiritual life and experience of the believers. All that which was true of the Lord Jesus, excepting His deity, is going to be written in our spiritual experience." The life of every believer is intended to be a rewriting of the history of the Lord Jesus. The Holy Spirit intends to write Jesus' life into believers so that all may be able to read.

The beginning of the biography is our being born anew, which, like Christ's beginnings, has its roots in eternity. Being born again is to receive eternal life, which is simply the presence of God. And it is this eternal life that governs everything in the believer's individual or corporate life. This is illustrated by the tree of life, representing Jesus as life, appearing at the beginning and ending of the Bible.

Jesus' earthly life was divided into three sections: babyhood, childhood and manhood. Each of these sections will be repeated in the believers' experience, each is illustrated by a different section of the Bible, and each will issue in life. Babyhood, illustrated by Abel, Enoch and Noah, represents the beginning of life based on justification by faith, or in simpler terms, a right standing with God. Childhood, illustrated by Abraham through Moses, represents being made complete by the work of the Holy Spirit, just as Jesus was made perfect in his human life. Manhood, illustrated by the Old Testament prophets and by Jesus' ministry after His baptism, is the travail of life and involves intense conflict to bring in the fullness of the divine life.

Mary, who is a servant of God to bring forth Christ, illustrates the next chapter in the biography. She is a picture of real service to God: "Service is bringing God back where we are." With Mary we see the operation of the cross in her costly suffering and the operation of the Holy Spirit who enabled her to serve to bring forth Christ. Just as the Son did not remain in his place in eternity but became a lowly man, so Mary went down to the lowest place by accepting God's arrangement to conceive the child Jesus out of wedlock. This costly suffering was part of her service to God. The result was that Christ was brought into the world and was brought closer to His rightful place. This story will be repeated in us.

The biography's next chapter involves Jesus' baptism, anointing and temptation. Jesus' baptism represented judgment and death to the whole race of mankind, which was discredited before God. When Jesus came out of the water, he was accredited by God and stood under an opened heaven. Only after His baptism was Jesus anointed by God. "When Jesus was anointed at the Jordan, that was the beginning of His life vocation, and that vocation was to be established upon a complete fellowship with His Father." Next, Jesus was tempted. Temptation has a history beginning with the two trees in the Garden of Eden. "The one tree, the tree of life, was a symbol of the divine life by which God wanted man to live, and the other tree, the tree of the knowledge of good and evil, was the symbol of man being sufficient in himself." This was the basis of Jesus' temptation. The devil wanted to turn Him from trusting in God to relying on His own strength. In the temptation concerning the bread, Jesus was tried about relying on the Father's life. In the temptation concerning the temple, Jesus was tried about relying on worldly methods (in this case miracles) of fulfilling his vocation. In the temptation concerning the earthly kingdoms, Jesus was openly tempted to compromise with the prince of this world. These temptations, which are a part of Jesus' history, are repeated in our lives as we endeavor in our service to bring God into the world. This is the writing of the Holy Spirit's biography of Christ. Under this writing of the Holy Spirit, the life of every believer will become a rewriting of the History of Christ for all to see.

"Now the principle of being and growing is life. The means and method of being and growing is a seed, with life in it, in which the whole organism of its kind exists...The seed of every species has, within itself, all that characterizes the particular organism. The particular nature of that species, its shape, its size, its color, its form, its features, its capacities, are all there in the seed where the life is. Of course, that is the wonder of nature. It is an amazing thing: just a seed with its tiny germ of life in it, and then, when grown, developed and in full expression, coming true to type in all its features. It is a marvelous thing. That is God's method of being and growing. It is all there.

We have read passages in which the word 'begotten' is used concerning certain people, a certain type of creation, 'begotten of God.' The seed, the fertilizing principle, is the Word of God, and the life is the Spirit of God, who is the Spirit of life. Within the Word of God - of course specifically within the Word of truth in the Scriptures, but in anything that God says, that really comes from God to us—there are contained all the wonderful possibilities, potentialities, of what is of God, of what is like God, of God's nature, of God's mind, of God's features, of all the dimensions to which God would bring a life; the very shape of the life which God would produce."

—*Union with Christ*

Acknowledgments

I gratefully acknowledge help from many generous people for inspiration, materials and other resources for this work. I thank George and Jon Moreshead, Doug Riggs, and Titus Chu for kind access to their *Witness and Testimony* library and for inspiration to do this work. I thank Bill Barker, James Reetzke, Angus Gunn, Chuck Debelak, and George Moreshead for helpful conversations and emails that gave me many insights into T. Austin-Sparks' life and the Honor Oak Christian Fellowship Center. Thanks to John Myer for creating the cover and to Betsy McNaughton and Norm Minahan for editorial emmendations.

I give special thanks to Kingsway Publications, Destiny Image Publishers, Clements Publishing, Faith Baptist Theological Seminary, James Reetzke and Dr. Robert Delnay for kind permission to quote their materials.

NOTES

(*A Witness and a Testimony* journal is abbreviated W&T)

Introduction

1. Austin-Sparks, *Stewardship of the Mystery,* vol. 1, p. 31.

Chapter 1: Early Years 1888-1926

1. Austin-Sparks, Theodore Ed. *A Witness and a Testimony.* London, Witness and Testimony, 1967, 23.
2. Interview with a Christian brother who knew Mr. Sparks.
3. Austin-Sparks, *That they all May Be One* Vol. 1, 124.
4. Torrey, R. A. *The Great Attraction.* "Reuben Archer Torrey - Free Online Sermons, Christian Writings, Stories, etc." Accessed August 10, 2004. http://articles.christiansunite.com/preacher34-1.shtml.
5. W&T, 1970, 25.
6. Gunn, Angus M. *Theodore Austin-Sparks, Reflections on His Life and Work.* Toronto: Clements, 2001, 2.
7. W&T, 1969, 25.
8. Austin-Sparks, *Our Warfare,* 70.
9. Kinnear, Angus. *Biography, T. Austin-Sparks.* Shippensburg, Pennsylvania: Destiny Image, 1983.
10. W&T, 1968, 43.
11. W&T, 1967, 138.
12. Austin-Sparks, *The Incense Bearers,* 4.
13. W&T, 1946, 38.
14. Delnay, Robert. *What Happened to Keswick?* Ankeny, Iowa: Faith Baptist Theological Seminary, 2002.
15. Reetzke, James. *T. Austin-Sparks, A Brief History of the Lord's Recovery.* Chicago: Chicago Bibles and Books, 2001, 50.
16. W&T, 1970, 25
17. Reetzke, 50.
18. W&T, 1926, 3
19. W&T, 1926, 2
20. W&T, 1926, 26.
21. W&T, 1926,2
22, W&T, 1926, 2
23. Austin-Sparks, *That They all May Be One* Vol. 1, 137.
24. W&T, 1971, 70.
25. W&T, 1926, 18

26. W&T, 1926, 27.
27. W&T, 1926, 35.
28. W&T, 1926, 48.
29. W&T, 1926, 71.
30. W&T, 1926, 83.
31. W&T, 1926, 83.
32. W&T, 1926, 108.
33. W&T, 1927, 7.
34. W&T, 1933, 2.
35. Reetzke, 52.
36. Reetzke, 52.
37. W&T, 1926, 120.

Chapter 2: A Sign to the World and a Ministry for All 1927-1939

1. W&T, 1927, 3.
2. W&T, 1927, p. 15.
3. W&T, 1927, 51.
4. W&T, 1926, 27.
5. W&T, 1927, 4.
6. Austin-Sparks, *The Service of God*, 7-9
7. Austin-Sparks, *The Service of God*, 4-5.
8. W&T, 1927, 133.
9. W&T, 1927, 54.
10. W&T, 1927, 67.
11. W&T, 1927, 68.
12. W&T, 1927, 84.
13. W&T, 1927, 100.
14. W&T, 1927, 147.
15. W&T, 1927, 148.
16. W&T, 1928, 10.
17. W&T, 1928, 3.
18. W&T, 1928, 4.
19. W&T, 1928, 2-3.
20. W&T, 1928, 18.
21. Gunn, 52.
22. W&T, 1929, 22.
23. W&T, 1930, 2.
24. W&T, 1931, 79.
25. W&T, 1931, 51.
26. W&T, 1929, 5-6.
27. Reetzke, 2.
28. W&T, 1929, 118.

29. W&T, 1930, 78.
30. W&T, 1930, 118.
31. W&T, 1933, 2.
32. Reetzke, 2.
33. Kinnear, Angus. *The Story of Watchman Nee: Against the Tide*. Wheaton, Illinois: Tyndale House, 1973, 152.
34. Nee, Watchman, Collected Works of Watchman Nee, Volume 11. Anaheim, California: Living Stream Ministry, 1992, 857.
35. Kinnear, *Against the Tide*, 188.
36. Kinnear, *Against the Tide*, 190.

Chapter 3: Wartime Interlude 1940-1947

1. W&T, 1944, 1.
2. W&T, 1944, 51.
3. Austin-Sparks, *The School of Christ*, 33.
4. W&T, 1940, 57.
5. W&T, 1940, 135.
6. W&T, 1940, 162.
7. Austin-Sparks, *God's Spiritual House*, 50.
8. W&T, 1941, 30.
9. W&T, 1941, 36.
10. W&T, 1941, 67.
11. W&T, 1941, 65.
12. W&T, 1941, 129.
13. W&T, 1941, 131.
14. W&T, 1942, 1.
15. W&T, 1942, 2.
16. W&T, 1942, 82.
17. W&T, 1942, 64.
18. W&T, 1944, 1.
19. W&T, 1943, 64.
20. W&T, 1944, 20.
21. W&T, 1944, 31.
22. W&T, 1944, 41.
23. W&T, 1944, 51.
24. W&T, 1944, 52.
25. W&T, 1945, 1.
26. W&T, 1945, 45.
27. W&T, 1945, 54.
28. Graham, Billy. *Just As I Am*. Toronto, Ontario: HarperCollins, 1997, 100.
29. W&T, 1946, 1.

30. W&T, 1946, 38.
31. W&T, 1947, 1.
32. Interview with a Christian brother who knew Mr. Sparks.
33. W&T, 1948, 25.
34. Interview with George Moreshead.

Chapter 4: Expansion and Enriching 1948 – 1958

1. W&T, 1948, 47.
2. W&T, 1948, 114.
3. Interview with Angus Gunn
4. Interview with Angus Gunn
5. W&T, 1948, 49.
6. W&T, Insert to May 1950 issue.
7. W&T, 1951, 1.
8. W&T, 1951, 97.
9. W&T, Insert to the September 1951 issue.
10. W&T, 1956, 49.
11. W&T, 1952, 1.
12. W&T, 1952, 49.
13. W&T, 1952, 50.
14. W&T, 1952, 121.
15. W&T, 1952, 122.
16. W&T, 1953, 97.
17. W&T, 1953, 98.
18. W&T, 1953, 122.
19. W&T, 1955, 1.
20. Interview with George Moreshead.
21. Reetzke, 81.
22. W&T, 1956, 49.
23. W&T, 1956, 51.
24. W&T, 1956, 50.
25. W&T, 1956, 1-2.
26. W&T, 1956, 27.
27. W&T, 1956, 29.
28. W&T, 1956, 30.
29. W&T, 1956, 32.
30. W&T, 1956, 51.
31. W&T, 1956, 100.
32. W&T, 1956, 122.
33. W&T, 1957, 49-51.
34. W&T, 1957, 73.
35. W&T, 1958, 1.

36. W&T, 1958, 26.
37. Reetzke, 79.
38. W&T, 1958, 121.
39. W&T, 1958, 122.
40. W&T, 1958, 123.
41. W&T, 1958, 124.
42. W&T, 1958, 125.
43. W&T, 1959, 2.
44. W&T, 1959, 3.
45. W&T, 1959, 25.
46. W&T, 1959, 50.
47. Reetzke, 44.
48. Lee, Witness. *Life-Study of Colossians*. Anaheim, California: Living Stream Ministry, 1984, 133-134.
49. Lee, Witness. *God's New Testament Economy*. Anaheim, California: Living Stream Ministry, 1986, 283.
50. Reetzke, 44.

Chapter 5: Alone, Yet in Christ 1959 – 1971

1. W&T, 1959, 2.
2. W&T, 1965, 121.
3. Reetzke, 78.
4. W&T, 1962, 118.
5. W&T, 1963, 2.
6. Reetzke, 78.
7. W&T, 1955 notice.
8. W&T, 1963, 1.
9. W&T, 1969, 49.
10. W&T, 1963, 106.
11. W&T, 1964, 1.
12. W&T, 1965, 122.
13. W&T, 1966, 121.
14. W&T, 1967, 2.
15. Gunn, 8.
16. Austin-Sparks, *Our Warfare*, 58.
17. Austin-Sparks, *The School of Christ*, 33.
18. W&T, 1969, 18 and 45.
19. Interview with a Christian brother who knew Mr. Sparks.
20. W&T, 1963, 105.
21. W&T, 1970, 52.
22. Austin-Sparks, *That They All May Be One* Vol. 1, 7.
23. Austin-Sparks, *That They All May Be One* Vol. 1, 5.

24. Austin-Sparks, *That They All May Be One* Vol. 1, 6
25. W&T, 1967, 2.
26. W&T, 1971, 69.
27. W&T, 1966, 74 and 1970, 121.
28. W&T, 1966, 97.
29. Austin-Sparks, *Recovering of the Lord's Testimony in Fullness*, 109.
30. W&T, 1966, 25.
31. W&T, 1966, 74.
32. W&T, 1968, 94.
33. W&T, 1969, 25.
34. W&T, 1970, 122.
35. W&T, 1959, 97.
36. W&T, 1961, 50.
37. W&T, 1962, 2.
38. W&T, 1962, 118.
39. W&T, 1963, 106.
40. W&T, 1965, 1.
41. W&T, 1966, 1.
42. W&T, 1966, 73.
43. W&T, 1967, 2.
44. W&T, 1967, 121.
45. W&T, 1969, 25.
46. W&T, 1960, 2.
47. W&T, 1961, 25.
48. W&T, 1961, 26.
49. W&T, 1962, 69.
50. W&T, 1963, 49.
51. W&T, 1963, 51.
52. W&T, 1970, 49.
53. W&T, 1960, 26.
54. W&T, 1960, 49.
55. W&T, 1960, 73.
56. W&T, 1970, 25.
57. W&T, 1961, 121.
58. W&T, 1963, 27.
59. W&T, 1966, 122.
60. W&T, 1968, 93.
61. W&T, 1969, 49.
62. W&T, 1970, 122.
63. W&T, 1971, 73.
64. Nee, Watchman. *A Table in the Wilderness*. Wheaton, Illinois: Tyndale House, 1978, last day.

65. W&T, 1971, March Insert

66. Includes interviews with Angus Gunn and George Moreshead, and impressions recorded in *A Witness and a Testimony* and other sources.

67. Nee, Watchman, Collected Works of Watchman Nee, Volume 45. Anaheim, California: Living Stream Ministry, 1992, 996.

68. Nee, Watchman, Collected Works of Watchman Nee, Volume 59. Anaheim, California: Living Stream Ministry, 1992, 6.

PRINCIPAL SOURCES

*Partial List of titles by Theodore Austin-Sparks:

Incorporation into Christ, 1926
The Holy Spirit and the Cross, the Church and the Coming Again of the Lord Jesus, 1926
The Release of the Lord, 1928
The Divine Reactions, 1929
The Body of Christ, 1932
In Touch with the Throne, 1934
We Beheld His Glory, 1935
The Centrality of Jesus Christ, 1936
The Incense Bearer, 1936
The City Which Hath Foundations, 1937
The Battle For Life, 1937
The Stewardship of the Mystery, Volume 1, 1937
The Stewardship of the Mystery, Volume 2, 1938
What is Man, 1939
The Law of the Spirit of Life in Christ Jesus, 1940
God's Spiritual House, 1941
The School of Christ, 1942
The Centrality and Universality of the Cross of Christ, 1943
God's End and God's Way, 1945
What is a Christian, 1945
Four Greatnesses of Divine Revelation, 1946
Prophetic Ministry, 1948
Attaining unto the First Three, 1950
Union with Christ, 1952
Some Principles of the House of God, 1952
The Recovering of the Lord's Testimony in Fullness, 1953
Pioneers of the Heavenly Way, 1953
The Gold of the Sanctuary, 1953
His Great Love, 1953

The Gospel According to Paul, 1955
The Spiritual Meaning of Service, 1955
God's Reactions to Man's Defections, 1956
The Israel of God, 1957
Rivers of Living Water, 1957
The God of the Amen, 1958
The Alpha and the Omega, 1958
Our Warfare, 1960
Discipleship in the School of Christ, 1962
The On-High Calling, 1964
The Holy City, New Jerusalem, 1967
The Holy Spirit's Biography of Christ, 1970

Bibliography

Austin-Sparks, Theodore Ed. *A Witness and a Testimony*. London, Witness and Testimony, 1926 – 1971.

Delnay, Robert. *What Happened to Keswick?* Ankeny, Iowa: Faith Baptist Theological Seminary, 2002.

Foster, Harry Ed. *Toward the Mark*, London: Witness and Testimony, 1972-1987.

Graham, Billy. *Just As I Am*. Toronto, Ontario: Harper-Collins, 1997.

Gunn, Angus M. *Theodore Austin-Sparks, Reflections on His Life and Work*. Toronto: Clements, 2001.

Kinnear, Angus. *The Story of Watchman Nee: Against the Tide*. Wheaton, Illinois: Tyndale House, 1973.

Kinnear, Angus. *Biography, T. Austin-Sparks*. Shippensburg, Pennsylvania: Destiny Image, 1983.

Lee, Witness. *God's New Testament Economy*. Anaheim, California: Living Stream Ministry, 1986.

Lee, Witness. *Life-Study of Colossians*. Anaheim, California: Living Stream Ministry, 1984.

Nee, Watchman, Collected Works of Watchman Nee, Volumes 11, 45, 59 . Anaheim, California: Living Stream Ministry, 1992.

Nee, Watchman. *A Table in the Wilderness*. Wheaton, Illinois: Tyndale House, 1978.

Reetzke, James. *T. Austin-Sparks, A Brief History of the Lord's Recovery*. Chicago: Chicago Bibles and Books, 2001.

Torrey, R. A. *The Great Attraction*. "Reuben Archer Torrey - Free Online Sermons, Christian Writings, Stories, etc." Accessed August 10, 2004. http://articles.christiansunite.com/preacher34-1.shtml.

Author's Interviews and Correspondence

George Moreshead, St. Louis, Missouri; Angus Gunn, Vancouver, British Columbia; Douglas Riggs, Tulsa, Oklahoma.

- Some of these titles are published as books and some are series of messages published in *A Witness and a Testimony*. Not all are in print. Some can be ordered from Seedsowers at http://www.seedsowers.com. Others may be obtained at no charge by request from Emmanuel Church 12000 E 14th St, Tulsa, OK 74128-5016 USA. Others can be found online at http://www.austin-sparks.net.

INDEX